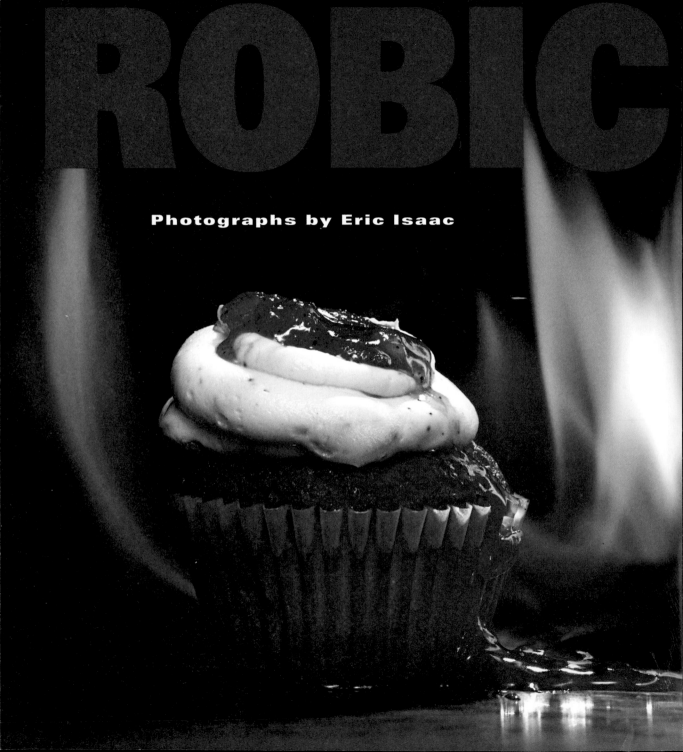

ROBIC

Photographs by Eric Isaac

ELLI'S CUPCAKES

A LOVE STORY, WITH

WITH 50 DECIDEDLY GROWN-UP RECIPES

ALLISON & MATT ROBICELLI

Viking Studio

VIKING STUDIO
Published by the Penguin Group
Penguin Group (USA) LLC
375 Hudson Street, New York, New York 10014

USA | Canada | UK | Ireland | Australia | New Zealand | India | South Africa | China
penguin.com
A Penguin Random House Company

First published by Viking Studio, a member of Penguin Group (USA) LLC, 2013

Photographs by Eric Isaac Photography

ISBN 978-0-670-78587-2

Printed in the United States of America

10 9 8 7 6 5 4 3 2 1

Set in Univers LT Std
Designed by Renato Stanisic

PUBLISHER'S NOTE
The recipes contained in this book are to be followed exactly as written. The
Publisher is not responsible for your specific health or allergy needs that may
require medical supervision. The Publisher is not responsible for any adverse
reactions to the recipes contained in this book.

FOR ATTICUS & TOBY

because you inspire us to try, to be brave, to attempt to become
the people we hope you boys will be when you grow up.
You show us the possibility and magic in the everyday,
and you are the only thing that's ever truly mattered.

"It's such a fine line between stupid and clever."
—*This Is Spinal Tap*

Preface

Thank you for opening this cookbook! I know there are many, *many* people out there thinking, "Ugh. This is just what America needs—another fucking cupcake cookbook," so honestly, just getting you to the opening page is a great start. I mean, you could be reading *any* cookbook right now: *Jacques Pépin's Techniques,* Guy Fieri's *Slamma Jamma Porkorama, 101 Jell-O Shots for Passover.* Yet here you are with *us,* and that's incredibly special. Welcome! Your presence is appreciated!

As the title suggests, this book is about more than just recipes. Robicelli's is far more than just a brand—it's the name of the family Matt and I started the night we met and fell in love. And because right now, as you and I are entering into a relationship of sorts where I talk and you listen, it seems only right that I give you a quick primer before you metaphorically "jump into bed with us." Unless you made it through the Jell-O shot book first, in which case you're free to take off your pants and meet us in whatever damn chapter you'd like.

The first thing you need to know is that our life is about so much more than cupcakes, and so is this book. As much as we're writing this to teach you how to make our world-famous buttercream or to answer questions like "how do I select a good wine for baking?" we're also here to tell you about other things we've learned along the way: what it's like to be a struggling mom-and-pop business in the worst economy since the Great Depression, how to keep your sanity when hitting rock bottom, why you should keep at least one "emergency cupcake" in your home at all times, or why we named a collection of cupcakes after *The Golden Girls* (hint: because it's the greatest television show in human history and so tremendously awesome that I don't understand why my eyes don't literally melt when I watch it). Okay, maybe that was more of a straight answer than a hint, but let's be honest here—the answer was totally obvious. Not like all the questions I'm going to be posing later, such as what the different types of butter and cocoa powder are. The answers to those questions are going to shake the very fiber of your being.

Second thing you need to know is that we've both spent just about our entire lives in Brooklyn, meaning that yes, there will be plenty of foul language in this book. Four-letter words, seven-letter words—we're also planning to make up some brand-spanking-new ones just for this book because this is kinda a big deal for us. While there are people out there who may take issue with the cursing, I need to remind you that this is pretty much a cornerstone of our native tongue. I could argue that I find it just as offensive when people butcher the English language by saying things like "y'all," "arsle," "hella," or "Kardashian." If it wasn't for curse words and grandiose hand gestures, I don't know if Brooklynites would even be able to communicate. In fact, I had requested that holograms of me making dramatic hand gestures be included in the book, but my publisher said it was "too expensive," which is total fucking bullshit.

Matt says: *You can't put a price on awesome, motherfuckers!*

And finally, know that we love you. Yes, *you*. Some of you are just discovering us; many don't know our full story except for the fact that we're two of the most lauded cupcake bakers in the country. None of this happened overnight, none of it was easy, and none of it would have happened if it wasn't for people just like you supporting us. We've had only one dream in our lives, and that was to make millions of people happy. If you make one or two of our recipes, share them with friends, help us make more people smile, then we love you for it. Thank you.

So, welcome to this book. *Robicelli's: A Love Story, with Cupcakes* is more than just, well, a love story with cupcakes. It's a recession survival story. It's about being as brave as you can when life throws its worst at you, and coming out on top. It's about challenging yourself, laughing at yourself, making mistakes and forgiving yourself for them. It's falling on your face over and over again and not letting that stop you. It's about never giving up on what you love, no matter how bad things seem to get.

And in between all that, it's about cupcakes. And yes, they are ridiculously delicious.

Contents

A Love Letter
to Cupcakes

**Dear Cupcake Haters, Cupcake-Hating Media,
Cupcake Conspiracy Theorists, Etc.,**

We get it, okay? We get why you hate cupcakes. We get how your toes curl at the "tweeness" of them, how you have a biological impulse to reject any edible that comes in colors not found in nature, how you have a natural suspicion of food that can be customized to feature a cutout of Justin Bieber's head on top of it.

We accept this. We understand. We agree.

Do you know what's *not* okay? Generalizing and dismissing the entire genre. Just because there are plenty of mindless, gimmicky, cutesy-wootsy bakeries out there whose saccharine sweetness is only outdone by the glitter-enhanced pure-sugar bombs they create does not mean that there are not literally thousands of excellent bakeries all across the world that are making something exceptional. If you could get over your shit for five minutes, go inside one of these places, and try something, you'd see that.

In case you've never seen the list of things that are irrefutably wonderful in the world, here's an excerpt of the first five entries:

1. Baby animals
2. Regular ol' babies
3. Cats in funny outfits like they think they're people or something!
4. Watching a guy get hit in the nuts
5. Cake

Please tell me of one child you know who has anxiously looked forward to blowing out the candles on his hunk of small-batch farmstead birthday cheese. A happy couple who eschewed a delicious tiered wedding cake for a celebratory artisan pickle bar. An adorable grandma who has invited her loved ones over to catch up over some locally sourced spelt crackers and kombucha.

Everyone likes cake! Any time something really awesome is going down, cake gets involved: birthdays, bar mitzvahs, going-away parties, good-intentioned kinky sex that doesn't work out as well as *Cosmo* implied that it would, weddings—the list is endless. Cake means something wonderful has happened; cake makes everyone smile a little on the inside.

Problem is, you normally have to buy a whole cake to get in on the action. But now, by the grace of God, we no longer need to wait for a special occasion, nor do we have to shamefully eat an entire cake by ourselves while watching TV movies and crying. We can buy a piece of cake meant to serve only one person! When you're having a bad day, you can buy a cupcake to turn the day around and make yourself feel special. You can call an old friend, ask him or her to meet you over a cupcake and a few cups of coffee, and just talk. You can buy several for the office to win the love of your coworkers.

Who of you has a problem with that? Who hates joy and happiness and catching up with people you love? If anything, the most maddening thing about this whole cupcake nonsense is that I can't believe it took someone so long to think of this. It's really such a smart idea.

Yet despite this logic, the media have been wondering what brand-new sweet is going to knock the glorious, beloved cupcake off its proverbial perch, when universally it will be rejected by every red-blooded American and reporters can finally leave cupcakes in the past! "Surely it's only a trend," they say. I mean, it's a trend that's been going on for close to twenty years now, but that just means it's all about to go south soon. Unlike fucking *normal* foods, desserts secretly hate one another and are incessantly plotting how to destroy all their competitors! Especially the Napoleons!

You don't see people getting this pissed off about sandwiches, do you? What do you think sandwiches are? They're just an entire meal made portable and personal size. How about burgers, which are portable steak? Or buying a slice of pizza instead of getting the entire pie? All the same logic. Yet I've never once seen a food writer say that burgers as we know them are over because he stopped at McDonald's for lunch or wondering what the "next" sandwich would be.

Maybe it's because of the sprinkles thing. Or because some people are just allergic to joy and too myopic to understand. Or maybe because for the first time in forever an entire arm of the food-service business is being owned and operated predominantly by women, and lord knows we can't have that. That's right, I said it. You hate cupcakes and therefore you're a sexist pig just like A. C. Slater. You should go put on some Z. Cavaricci pants, sit in a corner, and feel terrible about yourself. (You know what makes us feel better when we feel like that? Cupcakes. You may want to turn to page 43 and we can help you out.)

Cupcake haters, you're beginning to sound like that crazy old man who sits in front of the diner yelling about how Asian people are taking over the country and he has the microfilm in his bread box to prove it. You can either bitch about something or fix it. We're trying to do the latter.

We decided to buck the "stupid cupcake trend" that we so hated and do things our way. Nothing pink and cutesy and covered with sprinkles and ever so adorable. Nothing that tastes like asbestos or pure sugar. We don't use food coloring (and absolutely will *not* make "red velvet"). We don't rely on making cupcakes look like fuzzy bunnies or puppy doggies to help them sell. We don't cloak ourselves in a borderline condecending-girly aesthetic. In fact, one of us is a dude, and a gigantic behemoth of one who could probably take you down with one punch if he has enough gin in him.

Matt says: *Gin makes me fighty!*

What we *do* is think the same way we did back when we were making desserts for fancy-pants restaurants—balancing flavors and textures, relying on *flavor* instead of pure sugar, creating sweets that were both thoughtful and delicious. We design recipes around great ingredients and make just about everything in our kitchen from scratch—candies, compotes, the whole shebang.

Cupcakes are *not supposed to be stupid*! They should be so much more than just aesthetics, so much more than a cutesy, polka-dot novelty. They should be a small piece of the greatest cake you have ever had in your entire fucking life. That's all.

Maybe you all could put down the torches and pitchforks and try giving cupcakes another chance? Go out and try a few in your neighborhood. Find some you love and tell everyone you know about them. Reward the thousands of bakeries that make a spectacular product, and soon enough people will stop relying on red dye 40 to stand out and start relying on nothing but quality. If you demand better from your food, you'll begin to find better options more often. If you hit a dead end, try out a few of these recipes and see what we're talking about. They're so good, someone decided there needed to be a book about them!

And if that's too much to ask? Then just shut the fuck up already and let other people be happy. It's cupcakes, people. Not anything important, like sports or something.

Hugs and kisses, Allison and Matt

WHY WE READ THINGS THROUGH BEFORE WE BAKE

So let's say you bought this book specifically for our famous Chicken 'n' Waffles recipe. You go home, skip the intro and all the other stuff that I worked so hard on for the better part of *two freaking years,* and go straight to baking. You decide to start by making the cake and frosting it, then right when you're ready to start on the chicken, the entire point of the cupcake, you notice that you're supposed to soak it in buttermilk for *twenty-four hours* before starting anything. Or you promise your mom you're bringing fruitcake cupcakes to Christmas Eve dinner, then that morning you realize you needed to rehydrate all the fruit in brandy overnight. Or you're ready to make the buttercream for our blueberry port cupcake, only to learn that you need to reduce your blueberry port to a syrup and then chill it so it doesn't melt the butter when it goes in.

THIS IS WHY YOU READ THE ENTIRE FREAKING RECIPE BEFORE YOU GO JUMPING IN LIKE A LUNATIC AND DO SOMETHING STUPID.

There are some recipes in this book you can execute within an hour, some that take a few hours, some that take a day or two. There're some with a few components, and some with so many that you'll need to use every bowl you have in your kitchen. You wouldn't drive somewhere without reading the directions first, you wouldn't go scuba diving without listening to directions from a professional, you wouldn't jump off a bridge onto a moving train just because you saw some guy do it on TV once and it didn't look *that* hard. So don't just go trying to do things without reading the directions—*all* the directions—first.

And while we're on the topic of being prepared . . .

WHY WE *MISE-EN-PLACE* BEFORE WE BAKE

Before we start any project, professional chefs make sure we have everything out, measured, and ready to go. We call this *meis-en-place,* which is French for "everything in its place." My father calls this "getting all your shit together," because he has an irrational fear of the French. I think a poodle bit him once or something—I don't fucking know. I just deal with it and understand that we say things like "freedom fries" at my parents' house.

Whatever you want to call it, *mise-en-place* is important. Very often in cooking, *especially* when you're working with sugar, the time you have to add an ingredient is just a matter of seconds. If you're making caramel and you don't have your cream ready by the time the sugar is done, the whole thing will burn and you'll have to start again from the beginning. Plus, getting everything ready is going to make your time in the kitchen exponentially easier and more enjoyable, which is the whole point of doing it in the first place. If you don't enjoy baking, you just shouldn't do it; leave it to the professionals. Otherwise, we'll all go broke and you won't have anyone to write cookbooks for you.

THINGS YOU NEED

When you're buying kitchen equipment, it's not always necessary to break the bank, but don't cheap out either. You're much better off buying a piece of equipment that's going to be guaranteed to work every time you need it rather than choosing something that's a fraction of the price but will need to be continually replaced or, worse than that, fail while you're in the middle of a recipe.

STAND MIXER

If you are going to attempt to make our famous French buttercream, then you need a stand mixer. This is absolutely, 100 percent nonnegotiable. If you try to do it with a handheld one, you run a very real risk of burning yourself horribly, and nothing sucks the joy out of a day of cupcakin' quite like skin grafts.

HAND MIXER

In the event you're not a serious baker and just bought this book for the sexy pictures, foul language, and perhaps for killing spiders, you probably have no intention of going out and buying a crazy expensive stand mixer just to make our cupcakes. However, you most definitely have a handheld mixer—I don't even remember buying one in my lifetime, yet there are like six of them in my apartment. Go check your cupboard right now—it's there. Probably came with your house.

If you don't want to get any kind of mixer, you can make the cake parts with a whisk and a bit of elbow grease, but if your arm *literally* falls off when making American Frosting, don't hold us accountable. And also don't tell people that you got your stumpy-ass arm in their frosting, because that's just gross.

MEASURING CUPS AND SPOONS

We use lots of weights in our kitchen, but we know most home cooks don't. That's totally okay—we've converted everything for you. For dry ingredients, use solid metal measuring cups with a strong handle, scoop out your ingredient, shake back and forth *lightly* to settle, then scrape straight across the top with the back of a butter knife to level. *No packing anything down!* (Unless we explicitly say to do so.) Same deal with measuring spoons.

You'll also need a special measuring cup just for liquids. Get one that's at least four cups, see-through, and microwavable because we do a lot of heating things up and melting things in there. We love classic Pyrex and the OXO angled model.

CANDY THERMOMETER

This is the next piece of equipment that's nonnegotiable if you're attempting French buttercream. Working with molten sugar is just like being in chem lab back in high school—there is a ton going on at the molecular level that you cannot see, and cannot judge by sight or timing. It's a finicky material that acts differently every day due to things like humidity, barometric pressure, acidity, and altitude. I could explain further, but then we'd be venturing into the "nerd book" category, and it's specifically written out in my author contract that I'm writing a cookbook for the cool kids out there who wear leather jackets and shoot dice on street corners.[*]

There are two ways to know if your sugar is done, the first being by taking a small ball of molten sugar, dropping it in water, then examining the viscosity by rolling the ball between your fingertips. Why do we recommend you buy a candy thermometer over this other, non-special-equipment-requiring method? Because unless you no longer have any feeling left in your hands like us pros, this method is dangerous. It is an outdated and imprecise technique that pastry chefs used to determine temperature in the days before candy thermometers. Sure, it looks badass, but those guys would also stuff leeches into their pants if they felt feverish so all the "devil blood" would get sucked out of them. We live in the twenty-first century now. There's no need for amateurs to be rolling hot sugar in their hands and putting animals in their pants.

Matt says: *Unless you're into that stuff. We're looking at you, Florida.*

When you see pastry chefs use this method on TV, they're really doing it to illustrate why we call the stages soft ball and hard ball, etc. In the kitchen, we all use thermometers. When it comes straight down to it, thermometers are more accurate than people. In due time, we'll all be replaced by the thermometers, who will rule our land with an iron fist as they force humanity into the ground to mine for their precious mercury.

When picking a candy thermometer, the only hard rule is that it *must* clip onto the side of the pan. Make sure what you're buying is specified as a "candy/fry thermometer"—a regular old probe thermometer you use for roasts just isn't going to cut it. Analog thermometers are the cheapest option and easiest to clean (just put them in a pot of boiling water). We prefer the type that is encased in stainless steel, because it has a guard on the bottom that prevents direct contact between the bulb and the pan. You want the bulb of your thermometer to be suspended in the molten sugar to get an accurate temp—otherwise you're getting the temperature of the pan, everything will go wrong, you'll throw it out and try again just to have everything go wrong a second time, end up just using that canned crap frosting and praying that nobody notices. (Of course, everyone *will* notice, and you'll be branded a liar for the rest of your life. See how quickly your entire life went south, all because you picked the wrong thermometer?)

---

*If you want to be a nerd, I suggest you get what every chef I know considers our bible: **On Food and Cooking** *by Harold McGee. I also highly recommend any books written by Shirley O. Corriher. You can never know too much, and very often I put on my glasses, cuddle up under my tauntaun blanket, and study food-science books until the sun comes up. I can't always be jumping sharks on my motorcycle, you know.*

If you have lousy eyesight, or plan to do a lot of candy making/ sugar work and want perfectly precise temperatures, you may want to invest in a digital version. It requires a little extra care and needs to be cleaned by hand so as not to get the entire thing wet, but you really can't beat the feeling of security you get when you just *know* your sugar is done. Kinda like the feeling I got the first time I wore Spanx.

Matt says: Me too!

NONREACTIVE CANDY POT

By this, we mean a four-quart stainless steel saucepan that flutes out a bit at the top. There's a good reason for that lip: when tempering hot sugar syrup into a stand mixer with all its parts moving, that lip will help keep the edge of the pot steady while you slowly pour in the sugar. Make sure the pot is not so heavy that you can't easily lift it if it's full of scalding-hot sugar.

Matt says: We're fully aware we're making this hot sugar stuff sound absolutely terrifying, but trust us, once you get the hang of it, it's easy. We just don't want anyone to get all caught up in the excitement of cupcake baking, start jumping and dancing and flinging hot sugar around, horribly disfiguring all their friends, then suing us. Also, if you were coincidentally looking for a way to "accidentally" horribly disfigure all your friends, we heavily discourage it, thereby releasing ourselves from all liability potentially incurred by this entire paragraph.

MICROPLANE GRATER

This is what we use to grate nutmeg, and yes, you really do need to grate that fresh. We also use it for citrus zest and shaving chocolate.

SIFTER

You don't need one of those weird little flour sifters with the hand crank that makes you look like a little dancing monkey. We use a plain old wire-mesh strainer, the same kind you probably have lying around your house right now. We just saved you about four bucks. This book just keeps paying for itself!

REALLY BIG BOWL

We sift everything together into a big bowl, then lightly stir it together so all the ingredients are combined *before* we add them to our liquid ingredients. You've got a big bowl lying around somewhere. If you don't, go buy one. It's good for popcorn, really big salads, and using as a makeshift helmet during an impromptu slap-boxing match.

CHEF'S KNIFE

This is one item that we implore you to spend good money on—buy the right one, and it will last you so long you can be buried with it. Another plus: That will look totally badass at your funeral.

We like Wüstof, we like Henckels, and personally, we use Shun. All of these will run you well over $100 for a single chef's knife. But before you go look them up on the Internet and pass out over the fact that a nice set of Shuns will run you several

WHY WE SIFT

1. Flour, sugar-they're both teeny tiny specks of things. Look through a microscope and you'll see this:

Yes, they actually wear microscopic T-shirts. It's <u>adorable!</u>

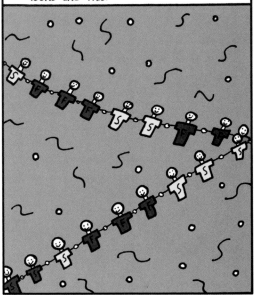

2. Flour, as you know, is starchy, so when it gets wet, it gets sticky. In fact, it's library paste. Now say we don't sift. Our mix looks like this:

3. Get it wet, it turns into . . .

. . . LUMPS!

4. But we sift and lightly stir to distribute everything equally . . .

Story: Allison Robicelli Art: Abby Denson

thousand dollars, know that you really need only spend a small fortune on a 10-inch chef's knife, as it's the workhorse of the group and you'll do everything with it. A home cook doesn't need a $200 bread knife, or a special knife "just for vegetables," or $600 worth of steak knives (unless you want everyone to know how rich you are, in which case, more power to you!).

BIG FAT HEATPROOF SPATULA

More than once I've grabbed a spatula to use on the stove, just to realize I've accidentally grabbed a non-heatproof one and ended up with a destroyed spatula and melted plastic in my food. This is why I say that when buying a spatula, always be sure it's heatproof. When working with batters, we always want to use as few motions as possible so that we don't develop the gluten in the flour, or deflate foams we've whipped. A nice big spatula has lots of surface area to help you fold, scrape, and do everything else with fewer motions.

OVEN THERMOMETER

I think someone did a study once that proved that 112 percent of ovens are calibrated to the wrong temperature. Don't ask me to prove it—I have no time to be doing your Googling—but the point is that every oven has hot spots, cold spots, runs a few degrees hotter or cooler than what it says on the dial. It's a good idea to invest in an oven thermometer to keep track of what's going on in there. To check for hot/cold spots, a great trick is to layer some baking sheets with white bread and bake on the center rack of your oven at 350°F until they brown.

Those places where the bread burned are hot spots—watch out for those! Make sure you rotate your pans halfway through, and constantly keep your eye on what you're baking, particularly in the last five minutes of cooking time.

Matt says: *If you ask a chef how long to cook something, we all say "until it's done." And that's not a joke—that's exactly how long you cook something. Cooking times are always guidelines—every stove, every oven puts out heat differently; things change based on altitude, if the barometric pressure is high that day—there are so many variables that if we listed them all, it would be insanely boring for you to read. Point is, chefs know when food is done because we're constantly paying attention to it, letting it tell us when it's ready. You should do that too.*

CUPCAKE PANS

We use plain old standard 12-cup cupcake pans. The ones we used in testing these recipes were nonstick aluminum, and the baking times reflect that. If you're just starting out and buying all-new baking supplies, go ahead and buy that type. But if you've already got pans, or like using silicone, or are just trying something out once and using disposable pans, by all means go forth and bake. However, know that this will affect the cooking times we've noted, so keep an eye on things and take your own notes.

Because many of our cupcakes involve fillings, soaks, and other types of manipulation, they really don't lend themselves to mini pans (though if you're just baking off straight cake and topping it with buttercream, a mini pan would do—just cut the cooking time by two thirds and check regularly).

We do not use the "jumbo" pans to make those gigantic monstrosities of cupcakes that people are now beginning to believe are supposed to be standard size. Next time you see one of those at a warehouse store or megamart, check out the nutritional label for a minute. Those "cupcakes" are actually *two* servings. What that means is you need to look at the calorie count, the fat, the sugar, and all the other stuff you'd normally like to ignore—then double it. Now, I'm not saying our cupcakes are good for you—they absolutely are not. But we firmly stand by our belief that dessert should be one insanely indulgent serving, and if you want more than one (like I always do), that's up to you. We're not about fine print or deceiving people—we have far too much respect for our customers to do that.

We also don't make those giant "big top" cupcakes because when you make a gigantic cupcake, it's called a fucking cake.

PASTRY BRUSH

In the past few years manufacturers have come out with silicone brushes that are pretty nice for working with sugar: You don't have to worry about losing bristles and having them end up in your food; they clean easily in the dishwasher; they stand up to high heat. We're big fans of the ones OXO makes.

PASTRY BAG AND TIPS

We pipe all our buttercream because piping makes it exponentially easier for us, not to mention that it makes the cupcakes all sexified. We also use disposable piping bags that you can pick up either online or at a cake decorating store—those cloth ones are a *massive* pain in the ass to clean, especially if you don't have a washing machine or dishwasher.

I'm sure many of you are familiar with the trick of using a zip-top bag to pipe, but we've always found this technique extremely awkward. If you're going to go through all that trouble, you're better off just buying a pack of the disposable bags, because each one will probably run you less than fifty cents and save you a whole lot of headaches.

We use two different styles of tips: a plain, wide open pastry tip and a fluted open star tip (#8, if you want to be twinsies with us!). We use the plain tip for any cupcake that we're dipping in chocolate fudge, because that tip gives the cupcake a nice flat surface area for the coating to cling to, and the fudge looks silky smooth and gorgeous once it sets.

For the rest, we use a fluted tip for a good reason. Many of our cupcakes have a liquid component on top, like a fruit compote, or a sauce like caramel or ganache. The ridges made by the fluted tip not only create little nooks and crannies for these toppings to stick to, but they also act like chutes so that all the extra runny liquid flows down into the cake rather than dripping off onto the counter. This enhances the flavor and creates a subtle textural contrast in some parts of the cake that we really love—sometimes soft, sometimes sticky, sometimes gooey. A pastry chef I once worked with told me that it's the tiny, barely noticeable touches that make the difference between an excellent dish and a brilliant one. Whenever we see a moment we can add just a little something extra, we grab it.

WOODEN SPOONS
Good for stirring things!

TASTING SPOONS
This one is going to throw you a bit, so I'm going to make sure I mention it several more times in this book: You need to taste things as you go. Yes, this is baking, and things are supposed to be precise. *However*, all ingredients are not equal. You could have two identical-looking strawberries in your hands and while one could be sweet and succulent and feel like everything that's wonderful about summer in one glorious bite, the other one could taste like a whole lot of nothing. Plus, plenty of flavorings come down to personal taste. Me, I like my salted caramels *salty*, my ghost pepper—peach compote *spicy*, my cranberry compotes tart to the point where you suck your cheeks in so hard that your head turns inside out. But I'm not everyone. At points in the book you will be instructed to taste while you slowly add sugar, extracts, spices, etc. You can always add more if you'd like, but you can't easily fix things if you go overboard.

FORK
For stabbing. Cupcakes and pastry dough, not people. We haven't written that type of book (yet).

Professionally this is called "docking," but that doesn't sound as fun as "stabbing," so that's the terminology we use (see page 13 for photographs).

BAKING SHEETS

Buy baking sheets that are 13 × 18 inches with a 1-inch lip. Shiny silver metal, no color coating. Even better if you buy one that can fit a wire cooling rack on it.

COOLING RACK

Not just for cooling as the name implies! We line a baking sheet with aluminum foil or plastic wrap, put the cooling rack on top, and put our cupcakes on top before soaking them with syrup or liquid. This way the counter doesn't get messy, the bottoms don't sit in the liquid, and the paper liners don't get all soggy and messy. And easy cleanup to boot! *Brilliance!*

WHISK

Get an OXO 11-inch balloon whisk. Most of the times we use a whisk, timing is of the essence, meaning we're going fast and we're going hard. The padding on the OXO will make sure it's not too uncomfortable, nor will the whisk go flying out of your hands and stab anyone in the eye. You never really live down a nickname like "Ol' Whisk Face."

MICROWAVE

In our opinion, this is the best, and safest, way to melt chocolate. We use our microwave to melt butter, soften ganaches and jams, heat up liquids—it's completely indispensable in the Robicelli's kitchen. If you don't own a microwave, that means that somehow this book has traveled through time and you are reading it in 1938. If that is the case, we will need you to go back to the bookstore where you found this, buy every copy of Action Comics #1 they have, then bury them in an airtight trunk at the corner of 21st Street and 4th Avenue in Brooklyn. In exchange, leave a note and we'll name a cupcake after you!

NONSTICK COOKING MATS/PARCHMENT PAPER

Nonstick mats are fantastic for making candy at home, but not essential. Professionally, we line everything with parchment paper, but in the professional kitchen we get it delivered in giant flat sheets. If you're buying parchment at the supermarket, it's going to come in a roll, then when you try to line a pan or lay it flat, it's going to roll back up on you. It's incredibly, incredibly stupid. If you're going to use it, make sure you roll it tightly the *opposite* way before you try to use it, then make it stick to your pan or counter with a spritz of cooking spray. (Don't ask me how long it took me to figure that one out.)

FOOD PROCESSOR

Not essential for *everything,* but there are recipes in this book that you may not be able to easily execute without a food processor. Again, read through every recipe from start to finish before you go buy ingredients—wouldn't want anyone to get stuck.

Allison says: *Easy way to make holes in your cupcakes so you can fill them: just push a regular pastry tip about two thirds of the way through the cupcake, twist, and remove. Reserve cake scraps in a plastic bag to use as bribe material for your children/spouse/roommate. (Please reference the works of B. F. Skinner for other ways you can use the items in this book to trick people into doing your bidding!)*

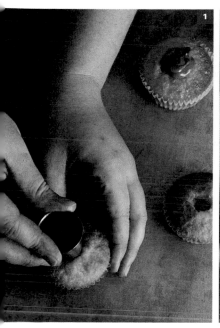

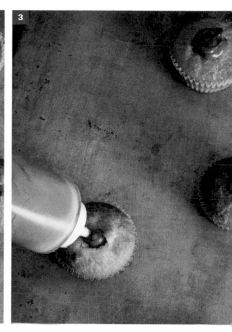

SQUEEZE BOTTLE

These are cheap—you can find them at any dollar store marketed as containers for mustard and barbecue sauce. They make filling cupcakes with jam or custard supereasy. All you need to do is use a pair of scissors to cut the nozzle down a bit so it ends up a tad wider. You can also store leftover caramel, butterscotch, wine reductions, or any of the other dessert sauces in these bottles, then keep them in the fridge so you can drizzle the toppings onto fruit salads or ice cream. Just make sure you label bottles so no one ends up putting salted caramel all over a hot dog (this means *you*, Matt).

INGREDIENTS
BUTTER

If you thought "butter is butter," you are SO STUPID. There is a *tremendous* amount you need to know about butter. From this point forward, you'll classify your life into "before and after I learned all that crap about butter." Buckle up, folks, and prepare to have your minds blown!

Contrary to popular belief, butter is not just a solid block of fat. What most of us use on a daily basis is about 80 percent fat, 19 percent water, and 1 percent milk protein solids. Different types of butter, different proportions. Does this matter in the context of this book? Most of the time, yes. You go screwing around with butter, everything can go horribly wrong—you feed subpar cupcakes to your friends and you just *know* what judgmental assholes they can be. So let's review.

Plain Ol' Butter

This is the stuff you find sold as sticks in the market, and because it's super readily available, it's what we use in this book. Available in salted and unsalted, the variety we always use when we bake is unsalted. Because *we* get to say how much seasoning goes into our food, not *you*—you got that, butter!

Whipped Butter

This is butter that's been pumped full of nitrogen gas, thereby making it easily spreadable at room temperature. *Do not use this for baking.* This is fine to use for sautéing, and personally I like tossing a spoonful of this with some kosher salt on top of nuts fresh out of the oven because it melts quickly. Just know that exact measurements don't apply to this product, so if you're using this for anything, use your best judgment.

Cultured/European Butter

If you're trying to make a go of being one of those people who's a totally insufferable asshole, this is the only butter you should ever use. Every time you're at a restaurant and the waiter sets down the bread basket, I want you to wave away his paltry little butter dish and say just loudly enough for other diners to hear: "Oh no, we won't be needing that! We eat only *European* butter. Once you've tried it, it's impossible to go back to this flavorless, pedestrian stuff." Then you can sit back contented, knowing that everyone around you is totally impressed that you are so fucking important that even average butter is beneath you.

If you're not trying to be an insufferable asshole . . . I'd still pick up this butter, because, honestly, it really is better than the American stuff. Back in olden times when farms (and yields) were considerably smaller, cream was collected from milk throughout the week and left to sit until there was enough to churn into butter. Over the course of a few days the cream would begin to ferment, imparting a more complicated flavor. Nowadays, European butter is made by adding cultures to the cream before the churning process. Not only does it taste better, but it also has a slightly higher butterfat content than the usual stuff you find in the supermarket.

In this book, we don't call for using European butter for two reasons: first, it's still not the most widely available product, and second, it's more expensive than American butter, and *God forbid* anyone ever runs a sale on the stuff. If, however, you don't mind ponying up the cash and want to try using it in our buttercream, we certainly wouldn't dissuade you.

Clarified Butter/Ghee

This is pretty much pure butterfat, butter with all the water and milk solids removed. The milk solids are what's responsible for butter's notoriously low smoke point (aka the temperature at which a fat burns). By clarifying butter first, we can sauté fruit, nuts, and other things without worrying the butter will burn before the food is done. We use this only for stove-top cooking, never for baking.

Matt says: *You can buy clarified butter, or you can make it the old-fashioned way by slowly melting butter over low heat, bubbling until the water evaporates, and skimming the milk solids that foam up at the top. Or you can do it the quick way: Melt the butter, put it into a plastic container, and pop it into the refrigerator until it resolidifies. Pop out all the butterfat that rose to the top, then pour out all the water and milk solids that sank to the bottom.*

Shit That's Not Actually Butter

"Buttery spread," "margarine," "I Can Totally Believe It's Not Butter But I'm Living a Lie!"—don't even think about using these in any manner with our recipes. Fat contents, ingredients—all completely different from butter, all won't behave the same in a recipe. You can play around with them all you want—we can't stop you—but straight substituting won't work. If you're looking for a way to make a healthy, low-fat dessert, try eating a peach. Those are delicious.

NATURE HATES US AND DOESN'T WANT US TO HAVE NICE THINGS

This does not refer just to my hair, which becomes a crime against nature once the humidity hits 30 percent. Butter and sugar, aka the two things that pretty much make up buttercream, *hate* the heat, *hate* the humidity. Sugar is hygroscopic, so it's going to soak up all the water that's floating around in the air on a humid day. Butter is going to get soft, and because it's not 100 percent pure fat, the water is going to begin to separate out of it. During most of the year we avoid this by adding xanthan and/or guar gum to our buttercream to keep it stable, and by storing cake in a refrigerated case.

However, maybe you live in the deep south, or you have to make cupcakes for an outdoor wedding in August. You've got a few options there:

1. Stick to American frosting: Not our favorite, but more stable because it's more sugar than fat, *and* it uses powdered sugar, which contains cornstarch, and that will help keep everything together.

2. Shortening: We really don't like to use shortening when we don't have to, but it's completely solid at room temperature, which helps make buttercream stable. Because it doesn't contain the water that butter does, it has a very waxy texture, so don't just go swapping all the butter out for it—we wouldn't go over 10 percent shortening replacement. Also, make sure you add it before the butter, giving it ample time to thoroughly blend well with the other ingredients.

Matt says: *You may have heard that refrigerating cakes dries them out—not always true. We designed all our cake recipes to be made with liquid fat—either oil or melted butter. This helps coat the starches in the flour, keeping our cakes moister and allowing them to be refrigerated/frozen without any negative effects. This "baked fresh daily" stuff you see in a lot of places is a gimmick: That hard rule applies only to bread and yeast-risen doughs. Otherwise, how would people make those giant wedding cakes "day of"?*

In the past few years there have been some decent organic butter-flavored shortenings finding their way into the market—both Spectrum Naturals and Earth Balance make good ones. However, almost all shortenings contain palm oil, controversial for environmental and human rights factors. I'm not here to preach about it—you can go research it on your own and make your own decisions. If you'd rather not use it for ethical reasons, there's always:

3. Coconut oil: All natural, solid at room temperature, and possibly really good for you, depending on what the talk shows are saying this week. Downside to this is that coconut oil has a very distinct flavor, so use it in buttercreams where there are other strong flavorings (such as in our Butterbrew, page 121). And again, don't replace more than 10 percent of the butter.

If the humidity is *really* bad, you probably want to skip baking all together, not just because standing next to a hot oven in the middle of the summer with 100 percent humidity is pretty much the worse hell we can imagine (we do it for a living—we know from experience). Your cakes will bake differently, your candies won't set, and your flour will get gummy. We can't stop you from baking if you're all gung ho for it, but be prepared to not have perfect results. It's not you—it's the weather. Don't feel bad.

Everyone sufficiently amped from learning about all the different types of butter? *Good!* Now let's learn about all the different types of sugar. This shit just doesn't end!

SUGAR

I could easily write an entirely separate book about the chemical compositions of different sugars, how they form molecular bonds and crystallize and find other ways to make my job difficult and ruin my life. In fact, you can argue that half of pastry making is just trying to control the wild beast that is sugar, coaxing and manipulating it to do your bidding. After centuries of turmoil, the human race has found techniques and tricks to make this easier, as we have the advantage of having both brains and opposable thumbs. Not feeling so high and mighty anymore, are you now, sugar?

There are three different major sugars we deal with in pastry making: sucrose, glucose, and fructose. We've spent years studying them and their reactions so you don't have to. Here's a quick rundown:

Granulated Sugar

Plain old white sugar, aka sucrose. It's been heavily processed, had all its natural molasses removed, and regardless of what the surgeon general might say, it's what makes life worth living. We use this in our cakes, our buttercream, and pretty much everything.

Brown Sugar

Like granulated sugar, but without all the molasses removed during processing. Molasses makes the sugar slightly acidic, so it's not interchangeable with regular sugar in baking because it will throw off all your leavening. We use unpacked light brown sugar in just about everything, so use that in any baked recipes. However, feel free to use dark in stove-top recipes like our butterscotch if you want more intense flavor.

Powdered Sugar

We call this 10X in the business because according to the box, this sugar is processed ten times to become so fine that it turns into a powder. About 3 percent of it is cornstarch, which keeps it from caking. This is the main component of most "American" buttercreams, which is what we at Robicelli's call "frosting."

Matt says: *In our eyes, to be a buttercream, your main component needs to be butter.*

Demerera Sugar

Aka turbinado or raw sugar. These are large crystals that haven't had their surface molasses washed off. Not to be used for baking sugar in this book, though we'll occasionally use them for sprinkling on top of cupcakes, like a finishing salt (more on finishing salt later. Bet you can't wait!).

Corn Syrup

Before you go jumping down our throats, know that the corn syrup you buy at the supermarket (and that we use) is not the evil high-fructose corn syrup that is the number-one threat to the future of our nation. Corn syrup is really glucose syrup, and glucose is one of the building blocks of regular sugar (sucrose). Without going into too much scientific detail (although I *really* want to), corn syrup aids in any instance when you're melting table sugar because it inhibits crystallization. HFCS is a totally different industrial-use product that's made in a lab; it has nothing to do with the stuff you're buying or using in this book. So you can chill out about it and rationalize that because there's no HFCS, this is all actually health food!

Molasses
One hundred percent pure sugarcane juice, without anything removed. We use Grandma's Original, which is minimally processed. As molasses is further processed, it loses much of its sweetness, eventually becoming blackstrap. Don't use that stuff.

Maple Syrup
I'm still shocked at how many people don't realize that the majority of what we are buying in the supermarket is *not*, in fact, maple syrup. Seriously, go check your pantry right now. What you've been using on your frozen waffles is pancake or table syrup, which is just high-fructose corn syrup with some artificial color and flavoring added. Of course, we don't use the stuff, opting instead for the more expensive, but far more delicious, pure maple syrup.

There are two types of syrup we use: Grade A is the top of the line and most expensive—when we are pouring syrup straight on top of our cupcakes, this is what we use. For baking or cooking, we use the darker and more intensely flavored grade B, which also has the benefit of being cheaper.

Honey
Chemically, honey is very similar to molasses. There are tons of different honeys available, the names of which refer not to the final flavor, but to the type of pollen the bees ate. We cook with classic clover honey, because it's the most popular variety and the taste everyone seems to love. You can use what you like, or what's on sale. Totally up to you.

Sugar Substitute
You can replace all the sugar in our cake recipes with sugar substitute if you want to eat a lower calorie cake *and* give yourself horrible diarrhea!

FLOUR
Use all-purpose flour for everything. Yes, there's cake flour and bread flour, southern White Lily flour, and blah, blah, blah. There's science and valid reasons why you can use each, but I'm choosing to keep this short and sweet because after all that butter and sugar business, I'm worried I'm just going to bore you to death and you'll all start

burning these books for fuel. Maybe I'll hook up with Ken Burns one day and we'll do an eight-part documentary on flour gluten; but, until then, we'll settle on the fact that everyone can find unbleached all-purpose flour in any supermarket, and we don't need to be driving everyone completely nuts. Know what? Let's just make a blanket statement to keep this easy for me here on out. Matt, can you take this one for me?

Matt says: *Use exactly the ingredients we specify in these recipes, and don't try to get creative with substituting different types of anything. You think you're fancy or something and the rules don't apply to you? Well, where the hell is your cookbook, buddy?*

Well done, Matt. Moving on . . .

Almond/Pecan/Etc. Flour

Commercial nut flours have absolutely no flour in them—they're actually just nuts ground superfine to resemble flour, then laid out flat and dried so the natural oils evaporate. When we grind our own nut flours, we add a few tablespoons of flour to absorb those oils, then aerate in a sieve. More on that later.

LEAVENING

Leavening comes down to two pillars of third-grade science: acids and bases. Remember making baking soda volcanoes? Same shit. When acids and bases react with each other, they create carbon dioxide, which is what makes it rise. Baking soda is pure alkali, and we use it in recipes where there's some acid to react with (like cocoa, buttermilk, honey, or brown sugar). Baking powder is a mixture of baking soda and cream of tartar (acid), and it reacts when it's mixed with a liquid. By the way, if you haven't made a baking soda volcano since you were a kid, you should get on that. Not only are volcanoes awesome at any age, but using your baking soda will help you test the leavening that's likely been sitting in your cabinet for ages for potency. Yup, it can turn into a dud after a while, and if it does, your cakes will fall flat and be ever so sad. :(

XANTHAN/GUAR GUM

They sound scary and toxic and potentially evil, but I swear that they're not. They're both totally natural products that we use to add extra stabilization to our famous French buttercream. Even though French is the best type of buttercream, it's also the least stable. Xanthan always goes in before we put in the sugar because it needs heat to activate, and it helps bind any water from the eggs.

Guar gum is an emulsifier that we use in emergencies if our buttercream "breaks," that is, it loses its emulsion. You'll know this has happened if you look at the buttercream and say, "Well that doesn't look right." Buttercream should look smooth and silky and just like the pictures. You can find both ingredients in the health food section of your supermarket or online.

SALT

Iodized Salt

Aka table salt, it is salt treated with iodine in order to prevent mental retardation and goiter due to iodine deficiency. While we appreciate salt looking out for us like that, we don't use this because it tastes funny.

Kosher Salt

We use this in everything. *Everything.* For baking, stove top, making facial scrubs, secretly dipping each other's toothbush bristles into when someone's not looking, late-night salt fights—you name it. Keep it on hand at all times in your kitchen, no matter what project you're tackling.

Finishing Salt

This is a *huuuuuge* category, but in a nutshell, finishing salt is the expensive stuff you see on the shelf that makes you say, "Ten dollars for *salt*?!?! Are you fucking *kidding* me?!?!" No, they're not kidding you, and yes, you should buy it. This salt isn't the stuff you cook with or sprinkle on top of cheap pizza. This is the stuff you use to *accentuate* amazing foods, like a mind-bendingly perfect rib-eye steak or, in our case, a cupcake that needs a little something to take it from being plain ol' delicious to pants-dropping sexy. Don't wince at the price tag, because with the minuscule amount you'll use at a time, a ten- to twenty-dollar box of salt is likely to last you a year or more. We have a few favorites: Occasionally we use Maldon for its big beautiful flakes, coarse grey salt from France, or a grinder that we fill with large crystals of Mediterranean sea salt.

CHOCOLATE

Chocolate

We use semisweet chocolate in everything because, well, we like it. Besides, it's a crowd-pleaser—not too dark, not too bland, *juuuuust* right. When making our ganaches and other things containing melted chocolate, it's important to use a very good chocolate that you really enjoy eating. Our favorite in the kitchen is made by Callebaut because it's delicious without being too expensive. You can find Callebaut in either blocks or chips at most cake or gourmet shops, or online. Other good brands are Scharffen Berger and Guittard. Please don't use the chocolate chips sold in the supermarket, which are filled with stabilizers to help them keep their shapes, or things labeled "baking chocolate," as they usually taste awful.

White Chocolate

Not technically chocolate at all—white chocolate is actually mostly cocoa butter, with some milk and vanilla mixed in for funzies. White chocolate is the big lying liar pants of the chocolate world. When looking for it in the store, you may find some unscrupulous candy shops trying to sell you "white coating chips," which are *not* white chocolate— they're oil and sugar and I don't know what else. Look at the ingredient label—if cocoa butter isn't the first ingredient, then you're eating a cheap impostor of a big lying liar pants, and that's just shameful, white coating chips. You should want more from your life than that.

Cocoa Powder

There are two types of cocoa: regular and Dutch process. Regular cocoa is acidic, which is why if you have ever tried to make something chocolate flavored by just sprinkling cocoa over it, you've probably ended up making a face like this:

This cocoa is meant for cooking only. Whenever you see a recipe that calls for cocoa powder, such as our chocolate cake recipe, it means plain ol' cocoa.

Dutch process is cocoa that's been treated with an alkali to neutralize its acidity. This is the cocoa you want to use if you're making chocolate buttercream or sprinkling it over something, because it tastes like powdered chocolate. In any place you're using cocoa that isn't being cooked, use Dutch process. Our favorite brand is the sinful Valrhona, which many chefs consider to be the best in the world. We're not ones to disagree with other chefs. They have knives.

Matt says: *Fun fact: It's called Dutch proccess because it was a method of processing invented by the Dutch. Whip that fascinating tidbit out at parties if you want to make sure that absolutely nobody will want to talk to you for the entire night.*

OILS

Canola Oil

This is one of the workhorse oils of the Robicelli's kitchen because it's Canadian, and we fucking *love* Canada. Neither of us has actually even been there, but Canada gave us both hockey and John Candy, and that's enough for us. The name "canola" actually stands for "***Can***adian ***o***il, ***l***ow ***a***cid." Why the convoluted name? Because the oil is made from rapeseed, and no one is buying "rape oil," no matter how many omega-3 fatty acids it contains.

Aside from being excessively polite and having an affinity for Molson, canola oil is also low in saturated fat; nearly flavorless, making it ideal for baking; and has a smoke point of 400°F, making it great for frying.

Grapeseed Oil

At home, we usually bake with grapeseed oil over canola. Grapeseed also has a high smoke point and is relatively neutral tasting, but between the two oils we personally prefer using grapeseed in homemade salad dressings, which is why we always have it on hand as our "house oil." However, this is a cupcake book and we're not making any salad dressings, so do whatever the fuck you want.

Nonstick Cooking Spray

What used to be just oil in a can has gotten *extremely* fancy over the years, so *please* make sure the one you're using is the totally neutral one with absolutely no bells or whistles. No "artificial butter flavor," no "garlic and herb," no "cool ranch"—**Plain**. **Ass**. **Spray**.

We also don't recommend the special "baking" spray that contains microscopic amounts of flour, since aside from baking we also use it for making homemade candies, and with all the work you're going to be putting into that you really don't want something as stupid as the freaking stuff you sprayed the pan with to be the thing that fucks it all up. Grapeseed or canola sprays are flavorless and versatile enough that you'll use them every day and won't let them go rancid in the back of that cabinet you only open once a year. You know the one—it's got a wok and a quesadilla maker and like forty-five bottles of barbecue sauces you've picked up at jam band festivals.

Olive Oil

Olive oil is great on a salad, but not great as an all-around go-to in the pastry kitchen because it has a *very* pronounced flavor that cannot be ignored. We bake with this only in recipes where we intend for that flavor to make a statement, or occasionally to drizzle over the top of a cupcake as a finishing oil (more on that in a bit).

Olive oil is very much like wine in that different regions produce different-flavored oils. Many specialty grocery stores will provide tasting stations that can help you select the right oil for you—my palate leans toward the buttery ones of Tunisia, but then again, I'm a food asshole (this is the proper nonabbreviated form of the word "foodie"). You can buy whatever you like at the market, but please make sure it's extra virgin.

Finishing Oil

Just as we covered in the "salt" portion, sometimes there's stuff just too delicate and fancy to be cooking with. This is the expensive oil you put a little drizzle of over some nice vegetables or, in our case, cupcakes.

OTHER STUFF

Vanilla

Vanilla beans come from orchids, which we can all agree are the prettiest flower ever. And that makes vanilla by proxy the prettiest flavor ever. It is lovely and delicate like a beautiful little ballerina, and you should treat it like the gentle flower it is. Always use pure vanilla extract—never imitation. When making a custard, spring for whole vanilla beans. And when you're done with the beans, dry them out and place them in a bowl with sugar—after a few weeks you'll have "vanilla sugar," which you can use for your coffee or cinnamon toast.

Extracts

Always make sure your flavor extracts state that they're "pure." You don't want to catch anything funny from the slutty ones.

Eggs

Use large eggs, always at room temperature. I credit studying how egg proteins react while being heated as the thing that solidified my love of cooking and made me want to be a professional chef. My three-hundred-page novel *Egg Proteins and Me: An Inappropriately Erotic Coming-of-Age Story* will be available next holiday season.

Milk

Regular whole milk is only 4 percent butterfat, meaning there's a negligible difference between that and 2 percent or skim. We go whole fat, all the goddamn time, because that's what true ballers do.

Coffee

Brew what you like. I can enjoy a fancy cup of Stumptown just as much as anyone, but as a native New Yorker, I also love a cup of Chock Full o'Nuts from a mobile coffee cart. I also drink a tremendous amount of Starbucks because there's a store within fifty feet of my apartment, and the people who work there are *so nice*. Plus if it wasn't for the fact that they served me about six cups of coffee every day for more than a year, this book might never have gotten written. I also probably wouldn't have had these horrible shakes for the past thirteen months.

Sweetened Condensed Milk

This is canned milk that's been boiled with sugar into a thick, almost syrupy milk concentrate. And goddamn is it freaking delicious. We use this to make dulce de leche, our tres leches soak, and certain candies. If you find yourself having any leftovers, it's amazing simply drizzled over some cut-up fruit or stirred into your coffee.

Wine/Hooch

Never, *ever* use cooking wine. I have absolutely no idea what the hell that stuff actually is, but cooking with Windex would probably yield a better product than using that crap. You can buy a decent bottle of wine for less than ten bucks, use a cup or two of it, then drink the rest while you're waiting for everything to bake (although don't buy something *too* expensive). Just don't forget you have things in the oven when you're calling your next-door neighbors to blab what you *really* think of them—because you don't want to bring over dry cupcakes when you're apologizing the next day. That's just insult to injury, folks.

The opposite rule applies to liquor—if you're cooking it, always go for the stuff on the cheaper end of the spectrum. The really good stuff goes down smooth, great for sipping on its own, but when it's in a mix with a bunch of other ingredients and baked, it gets lost. The harshness in the cheaper liquor that makes you work to get it down? That gets mellowed out considerably during baking, and enough of it sticks around to make its presence known in the finished product.

Matt says: *Contrary to popular belief, when you are baking with alcohol, the alcohol does not cook out completely—about 40 percent of it will remain. Does this mean our recipes will get you drunk? Well, you'd have to eat a lot of cupcakes, and even then, the answer is likely no. By the time the booze is mixed with all the other ingredients and divvied up among multiple cupcakes, you're looking at ingesting maybe, at most, a teaspoon of booze, which to begin with was only a small percentage of alcohol, and then on top of that 60 percent of it has been evaporated. So, sorry we're not as much fun as you were hoping.*

Let's say that's not enough for you, and you want to remove as much of the alcohol as you possibly can. Make a mixture that's 1:1 wine/booze to water. Put it in a large sauté pan with as much surface area as possible, and simmer on low for at least one hour until reduced by half. The water, along with the alcohol, will mostly evaporate, though not 100 percent. Also, don't attempt this with any cream-based liqueurs, as they will just curdle.

Peanut Butter/Other Nut Butters

We use a lot of peanut butter here, and our peanut butter buttercream is what one of our fans calls "as close as you can come to seeing God while on this earth." We'll disagree because saying that is horribly sacrilegious, and we ain't going to hell.

We use only natural peanut butters that have no added sweeteners. This way we can control the sugar and salt levels ourselves.

Bacon

Buy the good stuff. If you're going through all the trouble of making cupcakes from scratch, there's no point in putting sad, cheap bacon on top. If you know only bacon from the supermarket, you may not be aware that there's good stuff, but once you've tried it, you'll never be the same. Ask your butcher if he carries it, and ask for it sliced on the thicker side. If you have no choice but to buy from the market, try Boar's Head or an organic brand, thick cut, and no special extra seasonings. If you try to use turkey bacon or another "healthy bacon substitute," then you are totally missing the point of this book and probably should just stab me in the heart because I have obviously FAILED in reaching you.

FRUIT

You may think that real chefs use only fresh fruit, and that's simply not true. While I'd love to be able to have flawless fresh blueberries whenever I want, or August peaches every day of my life, most of the time our favorite fruits are good only a few weeks of the year, and the rest of the time they're giant watery orbs of suckitude. In most of our recipes, we're calling for frozen fruit, because good fruits are out of season more often than they are in season. If, however, you just happen to be making these recipes in that narrow window where said fruit is absolutely perfect, then by God, man, use it! Use it like an old French whore!

Bananas

We use a *ton* of bananas, and while conventional wisdom these days says you need to wait until the bananas are all black on the outside and turned to mush on the inside, we use the regular yellow ones. Really, buying bananas just to let them rot for a few days to bake a cake? Who's got time for that nonsense? Plus, the extra starch in a perfectly ripe yellow banana gives the cake a little more structure and bounce, which come in handy when we're filling our cupcakes with pudding or doing whatever other ridiculous thing we've decided on because we can't leave well enough alone.

Apples

It's really hard for me to pick my favorite apple for baking: I love Empires, Cortland, Winesaps, Granny Smiths. . . . We'll often mix them, depending on what's looking the best that day. Just make sure whatever variety is available to you is a "baking" or "cooking" apple; varieties like Red Delicious are meant for snacking only and disintegrate into a mealy disaster if you try to cook with them.

Pears

Use firm Bosc or Anjou pears for baking; Bartletts are great for eating, but too juicy for baking.

Even though we use varieties of apples and pears especially well suited for baking, they still release a decent amount of liquid when we shred them for cake. That's why before we use them, we drain and press them with a few paper towels and a weighted bowl for at least twenty minutes. This is also how we strain ricotta and sour cream as well.

Pumpkin/Butternut Squash

Most times of the year, all you'll be able to get is pumpkin in a can—and that's okay. But if you'd rather roast your own, don't buy the decorative jack-o'-lantern variety—get sugar pumpkins, which are less stringy and better tasting. Butternut squash is available year-round—if you're buying it whole, it should be rock hard.

To cook your squashes, split them in half and remove the seeds. Place them face down in a baking pan with ¼ inch of water, cover with aluminum foil, and bake at 400°F until the flesh is easily pierced with a knife. Then just cool, scoop out the pulp, mash until smooth, and either freeze it in pint containers or use it immediately.

Peaches

There are a few days of the year where peaches are absolutely so flawless, so sensual, that anyone who's cooking with them is *nuts.* If you find a perfect peach, you just eat it, preferably naked while lying in a field of grass, listening to smooth jazz and looking at rainbows. The rest of the summer you're going to find a lot of "meh" peaches, and these are the type you can cook with. To peel, cut an X in both the top and bottom skin of the peach, blanch the peach in boiling water for 90 seconds, then dunk it in ice water. When the peach is cool, you should be able to peel the skin right off. There is no shame in using frozen peaches, but we're not fond of the ones canned in corn syrup. If canned is your only option, try to buy the ones packed in juice and rinse well before using.

A NOTE ABOUT FOOD COLORING

As we've mentioned, we do not use any food colorings, and you won't find any called for in this book. We don't make cupcakes that look like little baby goats or Angry Birds, we don't use fondant, we don't use any sort of "edible decorations" that make the frosting look like somebody's grandpa. This isn't because we're health nuts or fear chemicals—it's because we think that our national standards for cake have gotten pretty silly.

When we judge the quality of a steak, we want to know about how the fat is marbled, or what breed the cattle was. We go to a restaurant and ask where the chef was trained, where he's traveled, what his influences are, and from where he sources his ingredients. However, when we judge a cake, our highest criteria is "How much does this cake actually look like Chewbacca?" We dye cakes to match our bridesmaids' dresses like they're shoes. We glorify cakes that are covered with petroleum extract and a sheet of a barely edible sugar and glycerin mixture—it could taste like sawdust and anchovy paste for all we know, but as long as it looks crazy on the outside, it's all good.

Personally, I've never craved the taste of a cake with a half cup of red dye 40 in it because it looked "wacky." I've never had the itching to dye a roast chicken blue just because it's my favorite color. I like my mom, but I've never been compelled to make a cupcake that looks like her so I could eat her face.

Our goal when launching Robicelli's was to get people to once again focus on what cupcakes *taste* like, not what they look like. And in the past four years, I actually think people are less shocked by the fact that we invented a cupcake that features fried chicken than they are by the fact we refuse to make red velvet.

Listen, if you want to use food dyes—artificial or natural—go right ahead. It's totally fine with us, really (you can find India Tree natural food dyes online or, even better, ask your local cake supply shop to order it for you). But please, from now on, promise us that you'll start judging the book and not just the cover, that you'll stop being willing to settle for half-assed desserts and eat only things made with a baker's full ass. That you'll stop being hoodwinked into eating cake of questionable virtue, stop buckling to cupcakes that have eyes and appear to be staring directly into your soul, commanding you to eat them. That you'll demand better for yourself because, after all, your life's way too short for you to be eating shitty cupcakes.

SO YOU FUCKED UP YOUR CUPCAKES!

We hope with every fiber of our beings that you make all the recipes in this book, each one is a gigantic success, and your neighborhood thinks the cupcakes are so good that they rename your street after you. We really do.

However, there may come a time where you leave your cupcakes in the oven for a minute too long and they're a bit dry. You underwhip your egg whites and your malted milk balls are less "ball" and more "puddle." The humidity causes your cake batter to look like soup. The peaches you bought were bland. Your sons have gotten buck naked and decorated each other with all of the expensive MAC makeup you treated yourself to for Mother's Day and are now running all over the house destroying your furniture, so you have to drop everything and run after them, and by the time you've gotten them ~~locked in a closet~~ in the bath, you remember that you left cookies in the oven and now they're "extra toasty."

Matt says: *If you burn the bottoms of your cookies, you can try to save them by running them over a Microplane grater and shaving off the burned parts. They might not be the prettiest ever, but they might still have a chance to fulfill their destiny of traveling through your digestive tract!*

It's okay. Really, it is. This isn't a Martha Stewart book. You don't have to be perfect.

Matt and I are professionals, which means only that we've already failed many, many, many times. Enough times to get good enough that we don't fail quite as often. We still have days where the weather messes up our cakes, where buttercreams break, but because we're pros, we know how to fix things on the fly. The more you bake, the more experience you get, the more you learn—well, then you'll eventually be able to do all those things too.

There are cupcakes that are relatively easy for beginners, like the Chocolate Peanut Butter Pretzel (page 102). There're cupcakes that take many hours and lots of different, more advanced techniques, like the Kiwanis (page 163). It's not important that what you make looks exactly like the pictures. What's important is that you try.

To make your life simpler, we've put ●━━◯ next to all our recipes. One ●━━◯ means the recipe is easy, three ●━━◯ is pro-level. And if there's a step you feel like skipping— like not making your own homemade candy for the top, or using store-bought strawberry rhubarb jam instead of our homemade version, go right ahead! Just because we're obsessive perfectionists who like to do things the hard way doesn't mean that saner minds shouldn't be able to make cupcakes too. We've put little "half-assed" suggestions at the end of some of our recipes to help you out and let you know if there are any shortcuts you can take (though, of course, we think the crazy-long and labor-intensive way is always the best way, because *we suffer for our art*).

However, let's say you make some mistakes you can't live with, but still don't want to toss all that hard work in the trash, or you have company coming over in a matter of minutes and they're expecting dessert. Well, we've got a secret that will save the day: Make a goddamn trifle!

Trifle is a traditional English dessert that has roots in the medieval German word "*Trüffel,*" which roughly translates to "I *totally* fucked up this cake and no one can ever know." You can also make a French "parfait," which is pretty much doing the same thing in fancy-ass wineglasses. Just layer cake, pudding or compote (especially if the cake is dry), toppings, buttercream, then repeat over and over until you reach the top. It will look beautiful, taste wonderful, and is easy to curl up with on the couch and eat with a giant wooden spoon.

 Matt says:
Don't forget that just as you can make some cupcakes without certain components, you can also make those components without making cupcakes. Why not make yourself some malted milk balls (see page 169) for snacking, apple butter (see page 211) for your morning toast, fig balsamic gastrique (see page 131) to go with dinner, or candied bacon (see page 65) to go with fucking __everything?__

SO YOU HAVE EXTRA STUFF

It's rare that you make a recipe with three or four components and you find you have *exactly* the right amount of custard, *exactly* the right amount of buttercream, *exactly* 3.5 pieces of a pecan to place on top of each cupcake. Or maybe you don't like a ton of buttercream on your cupcakes and find yourself with an extra pint.

Just about every "extra" in this book that goes into these cupcakes can be made on its own for other culinary uses, or mixed and matched to make new flavors. To help you out, we've added notes at the end of some recipes with ideas about how you can use up specific extra stuff, or what you can do with some of the components if you just feel like making them on your own. Here are some of our general favorite things to do when we have extra anything:

BUTTERCREAM

Put it in a freezer bag, squeeze the air out, seal, and freeze for up to four months. Next time you want to whip up a small cake, let the buttercream thaw on the countertop until room temperature, then beat it in a mixer on high until fluffy. Alternately, you can freeze it in ice cube trays and use it as "flavored butter" the next time you're making pancakes or waffles for brunch.

PUDDING

We just eat this. We've tried doing other things with it, like parfaits with fresh fruit, but I always end up eating the entire thing out of the storage container. If you can resist long enough to come up with a new use, let us know!

FRUIT COMPOTES

Pour on top of ice cream or stir into oatmeal or yogurt.

CANDIED BACON
Fold it into pancake batter.

BUTTERSCOTCH/CARAMEL/CHOCOLATE SAUCE
Store in the refrigerator in jars and drizzle it on shortbread cookies, ice cream, fresh fruit, fingers.

CUPCAKE TEMPERATURE

The best way to serve cupcakes is at room temperature. Problem with that is that French buttercream needs to set up and be stored in the refrigerator so it doesn't melt before serving. There's no blanket time to take them out of the refrigerator to bring them to room temperature—it depends on how hot it is outside. If you can easily poke your finger into the buttercream but it isn't too soft or melting, the cupcakes are probably ready to serve.

A NOTE ABOUT YIELDS

All the recipes in this book make about 24 cupcakes. I know that's a lot, and I'm sorry. With the amount of stuff we need to do with the fancy-ass buttercream and all the toppings and fillings and blah blah blah, 24 is pretty much the smallest we can scale them. If you don't have enough pans to bake all at once, executing them in batches is certainly fine—just make sure you wait a few minutes for the pans to cool before you go swapping out cupcakes and potentially searing your precious little fingers with hot metal.

In the event you absolutely don't want to make all 24 at a clip, bake off as many as you please, then freeze the remaining batter and buttercream for another time. That's right, just like Ted Williams, cupcakes can also be frozen in suspended animation! Place the batter in a freezer bag and squeeze out all the air. Do the same for the buttercream. When you want to bake, thaw both in the refrigerator, scoop the batter into pans and bake as originally directed, adding an addtional minute or two. Let the buttercream sit out on the counter while the cupcakes are baking, then hop back into the recipe like you never left.

BUTTERCREAM PROS AND CONS
FRENCH BUTTERCREAM
Pros:
Delicious. Like really, really, *really* fucking delicious. Like "Oh my God, I didn't know anything could actually taste that good" delicious.

Cons:

Need a stand mixer to make this. Totally nonnegotiable for both safety reasons (molten sugar) and practical reasons (the motor of a hand mixer isn't strong enough).

Not very stable; needs refrigeration for storage if not served on a day that's 68°F or less.

Requires more advanced baking skills.

Takes a lot of time.

AMERICAN FROSTING

Pros:

Cheaper.

Faster.

Thanks to the large amounts of powdered sugar in it (and the cornstarch in that sugar), very stable at room temperature and warmer climates.

No special equipment.

Any schmuck can make it.

Cons:

Not what we use, and don't you want to be twinsies with us?

Did we mention how fucking *ridiculously good* French buttercream is? We've tinkered with the American stuff to make it pretty damn delicious, but nothing comes close to the French stuff.

THERE ARE TOO MANY DAMN CUPCAKES IN THIS HOUSE, AND I'M TERRIFIED I MAY EAT THEM ALL

Many people don't realize that cupcakes freeze beautifully, which is essential in following the Robicelli's law of emergency cake (see page 231). They may not look as pretty coming out of the freezer as they did going in, but when you're eating cupcakes at 2:00 a.m. while listening to Air Supply songs and drinking red wine, do you really care?

Place the cupcakes on a plate and place them in the freezer until firm, about 20 minutes. Place them in a freezer bag, push out as much air as you can, seal, and return them to the freezer until you need them. You can also place them in an airtight container, but that takes up a bit more room, and if you're like us, your freezer is a perpetual disaster. You don't want to have to dig through everything and get clocked in the face by a frozen pork roast just to get to your special box of cupcakes buried all the way in the back. *But* they'll look pretty this way, so it's a good method if you're a fussy little princess.

FRENCH BUTTERCREAM

1. This is it-the star of the show, the main event, the most important part of our cupcakes-buttercream!

As this is French buttercream, this is *tres, tres serious*. You will pay attention, follow along, and execute these directions! *C'est sérieux!*

2. You need:

1 cup water

2 cups sugar

2 tbsp corn syrup

1/4 tsp cream of tartar

5 egg yolks

1 whole egg

1/8 tsp xanthan gum

1+1/2 lbs cold butter preferably European

Now let's do this! <u>Oeil du tigré, bitchés!</u>

3. In a heavy nonreactive saucepan, add water, then add sugar, corn syrup, and cream of tartar. The last two help keep the sugar from crystalizing.

← Candy thermometer. Nonnegotiable!

Put the pot on high heat. It's going to be there for a while. Be patient and keep your eye on it. Don't go walking away and watching TV or something.

4. Put the yolks and eggs in a <u>stand mixer</u> with the whisk attachment and turn to high. Just let it go! Eggs will triple in volume and go to the "ribbons" stage. You can't overwhip!

~Whee!

5. Wait on the sugar-looking for 235°F, aka "soft ball." When it happens, be ready to move quickly. Turn off the mixer and add the xanthan gum, turn back up to medium.

Remove the thermometer from the hot sugar. Lift with *two hands*. Rest the lip of the saucepan on the edge of the mixer bowl.

6. Slowly tilt and pour the sugar in a slooooow steady stream down the side of the bowl. Don't go too fast! If you do there will be chunks of scrambled eggs in your buttercream.

Story: Allison Robicelli Art: Abby Denson

7 Once the sugar is all in, turn the mixer to high. Beat until cool. Gauge this by putting the inside of your wrist to the outside of the bowl. It's more accurate than your hands. Switch out the whisk for the paddle. Next we're adding the butter. It's too heavy for the whisk and you'll end up breaking your stand mixer if you stay with the whisk.

8 Start cutting the butter into *thin pieces*—you could shave it with a cheese slicer if you'd like. Add the butter piece by piece—pain in the derriere, yes, but we're making an emulsion

9 See, if you dump all the butter in at once, the butter and eggs will never combine properly, and you'll have a "broken" buttercream. You'll be able to identify this easily—it'll be a chunky, watery, hot mess.
If your buttercream does break, you can fix it!

 Turn to medium high, then add a little more butter, piece by piece, until fixed.

Or try adding a little guar gum! This is very strong, so add a pinch and beat for a minute, then check.

10 Once your butter is added, turn the mixer to medium high to add some air—10, 20 seconds at most. *Quelle magnifique!* It should be fluffy and make you want to eat it with your fingers.

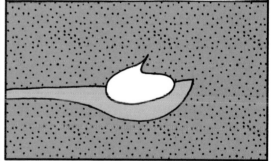

11 Once you have your base, there are so many ways to flavor it!

Coffee powder!
Vanilla beans!
Dutch cocoa!
Peanut butter!
Caramel!   Ham!
Ok, maybe not ham. Party pooper.

12 Congratulations! You did it! You made French buttercream! You are a god among men!

~FIN~

No one knows for certain when buttercream was invented, but we're pretty sure the French would take credit for it. Luxurious, decadent, um . . . buttery . . . it is truly one of life's most sinful indulgences and worth every painstaking, labor-intensive step it takes to make it the right way. But here in America, we don't have the time to be making French buttercream! We have beer to drink and football to watch! We can make buttercream stronger, faster, harder!

AMERICAN FROSTING

Because this is AMERICA, motherfuckers! We do buttercream on our own fucking terms!

1 You need:

3 sticks unsalted butter

2 cups 10x powdered sugar

8 ounces mascarpone cheese

1/4 cup heavy cream

Whoa! Whoah! What's with this fancy pants I-Tie cheese?

It tastes like solid cream and makes it taste less like pure sugar. Too patriotic for it? Try more butter.

2 Throw everything that isn't sugar into the bowl.

KID ROCK

TO THE EXTREME!!!!!

3 Beat the fuck out of that shit!!!

Beat it like we beat the Russians in ROCKY IV!

4 When that shit's fluffy, start adding your sugar a 1/4 cup at a time, eating a bit in between. Do it on low to keep the sugar from flying out of the bowl and getting on your primo duds. Can't let buttercream land a punch in this situash.

Story: Allison Robicelli Art: Abby Denson

5 Once it's all in, crank that shit and show it who's boss! Get it all fluffy like, then back off a minute to peep the action in the bowl. Is it too thick and mocking you?

6 Whip some cream in bit by bit to make it your bitch! That should do. It's good and spreadable. You can stop and know you've done your country proud.

7 That's all! Use this as directed, and frost your cupcakes with frosting so good Abraham Lincoln would gladly rise from the dead to high five you and go to town on your cupcakes. Because goddamn-this shit tastes like freedom . . .

. . . and freedom is delicious.

A Love Letter
to True Love

I never thought I'd ever fall in love. Torrid affairs? Casual flings? That was more my speed. But love? That was unforgivable. Love was for the weak, the spineless. Love was for girls who'd stand in the drugstore checkout, desperately ravaging magazines with headlines like:

"twelve surefire (non-stalkerish) ways to *MAKE HIM YOURS!*"
"heeeey fatty fatty fat fat! try this crash diet or *DIE ALONE!*"
"can't get a date? bleach your butthole and be *SEXY!*"

I grew up with Sally Ride and She-Ra. I was told that girls could be anything they wanted to be when they grew up. Then, suddenly, I felt I was expected to find the person who would "complete me," and I would put the rest of my aspirations on the back burner. I'd seen it a thousand times—the girl who dreams of being a senator or intergalactic crime-fighting ballerina, then she meets "the other half of her soul," and even though she swears to herself it will never happen to her, it happens anyway. She spends a few years chasing her dreams, then starts to get more and more interested in buying shit from Pottery Barn, and next thing you know she's popping out babies left and right. Slowly she ends up spending the rest of her life doing nothing but watching TV and shuttling her kids to peewee soccer games. I fucking *hate* soccer, and no man would ever force me into a life where I had to both watch and feign interest in it every week, no matter how hot and/or incredible in the sack he was.

Why did I need someone else to "complete" me? What was so goddamn wrong with me that I couldn't be a whole person myself? I wasn't going to surrender a life of potential adventure and general awesomeness to "some guy" and sit around waiting for real life to show up and crush all my dreams. I would be a renegade who answered to no one.

Like Mr. T, but with a nice rack. And white.

My parents, my friends—nobody got it. They thought I was insane and lonely and would die without love. Were they kidding? I had *plenty* of love in my life. I loved hardcore music, the New York Rangers, Monty Python, boneless Buffalo wings, Steve Martin, Calvin and Hobbes, crossword puzzles, the Chrysler building, musical theater, curling, *Caddyshack,* comfortable shoes, pudding, booze (lots of it), the classic sitcoms of the late 1980s, Scott Baio, God, America, and my cats (if they were speaking to me that day). These things alone provided a very fulfilling and quite well-rounded life. But above and beyond all this was my one great love, the one that no man could replace, and what one guy I dated said would be the thing to doom me to a lifetime of eternal loneliness: my job.

Cooking is not the sexy party that TV chefs make it out to be. It is hard, it is stinky, you sometimes cut off parts of your flesh that you were particularly attached to. Regardless, if it's your true calling, it's as addictive as any drug—particularly apt as so many of us in the industry are/were self-medicators. I loved it with my entire being because I could learn something new every day for the rest of my life, and still never know everything.

Cooking was also the perfect job for people like me—people who felt they didn't know where they belonged, felt disconnected from it all. Yet somehow working in tight quarters in blazing heat, burning and cutting ourselves to feed total strangers, keeping hours that prevented us from coexisting with the rest of society, operating high on adrenaline every single goddamn night—this wasn't a job to us, it was a lifestyle, a brotherhood. A sacred society with a profound mystical understanding shared only by those of us who worked late at night for almost no money, the mysterious men (and women) behind the curtain who kept New York City the most exciting place to eat in America. We were societal outcasts like pirates, but with 60 percent less gonorrhea.

Not a single guy I ever dated appreciated being second fiddle to the industry. There were no dates on Friday or Saturday nights, no romantic weekends out of town—just short phone calls on my cigarette breaks; quick rolls in the hay when I got home from work well past midnight, reeking of whatever I'd cooked that night (who needs to bleach your butthole when you smell like french fries and trout?), followed by passing the fuck out. Busy seasons would come, and I'd disappear for weeks at a time. The business, and my ambition, always came first.

Then Easter Sunday, 2005, happened. It was 1:00 a.m. I had just gotten off a busy night working the line. I ran to my apartment for a quick cleanup, put on some of my finest "seducin' clothes," slapped a fresh coat of paint on my flawless twenty-four-year-old face, and headed to the bar. There at the door with several of my friends was this giant of a man—six feet six inches tall, broadest shoulders I'd ever seen, red goatee. They

andez**FURNITUR**

A&H **FURNITURE CORP.**

718

95 Print
Brooklyn's the best in printing

Business Cards
Window Decals
Door Hangers
Postcards
Brochures
Graphic Design
Rack Cards
Letterheads

Tickets
Flyers
Caps
Signs
Invoices
Menus
Stickers
Envelopes

CD Inserts
NCR Forms
Banners
Car Decals
Posters
T-Shirts
Book Marks
Direct Mail

Road To Awe

Subway

Subway
The New York City Transit

station

Dominican Style Salon

SU
B
W
A
Y

Brooklyn
Wholesale
Printing

said, "You guys are finally in the same place. Allison, Matt. Matt, Allison. You guys are both chefs! How do you not know each other?"

Chef, eh? Ten bucks says this guy was probably an asshole.

Yeah, I know, two seconds ago I was talking about our sacred kinship and brotherhood and blah, blah, blah, and here I am putting up my dukes. You think the solution to a problem like this is for chefs to just date other chefs, right? *Wrong.* The reason you're in the business in the first place is because you're a fucked-up emotional disaster who's barely competent as a human being. Everyone else working with you? They're even worse. This is why nearly all chefs have a "never date another chef" rule.

Matt says: *Do they occasionally get drunk, have sex, and have awkward social encounters for the rest of their lives? All the fucking time!*

And sure enough, I was right. He was an asshole. Everything I'd say, he'd one-up me. I'd done an apprenticeship; he graduated at the top of his class at the French Culinary Institute. I was a pastry chef at twenty-four; he'd been a pastry chef at twenty-three. I'd cooked for Conan; he'd cooked for Regis. How do you beat cooking for Regis? You can't!

I may have thought he was a jerk, but it was still nice talking to someone who actually liked talking about food and didn't just smile and nod while secretly watching whatever ESPN was airing slightly over my head. By 2:00 a.m., we were tipsy, laughing, and ignoring every other person in the room. We went back to my place and read cookbooks (seriously). We shared an innocent kiss, but then laughed it off—we'd already learned our lessons the hard way and both swore we'd never get mixed up with another chef again. We started writing recipes together, realized we had undeniable chemistry, and talked about maybe opening a business together one day. By 9:00 a.m., I realized this guy wasn't actually an asshole—he'd just had his guard up too.

Then I couldn't stop thinking about him. Not in the business way—in the "tingly in my pants" way.

Shit.

Every night we'd end up on the phone, talking about work, about food, swapping war stories. We'd text all day from our respective kitchens. Still, I kept telling myself over and over, "Al, you don't like this guy. You know better. You and your life are awesome now; don't go falling in love and fucking it all up." No kissing, no touching, no ooey-gooey feelings or any other disgusting lame-ass shit like that.

Then three weeks later I had the type of morning I'd had many times before: waking up with a throbbing headache and the taste of whiskey in my mouth, no recollection of the night before, two hours late for work, completely naked, and with someone in bed with me. I knew the drill—roll over, give them the old "Hey! So yeah, last night was great. . . . Listen, I need to get to work, so you gotta get going, but I swear I'll call" bit, chug a liter of water, and go grovel at my boss's feet.

I rolled over and the person in bed with me was Matt. For the first time ever, despite the fact that I was pretty sure I was going to vomit, I was over-the-moon ecstatic.

Shitshitshitshitshitshitshitshitshit.

This was *not* happening to me! I had dreams and aspirations! I was going to take over New York, maybe work in restaurants around the globe, have adventures, and be perfectly happy being alone. I *liked* being alone. I didn't want anyone else in my little space. What if he started asking me to change, to give up my ambitions? What if I let down my guard and he got to know how fucked up I was inside, how no one could possibly love anyone as damaged as me? Then what? What was the point then?

Well, the funny thing is that when Mr. Right shows up, you don't actually have a choice. I mean, you *do* have choices, but you can almost actively hear fate telling you, "This is the guy. Just shut up, accept it, and keep going." Because when you meet the right guy, you realize how utterly fucking *wrong* you have been about love for your entire life.

It's not about completing *you,* about finding someone better who can patch up all your discrepancies as a human being. It's about you completing something else, about standing on the shoulders of giants (in my case, literally), becoming a part of something bigger than you could have ever been on your own. Alone, we were Matt and Allison—two kids from Brooklyn making their way in food. Together, we became the Robicellis—famous bakers, parents, business partners, husband and wife.

It doesn't feel like angels singing and colors getting brighter. There're no butterflies in your stomach. There's instant ease, immediate comfort. After one hour of talking to Matt, I didn't know this man would be my husband. But I do remember saying to myself, "I want this man to be my best friend." And he is.

Matt says: *And here, we begin our story. It's a long, long, loooooooooong story, and Allison and I are still writing it together every day of our lives. Fortunately for you, this story is also delicious.*

Dom Deluise

The Dom DeLuise is our cannoli-inspired cupcake, which was really a "must" for us for reasons beyond the fact that we're from southwest Brooklyn.

In the weeks after we first met, I told myself the reason I thought about Matt a thousand times a day was because for the first time ever, I had a friend who was as obsessed with food as I was. It absolutely wasn't because we were both madly in love with each other, as every person who knew both of us had already figured out.

I'm not that smart. Sue me.

One day I learned we were both off from work and decided to go out and buy him a bunch of my favorite foods "just because." I showed up at his house with a huge bag of antipasto, a pan of chicken parmigiana, and a box of my favorite dessert—cannoli. We ate nearly everything I brought while hanging out on the couch and watching old episodes of *Full House*. (*How* in God's name did I not realize I was in love with this guy? Al, you are so, so stupid.)

While I was oblivious, Matt wasn't. I'll let him tell you the next part.

Matt says: I didn't actually have a day off—I was taking a sick day because I had a stomach virus, but I didn't have the heart to tell Al that when she showed up. I still ate all the food she brought: the dried sausage, the oil-cured olives, the sharp provolone, the cannolis. I was running upstairs every twenty minutes "to check on the dog," but in reality, I was throwing up.

I knew that I was crazy about Allison the moment I laid eyes on her. But at some point while lying there on the cold tile floor with my head inside a toilet, I realized that this was the woman I wanted to spend the rest of my life with. For one thing, she somehow psychically knew to bring me chicken parmigiana, which is my favorite food of all time. Two, she also had an encyclopedic knowledge of Full House. *And three, never had I been so driven to repeatedly cause myself to violently throw up just to impress a girl.*

Matt's not that smart either.

Pistachio Cake

> **2 cups sugar**
> **¾ cup shelled raw pistachios**
> **10 tablespoons (1¼ sticks) unsalted butter**

4 large eggs

2 large egg whites

1 cup milk

2 teaspoons pure vanilla extract

1 teaspoon kosher salt

1⅓ cups all-purpose flour

2 teaspoons baking powder

Cannoli Buttercream

One recipe French Buttercream (page 32) or American Frosting (page 34)

1 cup ricotta, strained and pressed

½ teaspoon pure vanilla extract

To Finish

¼ cup miniature chocolate chips

¼ cup shelled pistachios, roasted and chopped

¼ cup candied citron or orange zest, finely diced (optional)

PISTACHIO CAKE

Preheat the oven to 350°F. Line cupcake pans with 24 baking cups.

Place the sugar and pistachios in a food processor and process until the pistachios are finely ground. Set aside.

Melt the butter in a microwave at 60 percent power for 1½ to 2 minutes. Keep the butter warm; do not allow it to sit and cool off.

In a stand mixer with the paddle attachment, beat the eggs and egg whites on medium-low speed for 2 minutes until lightly foamy.

Increase the mixer speed to medium-high. Pour the warm butter into the eggs slowly, so that the mixture tempers and the eggs do not scramble. Once the butter is added, reduce the speed to medium-low.

With the mixer running, add the milk, vanilla, and salt. Mix for 1 minute until well combined.

Sift together the flour and baking powder and stir into the pistachio mixture. Add to the batter. Mix on medium until just combined, about 10 seconds. Remove the bowl and paddle from the mixer and use the paddle to scrape the bottom and sides of the bowl, ensuring that everything is well mixed.

Scoop the batter into the prepared baking cups, filling them two thirds of the way.

Bake in the middle of the oven for 20 to 25 minutes, rotating the pan halfway through. The cupcakes are done when the centers spring back when you touch them.

Remove the cupcakes from the oven. Let cool completely.

CANNOLI BUTTERCREAM

For French buttercream (recommended): Prepare the recipe as directed on page 32. Add the pressed ricotta and vanilla and beat well until fully incorporated.

For American frosting: Prepare the recipe as directed on page 34, replacing the mascarpone with the pressed ricotta. Add the vanilla and beat well.

ASSEMBLY

Fill a pastry bag fitted with a plain or fluted tip with cannoli buttercream and pipe onto each pistachio cupcake.

Mix the chocolate chips, roasted pistachios, and candied citrus, if using, in a bowl and sprinkle on top of the cupcakes.

Allison says:
We named this for Dom DeLuise as an homage after he died—he was from our neck of the woods, graduated from McKinley Junior High just like I did, and wrote Eat This . . . : It'll Make You Feel Better, *which is one of my favorite cookbooks of all time. If you don't know who Dom DeLuise is, go rent* History of the World: Part I *immediately. (Also, please don't tell me if you didn't know who he was, because it makes me feel really old.)*

HALF-ASSED CORNER

Skip the citron if you can't find it—which, odds are, you won't be able to unless you live close to an Italian or Middle Eastern specialty store. It's not a make-or-break ingredient.

Tarte Bourdaloue

When we were first dating, we would stay up in bed for hours trying to come up with new interpretations of classic desserts. Bird chile and passion fruit pavlova; Stilton mousse with walnut Florentine; apple, currant, and Brie pot pie. But some classics we knew not to amp up with "bold flavors" because they were sacred. Such is the tarte bourdaloue. This was one of the first desserts Matt and I were both taught to make in our classical pastry training; it is the pride of any French patisserie worth its (artisanal) salt, and *you will treat it with some goddamn respect!* Traditionally, it's a buttery tart crust filled with poached pear and luxurious almond cream. However, no matter how mind blowing the tarte bourdaloue is, almost no one in this country knows what it is.

 French Matt says: You uncultured American swine!

So, in an effort to make this winning flavor combo a bit more popular this side of the pond, we broke tradition and messed with it a little to turn it into a cupcake—I mean, what's more American than cupcakes? Besides bald eagles, of course, but then again, you can't eat those (yet)!

Wine-Poached Pears

2 Bosc or Anjou pears, peeled, cored, and quartered

½ cup granulated sugar

1 cup white wine (pick something delicious, fruity, and not too expensive: ask the clerk at the wine store to help you)

Pear Cake

2 cups of peeled, shredded, drained, and pressed pears (about 2 large cooking pears; see page 26)

1 cup granulated sugar

1 cup brown sugar

1¼ cups canola or grapeseed oil

2¼ cups all-purpose flour, sifted

1 teaspoon baking powder

1 teaspoon baking soda

4 large eggs, beaten

1 teaspoon kosher salt
½ teaspoon cardamom
½ teaspoon freshly grated nutmeg

Roasted Almonds
½ cup whole almonds
½ teaspoon unsalted butter
½ teaspoon kosher salt

Almond Buttercream
One recipe French Buttercream (page 32) or American Frosting (page 34)
1½ teaspoons pure all-natural almond extract

POACHED PEARS

Place the pears and granulated sugar in a medium saucepan. Pour in the wine, then add enough water to cover the pears by at least ½ inch.

Simmer, uncovered, until the pears can be easily pierced with the tip of a knife, but are not mushy, 10 to 15 minutes.

Strain the pears, discarding the liquid, and set aside on a cutting board. Once completely cool, cut the pears into thin slices.

PEAR CAKE

Preheat the oven to 350°F. Line cupcake pans with 24 baking cups.

In a stand mixer with the paddle attachment, combine the pears, granulated sugar, and brown sugar, and mix on medium-low until well combined, about 1 minute.

With the mixer running, slowly pour in the oil. Continue mixing until combined. Stop the mixer, remove the bowl and paddle, and use the paddle to scrape the insides of the bowl, making sure everything is fully incorporated.

Sift together the flour, baking powder, baking soda, salt, cardamom, and nutmeg and add to the batter. Reattach the bowl and paddle to the mixer and mix on medium until just combined, then add the eggs and continue mixing until the batter is homogenous, about 10 to 20 seconds. Remove the bowl and paddle from the mixer and, once again, use the paddle to scrape the bottom and sides of the bowl, ensuring that everything is well mixed.

Scoop the batter into the prepared baking cups, filling them three quarters of the way.

Bake in the middle of the oven for 20 to 25 minutes, rotating the pan halfway through. The cupcakes are done when the centers spring back when you touch them.

Remove the cupcakes from the oven and let cool completely while you make the almonds and buttercream. Leave the oven on.

Matt says: Achtung! *Depending on the kind of pears you use, your cake batter may appear loose and watery. If this happens to you, add another ¼ cup flour, then let the batter sit in the refrigerator for 10 minutes or so to allow it to hydrate a bit before baking.*

ROASTED ALMONDS

Line a baking sheet with aluminum foil. Using a sturdy chef's knife, roughly chop the almonds.

Place in a hot oven until toasted, 5 to 7 minutes.

Remove the sheet from the oven and immediately add the butter and salt. Gather up the corners of the aluminum foil, pinch to seal, then vigorously shake to coat the almonds. Set aside to cool.

ALMOND BUTTERCREAM

Prepare the recipe for French buttercream as directed on page 32 or American frosting on page 34. Add the almond extract and beat well.

ASSEMBLY

Fill a pastry bag fitted with a fluted tip with the almond buttercream and pipe onto each pear cupcake.

Fan a few slices of pear across each cupcake. Sprinkle the chopped almonds on top.

SO YOU HAVE EXTRA . . .

Wine-poached pears
- Chop up and stir into oatmeal.
- Lay atop pancakes or French toast.
- Make a sandwich with Brie and bacon.
- Drop into a glass of prosecco for a fancy brunch cocktail.

Car Bomb

If you don't live in New York, you may not be aware of the evil we call Restaurant Week. It's a week where some of the best restaurants in town offer a prix fixe menu for a steep discount, hoping to inspire return business. I guess if you're a customer, you don't see what's evil about this. For the people who work in the restaurant biz, it is the most *god-awful experience* you are likely to have in your career. We normally spend the entire week doing prep for Saturday night. Restaurant Week is like Saturday night *every single night,* meaning we're working quadruple the hours at quadruple the speed for the same exact pay. We're going without sleep, making careless mistakes that result in trips to the hospital, plating things ages in advance, and trying to figure out how to make smaller portions and cheaper versions of our food look more expensive (oh shit, did I say that out loud?).

Matt and I had been dating for five weeks and practically living together when Restaurant Week hit. Matt was going full throttle, though I managed to escape that torture by taking my "dream job," which had day shifts. The day before it all started, we got a call that Matt's beloved grandfather was on his deathbed. His whole family had been summoned to Iowa, but thanks to Restaurant Week, Matt wouldn't get to go to say good-bye. Because his parents were going for a week, Matt had to stay at their house to take care of their elderly dog. I started my job at 7:00 a.m., but the job wasn't all that I had hoped for; in reality, it was like working in a sweatshop staffed exclusively with assholes (I lasted three weeks).

Restaurant Week finally came to a close, and Matt and I decided to meet up at the bar where we'd first met. We were completely physically, mentally, and emotionally exhausted, something we dealt with the only way we knew how to at twenty-four years old—by getting shitfaced. At some point, we ended up doing a few Car Bombs—a shot that involves layering Jameson whiskey and Baileys Irish cream in a shot glass, then dropping it into a pint of Guinness and chugging it as fast as you can. This story might be the first time in recorded history that anyone made a *good* decision after drinking one or two (or four) of those.

Matt turned to me and blurted out, "This was the worst week of my life. Not because my grandfather is dying, not because I made seven thousand individual apple tarts, not because I had to force-feed liverwust-wrapped pills to an incontinent basset hound. It was because I wasn't with you. And . . . I don't know. I know I want to spend the rest of my life with you. You okay with that?"

Apparently I said yes, because I woke up the following morning in Matt's arms with one of the worst headaches of my life and fuzzy memories of our doing many, *many* more car bombs. I didn't actually want to ask Matt "Did we get engaged last night?" because I would sound either heartless forgetting the moment we decided to spend the rest of our lives together or *really* clingy. I avoided the topic and played it cool until he asked me again later that day. And the next day. And the next day after that. Our wedding was years ago, but he still asks me to marry him at least once a week, maybe more.

So the moral of this story is that if people are telling you that you can't get someone stinking drunk and trap them into marriage, they are *completely* wrong!

Chocolate Guinness Stout Cake

¾ cup cocoa powder

⅔ cup scalding-hot Guinness stout

⅔ cup buttermilk

⅓ cup canola or grapeseed oil

1 large egg

1 large egg yolk

½ teaspoon kosher salt

1⅓ cups all-purpose flour

1¾ cups sugar

¾ teaspoon baking powder

½ teaspoon baking soda

Jameson Whiskey Ganache

½ cup chopped semisweet chocolate

½ cup heavy cream

¼ teaspoon sea salt

¼ cup Jameson whiskey

Baileys Buttercream

One recipe French Buttercream (page 32) or American Frosting (page 34)

¼ cup Baileys Irish cream

⅛ teaspoon guar gum (optional)

CHOCOLATE GUINNESS STOUT CAKE

Preheat the oven to 350°F. Line two cupcake pans with 24 baking cups.

Place the cocoa powder in the bowl of a stand mixer with the paddle attachment and pour the hot Guinness over. Mix on low speed until a thick paste forms and the mixture stops steaming, about 1 minute.

Increase the mixer speed to medium. In a 4-cup measuring cup, combine the buttermilk, canola oil, egg, egg yolk, and salt and mix lightly with a fork, ensuring the yolks are broken. Slowly pour into the bowl.

Stop the mixer, detach the paddle, and scrape the bottom of the bowl well to loosen any caked-on cocoa. Reattach the paddle and turn the mixer to medium, letting it run for 1 minute. Stop the mixer again.

Sift together the flour, sugar, baking powder, and baking soda and add to the batter. Mix on low speed until just combined. Remove the bowl and paddle, and use the paddle to scrape down the sides of the bowl, ensuring everything is mixed.

Matt says: *Guinness will foam up like crazy when you're heating it up. To keep this from happening, add ½ teaspoon of the oil called for in this recipe to the Guinness. It will reduce the surface tension just enough to keep the stout from exploding.*

Scoop the batter into the prepared baking cups, filling them two thirds of the way.

Bake in the middle of the oven for 20 to 25 minutes, rotating the pans halfway through. The cupcakes are done when the centers spring back when you touch them.

Remove the cupcakes from the oven. Let cool completely.

JAMESON WHISKEY GANACHE

Place the chocolate in a bowl and shake the bowl back and forth until the chocolate flattens out on top.

Heat the cream and sea salt in a medium saucepan until it comes to a boil.

Immediately pour the hot cream mixture over the chocolate and allow it to sit for 2 minutes while the chocolate melts. Add the Jameson.

Using a heatproof spatula, stir the cream and chocolate together until completely smooth.

Put a teaspoon of ganache on top of each cupcake and coat the tops using the back of a spoon. Place the cupcakes in the refrigerator to harden, about 15 minutes.

Leave the remainder of the ganache on the counter to use for garnish. The ganache should not be hot to the touch, but still be liquid. If it cools completely and becomes solid, microwave it on 50 percent power in 10-second intervals, stirring between each, until the desired consistency is reached.

BAILEYS BUTTERCREAM

For French buttercream (recommended): Prepare the recipe as directed on page 32. Once the butter is added, add the Baileys and mix on high to combine. Taste for seasoning and add more Baileys, a teaspoon at a time, until boozy enough for you. If the buttercream begins to separate due to the addition of too much liquid, add the guar gum.

For American frosting: Prepare the recipe as directed on page 34, replacing Baileys for the heavy cream. Once combined, taste and add more Baileys according to your preference.

ASSEMBLY

Fill a pastry bag fitted with a plain tip with the Baileys buttercream and pipe onto each chocolate cupcake.

Drizzle more Jameson whiskey ganache on top.

SO YOU HAVE EXTRA . . .

Jameson ganache

- Scoop with a melon baller and roll in Dutch-process cocoa or chopped nuts to make Jameson truffles.
- Reheat in the microwave and dip candied bacon (see page 65) into the warm ganache. Place in the refrigerator on a sheet of wax or parchment paper to set.
- Heat with milk to make Jameson-spiked hot chocolate.

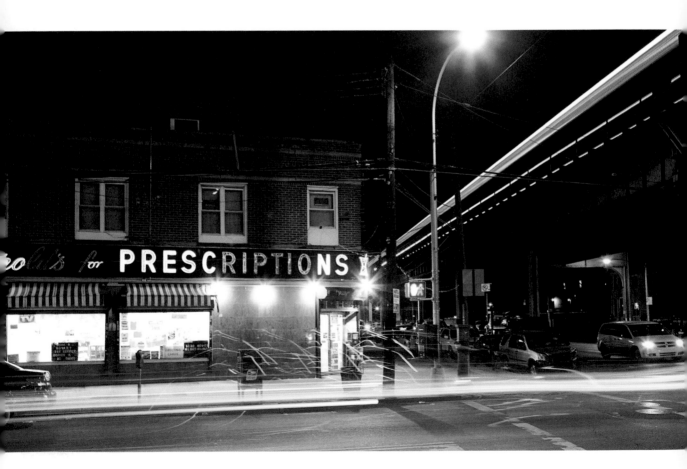

The Iona

You know you're getting old when you can eat cheese for dessert and enjoy it. Me, I can eat cheese for breakfast, lunch, and dinner, and often do. My doctor says I have to stop or I'll be dead by forty-five, but that old man can't stop me from living where I belong—*on the edge.* Matt was the only man I'd ever met who felt the same way. We've snuck fine cheese and accoutrement into movies, concerts, hockey games—anywhere a light nosh is appropriate. We like bringing in the good stuff so everyone around us knows how refined we are as we sit there in our PajamaJeans and Star Wars T-shirts.

One night while we were up in bed brainstorming cupcake flavors, Matt said we should do one based on a classic composed cheese plate: blue cheese, pears, walnuts, and port wine. I loved the idea but thought it wouldn't sell. A few weeks later, we were asked to make cupcakes based on the characters from the John Hughes classic *Pretty in Pink,* and decided this batshit idea would be perfect for Iona—crazy on the outside, yuppie in composition. Little did I know that not only would people buy it, but it would end up selling out three times the first weekend and eventually ended up putting us on the map as "pioneering cupcake auteurs." See the end of the recipe for a note from Matt on cheese selection.

Matt says: *The fact that there are "cupcake auteurs" is still hilarious.*

Port Wine Reduction

1½ cups port wine

Pear Olive Oil Cake

2 cups of peeled, shredded, drained, and pressed Bosc or Anjou pears (about 2 large cooking pears; see page 26)

1 cup granulated sugar

1 cup brown sugar

1 cup extra virgin olive oil

2¼ cups all-purpose flour, sifted

1 teaspoon baking powder

1 teaspoon baking soda

1 teaspoon kosher salt

4 large eggs, beaten

Blue Cheese Buttercream

1 recipe French Buttercream (page 32) or American Frosting (page 34)
½ cup (4 ounces) fine blue cheese
¼ teaspoon guar gum (optional)

Candied Walnuts

1 tablespoon unsalted butter
1 cup walnuts, chopped
⅓ cup sugar
1 teaspoon kosher salt
2 tablespoons water

PORT WINE REDUCTION

In a medium nonreactive saucepan, bring the port wine to a boil. Reduce the heat to medium-low, allowing the port to reduce to a syrup that coats the back of a spoon. Set aside to cool.

In the event you overreduce your port and it hardens when cool (happens to the best of us), add a few teaspoons of water and microwave on medium power in 10-second intervals until the reduction is liquid again. Mix well and let cool once more.

PEAR CAKE

Preheat the oven to 350°F. Line cupcake pans with 24 baking cups.

In a stand mixer with the paddle attachment, combine the pears, granulated sugar, and brown sugar, and mix on medium-low until well combined, about 1 minute.

With the mixer running, slowly pour in the olive oil. Continue mixing until combined. Stop the mixer, remove the bowl and paddle, and use the paddle to scrape the insides of the bowl, making sure everything is fully incorporated.

Sift together the flour, baking powder, baking soda, and salt and add to the batter. Reattach the bowl and paddle to the mixer and mix on medium until just combined, then add the eggs and continue mixing until the batter is homogenous, about 10 to 20 seconds. Remove the bowl and paddle from the mixer and, once again, use the paddle to scrape the bottom and sides of the bowl, ensuring that everything is well mixed.

Scoop the batter into the prepared baking cups, filling them three quarters of the way.

Bake in the middle of the oven for 20 to 25 minutes, rotating the pan halfway through. The cupcakes are done when the centers spring back when you touch them.

Remove the cupcakes from the oven and let cool completely while you make the buttercream and walnuts.

BLUE CHEESE BUTTERCREAM

For French buttercream (recommended): Prepare the recipe as directed on page 32 up to the soft ball stage. After adding the hot sugar to the eggs, wait for 2 minutes, then begin adding the blue cheese in small pieces. Once the mixture is completely cool, add the butter and continue as directed.

In the event the buttercream breaks, add ⅛ tsp of guar gum and beat on high until the buttercream becomes smooth. Add more guar gum pinch by pinch if necessary.

For American frosting: Prepare the recipe as directed on page 34, replacing the mascarpone with the blue cheese. Beat an additional minute before you begin adding the powdered sugar.

CANDIED WALNUTS

In a skillet over medium heat, melt the butter, then add the walnuts. Stir for 1 minute.

Add the sugar, salt, and water. Continue to cook, stirring constantly, until the sugar is melted and the nuts are completely candied, about 2 minutes. Remove from the heat and let cool completely.

ASSEMBLY

Fill a pastry bag fitted with a fluted tip with blue cheese buttercream and pipe onto each pear cupcake.

Sprinkle on the candied walnuts.

Drizzle about ½ teaspoon port wine reduction over each cupcake.

Matt says: *Don't just go picking up any blue cheese you see in the supermarket. In fact, unless you're shopping at a specialty grocery, we wouldn't suggest buying blue cheese at all. There are literally thousands of varieties of blue cheese produced all over the world, and most of them have nothing in common with that acrid Danish blue you'll find in your supermarket. If possible, find a local grocer or cheesemonger and tell him what you're using the cheese for—he'll be able to help you determine the proper cheese from those on hand, and a great grocer will even allow you to taste some so you can select the one you like best. Here's a list of some of the varieties we like, all common in specialty shops:*

> *Point Reyes Blue: Our favorite for this recipe. Not too subtle to disappear under all the other flavors, not too strong for those people who are terrified of blue cheese. And American to boot! U-S-A! U-S-A!*

> *Stilton: This is the classic blue often picked for the pear/blue/walnut/port cheese plate, and yes, it's pretty flawless as dessert cheeses go. We would use this more in the bakery if more of it would end up in the buttercream instead of in Allison's mouth. She's cost us hundreds of thousands in "missing cheese" costs.*

Cashel Blue: A creamy, mild Irish cheese that we describe as the perfect blue cheese for people who think they hate blue cheese. Seriously, if you're one of those hard-line "blue cheese is an abomination, and I don't care if you mix it with pears or cake or crack cocaine, I'm never going to like it!" types, ask your cheesemonger for a taste of this and see if it doesn't change your mind.

Gorgonzola Dolce: It is important to specify you are looking to buy "dolce," otherwise you may be sold Gorgonzola piccante, which is an entirely different cheese. "Dolce" means "sweet," and though this cheese isn't the traditional definition of that word, it is mellow and creamy, and perfectly complements any sweet accompaniments.

Roaring Forties Blue: From Australia, this cheese is a bit bolder, a bit firmer, but has a fantastic nuttiness that goes well with pears, as well as Vegemite sandwiches and kanga on the barbie.

SO YOU HAVE EXTRA . . .

Port wine reduction

- Keep in a jar in the refrigerator—it lasts for ages.
- Pour over vanilla ice cream.
- Make a grilled cheese with the reduction and Brie.

HALF-ASSED CORNER

Skip candying the walnuts and use plain roasted nuts instead.

A Love Letter to Bacon

The term "food porn" has never sat well with me, as I'm the type who's completely revolted by pornography. I've never seen how watching an oily, hairy man writhing all over a spray-tanned crystal-meth addict was supposed to get me, or anyone for that matter, in the romantic sort of way. Then I start thinking about these poor people degrading themselves on film, wondering if they have daddy issues, thinking about them starting off as wide-eyed kids hoofing it to Los Angeles with nothing but a suitcase and a dream, wondering how it all went wrong for them. Do they speak to their parents? Do they even have a family to go home to anymore? So no matter how delicious food looks, how sexy the photography is, I simply cannot bring myself to use the term "food porn." It is stupid, ugly, and kinda gross. Even though it's probably the most appropriate term for the story I'm about to tell you.

Before I met Matt, I had to downplay my love of food with the guys I would date. Not that I was ever one of those girls who would order only salads or would perpetually be on a diet. However, I learned the hard way that most men don't appreciate being totally neglected during a romantic dinner in favor of me giving my full undivided attention to a rack of baby back ribs.

Matt and I fell in love over food, yet it would be a few more weeks until I learned about Matt's first true love before me: bacon. His family is from Iowa, and he spent his childhood summers out at their family farm, feeding the pigs, cleaning the pens, cutting the umbilical cords of newborns. That's right, not only does the man bake cupcakes, my six-foot six-inch bear of a husband used to deliver adorable little baby piglets. *Awwwwwww.*

All those little piggies weren't just for cuddling and dressing up in tiny outfits and funny hats. No, eventually they grew into full-fledged hogs and swine, and were sold for meat. As much time as he spent out in the fields, he spent an equal amount of time in the farmhouse learning to cook at his grandmother's side. His lifelong love affair eventually inspired him to get the famous "Bacon" tattoo that covers his left forearm, years before the whole world went crazy and started making bacon everything: from air freshener to toothpaste to personal lubricant.

Matt says: *You think we're making that last one up because of the food porn parallel we've got going here. We really wish we were.*

We didn't have much time for proper dates at the beginning of our relationship because we both worked odd hours at restaurants. We'd usually end up at each other's places after shift, well after midnight. For reasons that I won't get into, we had swept everything off the dining room table onto the floor. While picking it up, I laid eyes on the dirtiest, filthiest magazine I had ever seen, just lying there on the carpet amid credit card statements and pharmacy receipts: the Burgers' Smokehouse catalog.

Never before had it occurred to this girl from Brooklyn that one could order meat from a catalog; but there it was splayed out in front of me. Thick whole country hams as juicy and tempting as a glamour girl's thighs. Delicate wisps of prosciutto, cresting and crashing all over one another in a giant, salty pork orgy. Full slabs of bacon wrapped in other kinds of bacon, served with bacon sauce. A centerfold of the naughtiest spiral ham, slathered in a gooey, glistening brown sugar glaze, its slices coyly fanning open to expose the succulent meat within, teasing me with just a slightest hint of crispy burned edges.

This was the first moment in my life when I realized that I was the kind of girl who was a little turned on by meat. This was also the moment when I figured out why I'd never had a relationship that lasted more than a few dates. Who the hell wants to date a girl who's mildly sexually aroused at the sight of ham?

Matt came into the room and found me on the floor, just sitting there silently, staring slack jawed while I thumbed through the pages. Almost as if he knew what I was thinking, he said, "It's my lifelong dream to one day eat one of those hams. And also to one day set some sort of world record for eating the most of something."

Matt says: *Which I did back in January 2011, when I ate 14.5 burgers in five minutes! Also, eating 14.5 burgers in five minutes is a horrible idea.*

I told him I'd never seen anything like it before, to which he replied, "Well then, I have something else you're going to enjoy." He helped me up slowly and walked me to his bedroom, laid me down on the bed, and proceeded to whip out the Amana Meat Shop & Smokehouse catalog from a stack he had on his nightstand. We lay there fawning over every single picture, talking about what kind of glazes we'd rub all over them if we were ever in a room with one of those bad boys. Next came the Smithfield hams, then New Braunfeds's, then the exotic game meats of Jackson Hole.

That's how we fell asleep that night. No sexy time, no funny business—just under a blanket, cuddled up in each other's arms, reading meat pornography. Knowing that I'm now married to a real man who will also occasionally pick eating a really good sandwich over intimacy? Well, there's nothing that's more of a turn-on than that.

Elvis'

We, of course, can take no credit for this one; this is all "the King."

Truth be told, we're not the biggest Elvis fans on earth, but you know who is? John Stamos. And maybe one day, John Stamos will eat one of these, then jump up and say, "My God! This is the best cupcake I have ever eaten in my entire life! I need to find the person who made this and run off with her straight away." And then I'll say, "But, John Stamos, I couldn't possibly—I'm a married woman!" And then John Stamos will say, "Well, can't we just make out a little? Maybe throw in some under-the-shirt action?" And I'll say, "Listen, John Stamos, maybe in another life, another time. In this time, despite whatever raging carnal desires we may have for each other, I belong to Matt Robicelli, and could never possibly love another man." Then John Stamos will cry a whole bunch and then, in consolation, I'll let him give me a two-hour backrub. Maybe if you make this cupcake, John Stamos will come to your house too!

Matt says: *WATCH YOURSELF, STAMOS.*

Roasted Candied Bacon
    1½ cups brown sugar
    12 slices thick-cut bacon

Banana Cake
    4 large, not overripe bananas
    1 cup granulated sugar
    1 cup brown sugar
    1¼ cups canola or grapeseed oil
    1½ teaspoons pure vanilla extract
    2 cups all-purpose flour, sifted
    1 teaspoon baking powder
    1 teaspoon baking soda
    1 teaspoon kosher salt
    ½ teaspoon ground cinnamon
    ½ teaspoon freshly grated nutmeg
    4 large eggs, beaten

Peanut Butter Buttercream
> One recipe French Buttercream (page 32) or American Frosting (page 34)
> ½ cup all-natural peanut butter
> 1 teaspoon kosher salt

ROASTED CANDIED BACON

Preheat the oven to 350°F. Line a baking sheet with aluminum foil, then place a wire cooling rack on top of it.

Place the brown sugar in a shallow pan. Dredge the bacon in the sugar on both sides to coat well, then place on the prepared baking sheet on top of the rack.

Bake for 15 to 20 minutes, until the bacon is a dark mahogany brown. Remove the sheet pan from the oven and let sit for a minimum of 10 minutes before you go anywhere near it. I know that all you want at this moment is to get your hands on a piece of that sweet, sweet candied bacon, but in this instance, you are faced with the possibility of *three* horrific types of burns: hot grease, hot sugar, hot metal. For the love of God, man! Show some self-control and walk away!

When the bacon is finally cool, remove it from the pan and coarsely chop, setting it aside in a bowl for later assembly. You can either throw out all the bacon fat/sugar drippings or reserve them for another use (see page 67).

BANANA CAKE

Preheat the oven to 350°F. Line cupcake pans with 24 baking cups.

In a stand mixer with the paddle attachment, combine the bananas, granulated sugar, and brown sugar and mix on medium-low until well combined, about 1 minute.

With the mixer running, slowly pour in the oil and vanilla. Continue mixing until combined. Stop the mixer, remove the bowl and paddle, and use the paddle to scrape the insides of the bowl, making sure everything is fully incorporated.

Sift together the flour, baking powder, baking soda, salt, cinnamon, and nutmeg and add to the batter. Reattach the bowl and paddle to the mixer and mix on medium until just combined, then add the eggs and continue mixing until the batter is homogenous, about 10 to 20 seconds. Remove the bowl and paddle from the mixer and, once again, use the paddle to scrape the bottom and sides of the bowl, ensuring that everything is well mixed.

Scoop the batter into the prepared baking cups, filling them two thirds of the way.

Bake in the middle of the oven for 20 to 25 minutes, rotating the pan halfway through. The cupcakes are done when the centers spring back when you touch them.

Remove the cupcakes from the oven and let cool completely while you make the buttercream.

PEANUT BUTTER BUTTERCREAM

For French buttercream (recommended): Prepare the recipe as directed on page 32. Once the butter is added, add the peanut butter and salt and mix on high to combine. Taste for seasoning. If desired, add more peanut butter, 1 tablespoon at a time, or a pinch more salt. Continue until, after tasting, your eyes roll into the back of your head.

For American frosting: Prepare the recipe as directed on page 34, reducing the sugar by 1 cup, replacing the mascarpone with the peanut butter, and adding the salt. Once combined, taste for seasoning.

ASSEMBLY

Fill a pastry bag fitted with a fluted tip with the peanut butter buttercream and pipe onto each banana cupcake.

Place candied bacon pieces on the top of each cupcake until all the bacon is used (or eaten).

Matt says: *What to do with all that leftover bacon fat and caramelized brown sugar that dripped onto your baking sheet? Crush it up and store in a jar to make the best damn condiment you've ever tried. Stir it into pancake or waffle batter, add to turkey meat loaves, shake with bourbon and ice, or just snort it like I do!*

The Maltz

You know what happens when a friend is expecting her boyfriend to finally propose and instead he comes over and, without explanation, dumps her? Months of the most depressing Facebook status updates ever. I'd comment almost every day, as did dozens of my friends, with a little hopeful note, but nothing seemed to help. Then one day an old high school friend, Ben Maltz, chimed in, "You know what will fix this? Some chocolate. Or some bourbon. Or bacon." Immediately, the act of jointly consoling our friend was completely abandoned as the lot of us began plotting a cupcake based on Maltz's wisdom. I like to think of this one as a sort of "divine intervention" number— because really, what can cure a broken heart better than chocolate, bourbon, and bacon? I can name only a few things, but none of them is really appropriate for this book. Or any book, really.

Chocolate Bourbon Cake
¾ cup cocoa powder
⅓ cup scalding-hot coffee
⅓ cup scalding-hot bourbon
⅔ cup buttermilk
⅓ cup canola or grapeseed oil
1 large egg
1 large egg yolk
½ teaspoon kosher salt
1⅓ cups all-purpose flour
1¾ cups sugar
¾ teaspoon baking powder
½ teaspoon baking soda

Chocolate Bourbon Buttercream
½ cup bourbon
¼ cup Dutch-process cocoa powder
One recipe French Buttercream (page 32) or American Frosting (page 34)

Candied Bacon
See roasted candied bacon, page 65

CHOCOLATE BOURBON CAKE

Preheat the oven to 350°F. Line two cupcake pans with 24 baking cups.

Place the cocoa powder in the bowl of a stand mixer with the paddle attachment and pour the hot coffee and bourbon over. Mix on low speed until a thick paste forms and the mixture stops steaming, about 1 minute.

Increase the mixer speed to medium. In a 4-cup measuring cup, combine the buttermilk, oil, egg, egg yolk, and salt and mix lightly with a fork, ensuring the yolks are broken. Slowly pour into the mixer bowl.

Stop the mixer, detach the paddle, and scrape the bottom of the bowl well to loosen any caked-on cocoa. Reattach the paddle and turn the mixer to medium, letting it run for 1 minute. Stop the mixer again.

Sift together the flour, sugar, baking powder, and baking soda and add to the batter. Mix on low speed until just combined. Remove the bowl and paddle and use the paddle to scrape down the sides of the bowl, ensuring everything is mixed.

Scoop the batter into the prepared baking cups, filling them two thirds of the way.

Bake in the middle of the oven for 20 to 25 minutes, rotating the pans halfway through. The cupcakes are done when the centers spring back when you touch them.

Remove the cupcakes from the oven. Let cool completely.

CHOCOLATE BOURBON BUTTERCREAM

Heat the bourbon in a small saucepan over high heat. Boil until reduced by half. Add the cocoa powder and stir into a paste. Let cool.

Prepare the French buttercream as directed on page 32 or American frosting on page 34. Add the bourbon paste and mix well until smooth.

ASSEMBLY

Roughly chop the candied bacon.

Fill a pastry bag fitted with a plain tip with the chocolate bourbon buttercream and pipe onto each chocolate cupcake.

Sprinkle a generous amount of candied bacon on top of each cupcake.

The Noah

The Noah came out of one of those times when we looked into the refrigerator, took stock of what we had, and thought, "How do we make something *awesome* out of this?" That day we had lots of apples, lots of goat cheese, lots of bacon, and lots of bourbon (well, we always have lots of bourbon, but for other reasons). It's easy to come up with amazing cupcakes when you have ingredients like that on hand. I mean, can you imagine if our fridge had been filled with moss, crab juice, and rocks? That would have been disastrous!

We asked Facebook what to name our new creation, and our friend Noah Fecks responded, "Orgasmatron." In an effort to keep our sidewalk menu PG, we named it after him instead. But trust me, once you taste this, you'll agree that "Orgasmatron" was probably a more appropriate name.

Bourbon–Brown Butter Sauce
- 8 tablespoons (1 stick) unsalted butter
- ½ cup brown sugar
- 1 teaspoon kosher salt
- ¼ cup bourbon
- ½ cup heavy cream

Apple Cake
- 2 cups of peeled, shredded, drained, and pressed apples (about 2 large cooking apples; see page 26)
- 1 cup granulated sugar
- 1 cup brown sugar
- 1¼ cups canola oil
- 2 cups all-purpose flour, sifted
- 1 teaspoon baking powder
- 1 teaspoon baking soda
- 1 teaspoon kosher salt
- ½ teaspoon ground cinnamon
- ¼ teaspoon ground ginger
- ½ teaspoon freshly grated nutmeg
- 4 large eggs, beaten

Goat Cheese Buttercream
One recipe French Buttercream (page 32) or American Frosting (page 34)
½ to ⅔ cup (4 to 6 ounces) goat cheese

Roasted Candied Bacon
See roasted candied bacon (page 65)

BOURBON–BROWN BUTTER SAUCE

Melt the butter in a medium saucepan over low heat, occasionally stirring from the bottom with a heatproof spatula until the butter begins to brown, about 4 minutes.

Add the brown sugar and salt, continuing to stir until well combined. Add the bourbon.

Raise the heat to medium-high and continue to cook until the mixture begins to boil and the brown sugar is completely dissolved. Remove the pan from the heat and stir in the cream. Return the pan to medium heat and continue cooking, stirring constantly, for 2 minutes. Set aside to cool.

APPLE CAKE

Preheat the oven to 350°F. Line cupcake pans with 24 baking cups.

In a stand mixer with the paddle attachment, combine the apples, granulated sugar, and brown sugar and mix on medium-low until well combined, about 1 minute.

Matt says:
By cooking your sugar sauce further after adding the cream, you help prevent the brown sugar from crystallizing and your sauce from becoming grainy once it cools. You can store any extra in the refrigerator for drizzling on ice cream or yogurt, or make large batches to drink with a straw.

With the mixer running, slowly pour in the oil. Continue mixing until combined. Stop the mixer, remove the bowl and paddle, and use the paddle to scrape the insides of the bowl, making sure everything is fully incorporated.

Sift together the flour, baking powder, baking soda, salt, cinnamon, ginger, and nutmeg and add to the apple mixture. Reattach the bowl and paddle to the mixer and mix on medium until just combined, then add the eggs and continue mixing until the batter is homogenous, about 10 to 20 seconds. Remove the bowl and paddle from the mixer and, once again, use the paddle to scrape the bottom and sides of the bowl, ensuring that everything is well mixed.

Scoop the batter into the prepared baking cups, filling them three quarters of the way.

Bake in the middle of the oven for 20 to 25 minutes, rotating the pan halfway through. The cupcakes are done when the centers spring back when you touch them.

Remove the cupcakes from the oven and let them cool completely while you make the buttercream.

Matt says: Achtung! *Depending on the kind of apples you use, your cake batter may appear loose and watery. If this happens to you, add another ¼ cup flour, then let the batter sit in the refrigerator for 10 minutes or so to allow it to hydrate a bit before baking.*

GOAT CHEESE BUTTERCREAM

For French Buttercream (recommended): Prepare the recipe as directed on page 32. While adding butter, also add the goat cheese.

For American frosting: Prepare the recipe as directed on page 34, replacing the mascarpone with goat cheese.

ASSEMBLY

Finely chop the candied bacon.

Fill a pastry bag fitted with a fluted tip with the goat cheese buttercream and pipe onto each apple cupcake.

Place candied bacon pieces on the top of each cupcake.

Using a teaspoon, drizzle the top of each cupcake with the bourbon—brown butter sauce.

SO YOU HAVE EXTRA . . .

Bourbon-brown butter sauce

- Pour over vanilla ice cream.
- Use in place of maple syrup at the breakfast table.
- Use as a glaze for ham steaks.

A Love Letter
to the East End

I have been going to East Hampton each summer to visit my aunt Rosemarie since I was a kid. Not, mind you, to the part filled with fancy mansions where every Christmas Billy Joel drunkenly drives his Mercedes through your front door. No, we summered entirely in the salty fisherman/starving artist/lesbian spiritual guru community, which, as you might imagine, is *far* more entertaining.

For me, it was never a land of fancy nightclubs or polo matches but rather thousands of acres of family farms bursting with the most delicious produce you'll ever taste, bays filled with fish and crustaceans we'd spend each day plucking from the pleasantly briny water for our dinner, and miles upon miles of vineyards producing wines that were perfect for steaming that day's oceanic bounty. Weekends in the Hamptons were about one thing to my family: feasting off the land in a way that still allowed us to enjoy such wonders as air conditioning and indoor plumbing. To a girl from Brooklyn who's terrified of all forms of wildlife (including small birds) and who has a steadfast refusal to poop in the woods during her lifetime, it was roughing it.

Matt and I were engaged during the summer of 2005, shortly before my twenty-fifth birthday. I thought the perfect way to celebrate both milestones would be a weekend in East Hampton. I could impress my former Boy Scout fiancé by showing him how to catch a blue crab or dig for clams, cook side by side with him at night, and then cap off the trip with a romantic tour down the main road of the North Fork, stopping at wineries and farm stands along the way as we said grown-up things like "this red has notes of pencil shavings and elderberries," and "this farm-stand cheese has a certain aroma of field moss and dew that evokes the early morning of (insert name of made-up town here), France."

I woke up on our first morning there and began to ready myself for a day of clamming, as all girls who are so freakishly pale that they are borderline see-through do: by slathering every inch of my body with SPF 10,000 sunblock. I asked Matt if he wanted me to put sunblock on his back for him, to which he replied that he didn't need to because his skin didn't get color. Having known the man for only four months, what choice did I have but to believe him? We hit the bay, grabbed our clamming rakes, and spent three hours in the water.

That weekend, Matt and I each learned something very important about each other. Matt learned that in any instance where he accidentally gets hit in the balls, I will laugh, *and* if he gets hit in the balls so hard that he starts throwing up, I will laugh to the point where I will start hyperventilating and almost pass out.

I learned that when someone says, "I don't need sunblock," he has no idea what the hell he is talking about and God will punish him for his stupidity by giving him acute sun poisoning, so that while his fiancée is cooking the romantic dinner she has planned for weeks, he will be lying on the cold bathroom floor with his head in the toilet. And while his fiancée is in the tasting rooms in every vineyard of the North Fork talking about pencil shavings and elderberries, he will be in the bathroom of each and every tasting room with, you guessed it, his head in the toilet. And on the day of her birthday, will his fiancée be off at a fancy restaurant toasting with champagne and slurping down oysters? No! She will be rubbing antibacterial lotion all over the idiot's back, which is now covered with open sores; bandaging his burns with numerous rolls of gauze; and holding him while he shivers and cries (in the most masculine way possible).

I bought several bottles of wine that weekend, none of which can be consumed by anyone with acute sun poisoning. Rather than wait a few weeks for him to recover so we could drink the wine properly, I used it to bake with. Though I don't doubt that many of you have already tried savory dishes with wine, I'm sure many of you haven't tried it in baked goods, which is a shame. All those funny flavors we talk about in wines—the deep notes of chocolate, aromas of blackberries and nectarines, bright flavors of citrus—those sound like the perfect complement to baked goods to me. These next cupcakes are an ode to the flavors of the eastern tip of Long Island, and a stark reminder that if you don't listen to your wife, she'll one day write in a book about your throwing up and crying.

And wear sunblock, folks. It's good for you.

The Duckwalk

Of all the wines produced at Duck Walk Vineyards, the one that is so spectacular, so memorable that you'll want to chug it out of the bottle and try to ride your neighbor's motorcycle like a dime-store ride is their velvety blueberry port. It's so good that I wouldn't recommend cooking with it—a wine this delicious deserves to be drunk on its own while listening to Coltrane and reading something insanely pretentious.

For this recipe, we simmer richly flavored wild Maine blueberries in a moderately priced port wine to make a richly flavored compote, then strain out the blueberries and reduce the remaining liquid to a thick syrup. But just because we're doctoring up a cheaper wine to make it seem shi shi doesn't give you carte blanche to go buying your port at the 99-cents store and expecting miracles. Go to your local wine shop and ask for a bottle that won't break the bank.

Port Blueberries, Three Ways
  2 cups frozen blueberries (we prefer Wyman's of Maine, but whatever
  brand you can find will be fine)
  3 cups port wine
  ¼ cup sugar

Vanilla Cake
  12 tablespoons (1½ sticks) unsalted butter
  4 large eggs
  1 cup milk
  1 teaspoon pure vanilla extract
  1 teaspoon kosher salt
  2 cups all-purpose flour
  1¾ cups sugar
  2 teaspoons baking powder

Blueberry Port Mascarpone Buttercream
  One recipe French Buttercream (page 32) or American Frosting (page 34)
  ½ cup (4 ounces) mascarpone
  Blueberry port syrup (from port blueberries, phase two, below)

PORT BLUEBERRIES, PHASE ONE

Put the blueberries, port, and sugar in a medium nonreactive saucepan and bring to a boil. Turn down the heat to low and let simmer while you make the cupcakes.

VANILLA CAKE

Preheat the oven to 350°F. Line cupcake pans with 24 baking cups.

Melt the butter in a microwave at 60 percent power for 1½ to 2 minutes. Keep the butter warm—do not allow it to sit and cool off.

In a stand mixer with the paddle attachment, beat the eggs on medium-low speed for 2 minutes until light yellow and lightly foamy.

Increase the mixer speed to medium-high. Pour the warm butter into the eggs slowly, so that the mixture tempers and the eggs do not scramble. Once the butter is added, reduce the speed back to medium-low.

With the mixer running, add the milk, vanilla, and salt. Mix for 1 minute until well combined.

Sift together the flour, sugar, and baking powder and add to the batter. Mix on medium until just combined, 10 to 20 seconds. Remove the bowl and paddle from the mixer and use the paddle to scrape the bottom and sides of the bowl, ensuring that everything is well mixed.

Scoop the batter into the prepared baking cups, filling them two thirds of the way.

Bake in the middle of the oven for 20 to 25 minutes, rotating the pan halfway through. The cupcakes are done when the centers spring back when you touch them.

Remove the cupcakes from the oven. Let cool for 5 minutes, then remove from the pan and place on a baking sheet.

Dip a pastry brush into the simmering blueberry port liquid and brush the top of each cupcake three times. Let cool.

PORT BLUEBERRIES, PHASE TWO

Strain the remaining blueberry port mixture, setting the blueberries aside and returning the liquid to the pan. Bring the heat up to high and boil until the liquid is reduced to a syrup that coats the back of a spoon, about 10 minutes. Pour the syrup into a bowl to cool.

BLUEBERRY PORT MASCARPONE BUTTERCREAM

Prepare the recipe for French buttercream as directed on page 32 or American frosting on page 34. Add the mascarpone after adding the butter. (Note that if you're making the

American frosting, yes, you are adding mascarpone twice. It will make the frosting supercreamy tasting and so good you'll probably cry, so make sure no one you want to impress is in the room.)

With the mixer running, stream about ¼ cup blueberry port syrup into the buttercream until the mixture is brilliantly blue. Taste and add more syrup according to your personal preference.

Mix any additional syrup back into the reserved port-simmered blueberries.

ASSEMBLY

Fill a pastry bag fitted with a fluted tip with blueberry port mascarpone buttercream and pipe onto each vanilla cupcake.

Using the back of a teaspoon, make an indent in the center of the buttercream. Fill with the port-simmered blueberries (about 2 teaspoons, depending on how rough you are with your indenting skills).

SO YOU HAVE EXTRA . . .

Port blueberries

- Pour over vanilla ice cream.
- Pour over warm Brie or Camembert cheese and serve with crackers.
- Mix into Greek yogurt.

HALF-ASSED CORNER

If you don't want to go through all the trouble of reducing the leftover blueberry port to add to the buttercream, this cupcake will still be delicious with plain mascarpone buttercream topped with a spoonful of the simmered blueberries.

The North Fork

I love blackberries, but they're what I call a "tricky" fruit. They'll look delicious, smell delicious, but then you eat one and it's so sour that your face completely inverts. Or you pop one into your mouth and it tastes like absolutely nothing at all. I've done some research, and I think that the window where a blackberry is totally perfect to eat on its own is exactly four hours and twenty-six minutes. If you perchance find yourself with a totally flawless basket of blackberries, then shovel them into your mouth raw with reckless abandon! However, if they're sour, or taste like packing peanuts, or all you can get your hands on are frozen blackberries, then why not simmer them in some sugar and red wine and make this cupcake?

We use wine from Long Island's North Fork—Castello di Borghese is one of our favorites—but feel free to use whichever cabernet you like.

Blackberry Cabernet Compote

- 1 pint fresh or frozen blackberries (if unavailable, try looking for a frozen mixed berry assortment)
- 1 cup blackberry jam
- ½ cup sugar
- 1 cup cabernet sauvignon

Chocolate Cabernet Cake

- ¾ cup cocoa powder
- 2 cups cabernet sauvignon reduced to ⅔ cup, scalding hot
- ⅔ cup buttermilk
- ⅓ cup canola or grapeseed oil
- 1 large egg
- 1 large egg yolk
- ½ teaspoon kosher salt
- 1⅓ cups all-purpose flour
- 1¾ cups sugar
- ¾ teaspoon baking powder
- ½ teaspoon baking soda

BLACKBERRY CABERNET BUTTERCREAM

One recipe French Buttercream (page 32) or American Frosting (page 34)

Blackberry cabernet compote reduction (from above)

BLACKBERRY CABERNET COMPOTE

In a medium heavy-bottomed, nonreactive saucepan, combine the blackberries, blackberry jam, sugar, and red wine and bring to a boil over high heat, stirring with a wooden spoon.

Reduce the heat to medium-low and simmer for 15 minutes.

Strain the compote into a bowl. Set the blackberries aside. Return the liquid to the pan and bring to a boil. Reduce the liquid until it coats the back of a spoon, about 5 minutes. Let cool completely.

CHOCOLATE CABERNET CAKE

Preheat the oven to 350°F. Line two cupcake pans with 24 baking cups.

Place the cocoa powder in the bowl of a stand mixer with a paddle attachment and pour the hot cabernet over. Mix on low speed until a thick paste forms and the mixture stops steaming, about 1 minute.

Increase the mixer speed to medium. In a 4-cup measuring cup, combine the buttermilk, oil, egg, egg yolk, and salt and mix lightly with a fork, ensuring the yolks are broken. Slowly pour into the mixer bowl.

Stop the mixer, detach the paddle, and scrape the bottom of the bowl well to loosen any caked-on cocoa. Reattach the paddle and turn the mixer to medium, letting it run for 1 minute. Stop the mixer again.

Sift together the flour, sugar, baking powder, and baking soda and add to the batter. Mix on low speed until just combined. Remove the bowl and paddle and use the paddle to scrape down the sides of the bowl, ensuring everything is mixed.

Scoop the batter into the prepared baking cups, filling them two thirds of the way.

Bake in the middle of the oven for 20 to 25 minutes, rotating the pans halfway through. The cupcakes are done when the centers spring back when you touch them.

Remove the cupcakes from the oven. Let cool completely.

BLACKBERRY CABERNET BUTTERCREAM

Prepare the recipe for French buttercream as directed on page 32 or American frosting on page 34. Drizzle in the blackberry cabernet reduction, 1 tablespoon at a time, tasting constantly, until the desired flavor is reached (about 3 tablespoons for us). Mix the remaining compote with the reserved blackberries.

ASSEMBLY

Fill a pastry bag fitted with a fluted tip with the blackberry cabernet buttercream and pipe onto each chocolate cupcake.

Using the back of a teaspoon, make a small indent in the center of the buttercream. Fill with the reserved blackberry cabernet compote—about 1 teaspoon—though you don't need to measure.

SO YOU HAVE EXTRA . . .

Blackberry cabernet compote

- Pour over vanilla ice cream.
- Mix with Greek yogurt.
- Stir into a glass of wine with some chopped fruit for an individual sangría.
- Add a touch of red wine or balsamic vinegar and serve alongside beef, duck, or venison.

Red Wine & Peaches

One of the nice things about making sangría is that you can pretend that it's healthy because there's fruit in it. Actually, red wine is good for you too, isn't it? Why haven't we replaced cereal and milk with fruit and wine?

Anyway, if you're ever looking for a great, simple summertime recipe, all you need to do is peel and cut up some peaches, toss them in a bit of sugar, and soak them in wine. That's it. Eat them out of the bowl. Serve them on ice cream. Spoon them on top of your afternoon yogurt so you can "drink on the job" without people knowing. Or, you can make some cupcakes, top with a touch of mascarpone buttercream and a nice helping of wine-soaked peaches, and you'll look like a world-class pastry chef with barely any effort.

Red Wine Peaches

4 medium, ripe white peaches, peeled and cut into ½-inch slices
½ cup sugar
2 cups fruity red wine, such as a Beaujolais or young pinot noir

Peach Cake

12 tablespoons (1½ sticks) unsalted butter
4 large eggs
½ cup peach juice (we like Ceres or Looza)
⅓ cup half-and-half
1 teaspoon kosher salt
2¼ cups all-purpose flour
1½ cups sugar
2 teaspoons baking powder
1 medium white peach, peeled and diced

Mascarpone Buttercream

One recipe French Buttercream (page 32) or American Frosting (page 34)
½ cup (4 ounces) mascarpone

RED WINE PEACHES

Toss the peach slices with the sugar. Place in a medium bowl.

Pour in 2 cups of the red wine, making sure the peaches are completely submerged. Cover the bowl with plastic wrap and let sit in the refrigerator for a minimum of 30 minutes.

Matt says:
If you want to remove the alcohol from the red wine before you begin, follow the directions provided on page 24. Or just use a bottle of nonalcoholic red wine and up the sugar by ¼ cup. That would probably be easier.

Using a sieve over a medium nonreactive saucepan, strain the peach-wine mixture. Set the peaches aside in another bowl and cover with ½ cup of the strained wine.

Place the saucepan with the remaining wine over high heat and reduce the wine until it becomes syrupy and coats the back of a spoon, about 20 minutes. Set aside at room temperature to cool.

PEACH CAKE

Preheat the oven to 350°F. Line cupcake pans with 24 baking cups.

Melt the butter in a microwave at 60 percent power for 1½ to 2 minutes. Keep the butter warm—do not allow it to sit and cool off.

In a stand mixer with the paddle attachment, beat the eggs on medium-low speed for 2 minutes until light yellow and lightly foamy.

Increase the mixer speed to medium-high. Pour the warm butter into the eggs slowly, so that the mixture tempers and the eggs do not scramble. Once the butter is added, reduce the speed back to medium-low.

With the mixer running, add the peach juice, half-and-half, and salt. Mix for 1 minute until well combined.

Sift together the flour, sugar, and baking powder, and add to the batter. Mix on medium until just combined, 10 to 20 seconds.

Add the diced peach and stir for 10 seconds. Remove the bowl and paddle from the mixer and, use the paddle to scrape the bottom and sides of the bowl, ensuring that everything is well mixed.

Scoop the batter into the prepared baking cups, filling them two thirds of the way.

Bake in the middle of the oven for 20 to 25 minutes, rotating the pan halfway through. The cupcakes are done when the centers spring back when you touch them.

Remove the cupcake from the oven. Let cool completely.

MASCARPONE BUTTERCREAM

Prepare the recipe for French Buttercream as directed on page 32 or American frosting on page 34. Add the mascarpone after adding the butter. (Note that this is additional mascarpone if you're making American frosting. Yes, that little extra is totally worth it.)

ASSEMBLY

Fill a pastry bag fitted with a plain tip with the mascarpone buttercream and pipe onto each peach cupcake.

Remove the peach slices from the wine and fan the slices across each cupcake. Drink the reserved wine.

Using a teaspoon, drizzle red wine reduction over the cupcakes. Serve immediately.

Matt says: *If you don't want to serve these immediately, then poach the peaches in red wine instead of just soaking them. Put the peaches, sugar, and wine in a saucepan, simmer for 5 minutes, remove the peaches to a plate, and reduce the wine to a syrup. The finished product won't have the exact texture we like so much in the raw soaked peaches, but it will still be one of the best cupcakes you've ever had in your entire life. (We lIke to aim high.)*

Cherries Jubilee

I think so many of us hate cherries because we've all had lousy cherries—those nasty gummy bits you find swirled into ice cream, or the fluorescent maraschino ones that taste like little balls of Silly Putty soaked in formaldehyde. Then there's that cherry pie filling that comes out of a can that totally defies scientific explanation. *Fresh* cherries, on the other hand, are kinda one of the most awesome things ever. So why don't more people bake with those instead of that crap that comes out of the can? *Goddamn cherry pits*. Making a whole pie or crumble with cherries takes damn well near forever.

So what makes our Cherries Jubilee an excellent proposition? These cherries are packed with flavor, and each cupcake gets only about three of them on top. Maximum flavor, minimum labor. Plus, you get to set the cherries on FIRE!

Vanilla Cake
12 tablespoons (1½ sticks) unsalted butter
4 large eggs
1 cup milk
1 teaspoon pure vanilla extract
1 teaspoon kosher salt
2 cups all-purpose flour
1¾ cups sugar
2 teaspoons baking powder

Cherries Jubilee
1½ pounds fresh dark red cherries, pitted, or two 14-ounce jars morello cherries, drained and well rinsed
Juice of ½ large lemon
⅓ cup granulated sugar
⅓ cup brown sugar
½ teaspoon kosher salt
½ cup kirsch, cherry brandy, cherry liqueur, or cognac
1 teaspoon pure vanilla extract

Cherry Vanilla Buttercream
One recipe French Buttercream (page 32) or American Frosting (page 34)
1 teaspoon pure vanilla extract
Cherries jubilee syrup (recipe follows)

VANILLA CAKE
Preheat the oven to 350°F. Line cupcake pans with 24 baking cups.

Melt the butter in a microwave at 60 percent power for 1½ to 2 minutes. Keep the butter warm—do not allow it to sit and cool off.

In a stand mixer with the paddle attachment, beat the eggs on medium-low speed for 2 minutes until light yellow and lightly foamy.

Increase the mixer speed to medium-high. Pour the warm butter into the eggs slowly, so that the mixture tempers and the eggs do not scramble. Once the butter is added, reduce the speed to medium-low.

With the mixer running, add the milk, vanilla, and salt. Mix for 1 minute until well combined.

Sift together the flour, sugar, and baking powder and add to the batter. Mix on medium until just combined, 10 to 20 seconds. Remove the bowl and paddle from the mixer and use the paddle to scrape the bottom and sides of the bowl, ensuring that everything is well mixed.

Scoop the batter into the prepared baking cups, filling them two thirds of the way.

Bake in the middle of the oven for 20 to 25 minutes, rotating the pan halfway through. The cupcakes are done when the centers spring back when you touch them.

Remove the cupcakes from the oven. Let cool for 5 minutes, then remove the cupcakes from the pan and place on a baking sheet.

CHERRIES JUBILEE AND SYRUP
In a large heavy bottomed, nonreactive skillet, cook the cherries, lemon juice, granulated sugar, brown sugar, and salt over medium-high heat, gently stirring with a wooden spoon.

When the cherries have released their juices and the sugar has dissolved, about 3 minutes, remove the pan from the heat and add the kirsch. Using a match or long-handled lighter, set the cherries on fire and return the pan to the burner, turning down the heat to low.

When the flame has died out, add the vanilla and gently stir again to make sure the cherries are coated.

Strain the cherries jubilee. Set the cherries aside and return the liquid to the pan. Turn the heat back to high.

Reduce the liquid until it becomes a thick syrup and coats the back of a spoon, 5 to 10 minutes. Set aside and cool completely.

CHERRIES JUBILEE BUTTERCREAM
Prepare the recipe for French buttercream as directed on page 32 or American frosting on page 34. Add the vanilla and beat well.

With the mixer running, stream about ¼ cup cherry jubilee syrup into the buttercream. Taste and add more syrup according to your personal preference.

Mix any additional syrup back into the reserved cherries.

ASSEMBLY
Fill a pastry bag fitted with a plain tip with the cherry vanilla buttercream and pipe onto each vanilla cupcake.

Place at least 3 cherries on top of each cupcake. Fill any gaps with additional cherries.

SO YOU HAVE EXTRA . . .
Cherries in syrup
- Store in an airtight container in your freezer.
- Make a milk shake with vanilla ice cream (and lots more brandy, if you'd like).
- Mix with a few tablespoons of red wine vinegar and serve with duck breast.

HALF-ASSED CORNER
Just use plain vanilla buttercream and top with the cherries.

A Love Letter
to Bad Luck

What most people don't realize about bad luck is that many times it's actually good luck in disguise. It would be far nicer (and more considerate) if it just showed up like good luck in the first place, instead of screwing up your entire goddamn life and making you completely and utterly fucking miserable for *ages* just to teach you some sort of "valuable character-building life lesson," but—hey!—in hindsight, it's good luck nonetheless. In fact, bad luck was exactly how we ended up baking cupcakes.

The first time I saw a "cupcakery," my initial thought was "What a brilliant idea!" because, well, it's an incredibly brilliant idea. I could go get a piece of cake and a cup of coffee whenever I wanted. Seriously, how could that go wrong? Everyone likes cake. Problem is, you normally have to buy a whole cake to get in on the action. But much like someone made pizza accessible by selling it by the slice rather than by the whole pie, so did the cupcake become a liberating dessert. A glorious little cake, sized for one! And I didn't have to share it with anyone!

Then I actually tried the cupcake, a little blue and white number that had the flavor and texture of asbestos slathered with a mixture of plaster and powdered sugar. I stared at this little cake, thinking, "I just don't get it. How can you screw up cake this badly?" In an instant, my dreams of taking thrice-weekly trips down the block to double-fist chocolate cake while drinking gallons of coffee went up in smoke, and I became one of those people who dismissed cupcakes as "ridiculous."

Matt and I would have the occasional cupcake here and there, some of them fantastic, but many of them, well, sad. Why was it so hard for people to make good cake? More than that, why were so many people going crazy over the bad ones? Why didn't anyone use

French buttercream? Why weren't people using fresh fruits or extracts that didn't taste like fermented cat urine? Why was everything fucking pink?

These were just things we said to each other, though. Neither Matt nor I had any intention of actually *doing* something to fix the problem—we simply wanted to complain about it. It's the American way.

We'd been talking about opening a business together since the night we met. We'd both tired of working long hours in fine dining, cooking for the types of people who made more money in a single day than we did in a month. But though we hated the industry, we still loved the job—working with interesting ingredients, trying new things, always challenging ourselves. Most of all, we loved making people happy, and nothing makes people as happy as dessert.

Matt says: *I could probably think of a few things.*

After a few twists and turns through the food world, we both ended up in the world of specialty gourmet retail and decided that was the solution: We would open a bona fide gourmet shop in our neighborhood in south Brooklyn, bringing sexy cheeses, expertly prepared foods, and well-made specialty food items to a blue-collar neighborhood that had never seen them before. Cupcakes? Never part of the plan. In fact, at that time had you told us that not only would we start making cupcakes, but that we would become two of the most famous "cupcake chefs" in the world, I would have slapped you so hard your grandma would have felt it.

Matt says: *Unless your grandma is dead, in which case, we're sorry for your loss.*

The market was booming, real-estate values were quadrupling, and gentrifiers were beginning to invade our little corner of Brooklyn—it was the ideal time for us to go into business for ourselves. We spent years living off the bare minimum, tucking all our money into a savings account, and working in the gourmet retail industry in various roles so we could learn as much as we could. Soon after our son Atticus's first birthday, while I was five months' pregnant with our second son, Toby, bad luck struck, and Matt lost his job. We decided *that* was the perfect time to go into business for ourselves.

Matt says: *We've established by this point in the book that we're absolutely insane, yes?*

We took every penny of our savings, some investment money from family and friends, and a second mortgage on my parents' house and took the leap. In September

2008, six weeks after the birth of our second child, we opened Robicelli's Gourmet Market on the Third Avenue shopping strip in Bay Ridge, Brooklyn.

And four days after our doors opened, the stock market crashed. In a matter of hours, everything was gone: our reserve funds to run the store, all the potential clientele we were marketing to, and our entire life savings.

Yay!

The business plan that I had spent months writing, the years of experience running other people's shops, the small-business classes we took, the advice we got from "experts" in the field—all were rendered completely *worthless* within a matter of hours. The main street of our neighborhood, which had been bustling with hundreds of people for as long as I'd been alive, was suddenly deserted and eerily quiet. The news was saying that the sky was falling and it was only a matter of time before everyone was going to lose their jobs. If people ventured outside, they might spend money in the neighborhood, so it was better they stayed locked indoors until the economy got better and they could go out again.

Matt says: *This sort of logic, obviously, did not help anyone. Except maybe Walmart.*

We were eeking by every month, barely paying our bills, amassing more and more debt just to keep our family fed. We turned to other local businesspeople for advice, and they were as panicked as we were—even those who had been in business thirty plus years had never seen Bay Ridge that bad. We couldn't fight the panic that had gripped America, no matter how hard we worked.

Then one day, the good luck finally showed his face. He walked straight through the door smelling of Marlboro Lights and wearing a New York Jets Windbreaker.

Several years earlier, when I was twenty-one and training myself to be a chef, I made cakes out of my parents' house for a local "old man" bar. One of those cakes was the moistest, most delicious carrot cake anyone had ever tasted. People don't usually go to bars for dessert, but I developed a cult following that was crazy for it. Even though I stopped baking for them a short time later to start my career in Manhattan, the staff there told me that every so often they'd still get people walking in, asking if the bar still served my carrot cake.

Well, one day a guy at the bar started reminiscing about that "great carrot cake you guys used to have here," and the bartenders told him that I'd returned to the neighborhood with my own place. The guy paid his tab and walked eleven blocks in the rainy March weather, stormed through our door, and demanded we make him a carrot cake for his birthday.

We weren't baking at the time—hell, I wasn't even at the shop at all. With an infant, a newly minted two-year-old, and not a dime for babysitters, I'd become a full-time stay-at-home mom while Matt ran the store. Still, we needed any money we could get, so I strapped the kids into the stroller, walked on over to the store, and put the kids behind the counter with their dad while I got to baking the man a birthday cake. The next week he came in again asking for another cake. Matt asked him if it was his birthday again, and he said, "If you guys made this cake every day, I'd buy it every day."

A few weeks later, during our usual Friday-night ~~screaming match about how we were broke and our family was going to end up on the street~~ meeting on ideas on how to save the business, I brought up the carrot cake. Regardless of how good it was, there was no way we could sell forty carrot cakes a day to cover the rent. But maybe if we made just a few individual pieces, "cupcakes," then we could tell the guys at that bar and they'd possibly come down for sandwiches! And if they liked the sandwiches, then they'd tell the guys at their jobs, and they'd all start ordering from us. Then word would keep spreading and our problems would all be solved.

Then, as is apt to happen in marriage, things started to get ultracompetitive. Matt had graduated at the top of his pastry class at the French Culinary Institute. He'd been the pastry chef at Lutèce and The Water Club; he'd cooked for the rich and famous; and it was going to be *my* cake that put the store on the map?! Oh no, no, no. Matt was insistent *he* was going to start making cupcakes too. In fact, his wouldn't be lame-ass "carrot." He'd make small versions of his famous chocolate peanut butter wedding cake, so good that he claims that every bride he'd ever made it for hugged him (I sincerely doubt this claim).

Matt says: *She can doubt all she wants—it's true. The cake was so good that some of those brides would hug me a little too long too. Wonder how those marriages are working out.*

So now it was more than just the carrot cake. We had two accomplished pastry chefs trying to one up each other with their "really, really, really small cakes." We never treated them like plain ol' run-of-the-mill cupcakes, and we've never strayed from that philosophy. People went crazy for them, and here you are all these years later, holding our cupcake cookbook in your hands. Fancy that.

Bad luck had backed us into a corner and forced us into doing *exactly* what we had been trying so unsuccessfully to do for years—bringing our fancy, highfalutin food ideas to *everybody*—not just the one-percenters eating in tony Manhattan restaurants. We had the bar guys come down, working moms, doctors, subway conductors, sewer workers, lawyers, meter maids, teachers, cops, and firefighters—it didn't matter who you were or how much money you made. Anyone who had a few bucks in their pocket got a chance to eat something really special, no matter what their social class.

Not only that, our strained marriage got the shot in the arm it desperately needed. The previous year had been all about diapers and spreadsheets and checkbook balances. Now we were lying in bed every night, talking about food, dreaming up new recipes, just as we had when we were first dating.

Sometimes bad luck needs to show up and smack you around a little bit to get you on the right path, so many years later you see that it really was good luck all along. But the most important thing that it did for us was teach us what to do when it shows up, because our story certainly doesn't end here. No, bad luck has kept coming again and again—after our business, after our family, after our sanity—and it has been painful every single time. We learn from it, we get up, and we keep going—because we're the Robicellis, motherfuckers! We understand by now with the gift of our hindsight that bad luck is what you make of it, good luck is where you find it, and at the end of the day, we end up better for both.

At least, this is what we keep telling ourselves.

Carrot Cake

This is it, folks—the one that started it all. Yet after a few years in the business and hundreds of cupcake flavors, this cupcake feels so . . . naked. There're no custards or fresh-made cookies or fried chicken, there aren't ten thousand steps and hours of preparation. This cupcake is so easy, we feel like we're cheating when we make it.

Our carrot cake is simple: carrots, spices, cream cheese, and roasted walnuts—and absolutely *no* raisins. I despise raisins with every fiber of my being. They are slimy and gross and think they can just show up wherever the fuck they want, assuming that everyone just loves them. Arrogant bastards. If you want to put raisins in your carrot cake, make sure you tell everyone it's a carrot *raisin* cake so you're not getting everyone all stoked about eating some cake, only to have them bite in, be rudely surprised, and end up hating you. That honestly would be the considerate way to do all your baking, but the raisin mafia ain't having it, because nobody ever buys the raisin cake. Tell me, raisins, if you're supposedly so good, then why the need to be so sneaky? Huh?

Carrot Cake

- 2 cups shredded carrots, packed
- 1 cup granulated sugar
- 1 cup brown sugar
- 1¼ cups canola or grapeseed oil
- 1 teaspoon pure vanilla extract
- 2¼ cups all-purpose flour, sifted
- 1 teaspoon baking powder
- 1 teaspoon baking soda
- 1 teaspoon kosher salt
- ¾ teaspoon ground cinnamon
- ½ teaspoon freshly grated nutmeg
- ½ teaspoon ground ginger
- ½ cup chopped walnuts (optional)
- ½ cup raisins (if you must)
- 4 large eggs, beaten

Roasted Walnuts

1 cup walnuts, roughly chopped
1 tablespoon unsalted butter
1½ teaspoons kosher salt

Cream Cheese Buttercream

One recipe French Buttercream (page 32) or American Frosting (page 34)
One 8-ounce package cream cheese
1 teaspoon pure vanilla extract
¼ teaspoon guar gum (optional)

CARROT CAKE

Preheat the oven to 350°F. Line a cupcake pan with 12 baking cups.

In a stand mixer with the paddle attachment, combine the carrots, granulated sugar, and brown sugar and mix on medium-low until well combined, about 1 minute.

With the mixer running, slowly pour in the oil and vanilla. Continue mixing until combined. Stop the mixer, remove the bowl and paddle, and use the paddle to scrape the insides of the bowl, making sure everything is fully incorporated.

Sift together the flour, baking powder, baking soda, salt, cinnamon, nutmeg, and ginger and add to the batter. Reattach the bowl and paddle to the mixer and mix on medium until just combined, then add the eggs and continue mixing until the batter is homogenous, about 10 to 20 seconds. Remove the bowl and paddle from the mixer and, once again, use the paddle to scrape the bottom and sides of the bowl, ensuring that everything is well mixed.

Add the walnuts, if using, and raisins, if you're a bastard, and mix them in by hand using the paddle attachment.

Scoop the batter into the prepared baking cups, filling them three quarters of the way.

Bake in the middle of the oven for 20 to 25 minutes, rotating the pan halfway through. The cupcakes are done when the centers spring back when you touch them.

Remove the cupcakes from the oven and let cool completely while you prepare the walnuts and buttercream. Leave the oven on.

ROASTED WALNUTS

Line a baking sheet with aluminum foil. Spread out the chopped walnuts and roast in the oven until you just begin to smell them, 7 to 10 minutes.

Remove the pan from the oven. Place the butter and salt on top of the walnuts, gather the corners of the aluminum foil together to enclose the walnuts in a pouch, then shake well for 1 minute to coat with butter and salt. Set aside to cool.

CREAM CHEESE BUTTERCREAM

For French buttercream: Prepare the recipe as directed on page 32. Once completed, add the cream cheese and vanilla and beat on high until well incorporated. If the cream cheese is particularly liquidy, it could cause the buttercream to "break." If that happens, add the guar gum and continue beating on high for 2 minutes until the mixture comes back together.

For American frosting: Prepare the recipe as directed on page 34, replacing the mascarpone with the cream cheese.

ASSEMBLY

Fill a pastry bag fitted with a fluted tip with the cream cheese buttercream and pipe onto each carrot cupcake.

Sprinkle the roasted walnuts on top.

Matt says:
You need to freshly grate carrots for this recipe— preshredded carrots have lost most of their moisture, and we account for that stuff in this recipe. If you really have a problem grating your own carrots— like if you can't even look at a box grater because you dated one for most of high school only to have it stand you up for prom—then soak the preshredded carrots overnight in a bowl of water, then drain well.

Chocolate Peanut Butter Pretzel

The first cupcake Matt ever added to the Robicelli's repertoire was the "CPB": chocolate cake and peanut butter buttercream topped with roasted peanuts and rich chocolate ganache. Sounds awesome, right? Of course it's awesome—how the hell can you screw something like that up? Of course, we eventually tired of awesome and needed to go past that to "mind blowing." So we decided to roll the entire damn thing in crushed-up pretzels and pour more chocolate over the top. You're welcome.

Chocolate Cake
- ¾ cup cocoa powder
- ⅔ cup scalding-hot coffee
- ⅔ cup buttermilk
- ⅓ cup canola or grapeseed oil
- 1 teaspoon pure vanilla extract
- 1 large egg
- 1 large egg yolk
- ½ teaspoon kosher salt
- 1⅓ cups all-purpose flour
- 1¾ cups sugar
- ¾ teaspoon baking powder
- ½ teaspoon baking soda

Peanut Butter Buttercream
- One recipe French Buttercream (page 32) or American Frosting (page 34)
- ½ cup all-natural peanut butter
- 1 teaspoon kosher salt

Classic Ganache
- ¼ cup chopped semisweet chocolate
- ¼ cup heavy cream
- Pinch sea salt

To Finish
1½ cups salted pretzels, such as rods or other thick varieties
¾ cup roasted peanuts

CHOCOLATE CAKE
Preheat the oven to 350°F. Line two cupcake pans with 24 baking cups.

Place the cocoa powder in the bowl of a stand mixer with the paddle attachment and pour the hot coffee over. Mix on low speed until a thick paste forms and the mixture stops steaming, about 1 minute.

Increase the mixer speed to medium. In a 4-cup measuring cup, combine the buttermilk, oil, vanilla, egg, egg yolk, and salt and mix lightly with a fork, ensuring the yolks are broken. Slowly pour into the mixer bowl.

Stop the mixer, detach the paddle, and scrape the bottom of the bowl well to loosen any caked-on cocoa. Reattach the paddle and turn the mixer to medium, letting it run for 1 minute. Stop the mixer again.

Sift together the flour, sugar, baking powder, and baking soda and add to the batter. Mix on low speed until just combined. Remove the bowl and paddle and use the paddle to scrape down the sides of the bowl, ensuring everything is mixed.

Scoop the batter into the prepared baking cups, filling them two thirds of the way.

Bake in the middle of the oven for 20 to 25 minutes, rotating the pans halfway through. The cupcakes are done when the centers spring back when you touch them.

Remove the cupcakes from the oven. Let cool completely.

PEANUT BUTTER BUTTERCREAM
For French buttercream (recommended): Prepare the recipe as specified on page 32. Once the butter is added, add the peanut butter and salt and mix on high to combine. Taste for seasoning. If desired, add more peanut butter, 1 tablespoon at a time, or a pinch more salt. Continue until, after tasting, your eyes roll into the back of your head.

For American frosting: Prepare the recipe as directed on page 34, reducing the sugar by ½ cup, replacing the mascarpone with the peanut butter, and adding the salt. Once combined, taste for seasoning. Add more sugar or peanut butter if desired.

CLASSIC GANACHE
Place the chocolate in a bowl and shake the bowl back and forth until the chocolate flattens out on top.

Heat the cream and sea salt in a medium saucepan until it comes to a boil.

Immediately pour the hot cream mixture over the chocolate and let sit for 2 minutes to allow the chocolate to melt.

Using a heatproof spatula, stir the cream mixture and chocolate together until completely smooth.

Allow to cool slightly before drizzling on the cupcakes. The ganache should not be hot to the touch; it should still be liquid. If it cools completely and becomes solid, microwave it on 50 percent power in 20-second intervals, stirring between each, until the desired consistency is reached.

ASSEMBLY

Fill a pastry bag fitted with a plain tip with the peanut butter buttercream and pipe onto each chocolate cupcake. Put the cupcakes in the refrigerator so the buttercream hardens, about 20 minutes.

Pulse the pretzels and peanuts in a food processor until they're coarse crumbs. Alternately, place in a strong zip-top bag and repeatedly smack the bag with a rolling pin, heavy skillet, or anything else you find enjoyable. Place the crumbs in a pie dish or baking pan.

Remove the cupcakes from the refrigerator and gently roll the sides of the buttercream in the pretzel mixture. Pour a handful of the mixture over the top of each cupcake and lightly pack on with your hand. Shake off any excess and set aside.

Drizzle the ganache across the top of each cupcake.

Tres Leches

This is the third cupcake we ever made, and the hundreds of flavors we've made since have been in an attempt to top it. It may be impossible. This very well might be our bestselling cupcake—it is certainly our most requested. One month I didn't put it on the menu and got 70 percent more threatening e-mails than I normally receive.

Be forewarned that if you make this for guests, they may keep showing up and demanding you make it for them again and again. You can easily solve this problem by buying them a copy of this book and telling them to make it for their damn selves. In fact, you could buy a copy of this book for *everyone* you know, just to be safe. Relatives, neighbors, babysitters, mechanics—this book is really a very good catchall gift. Looks like I solved your "what do I get everyone for Christmas this year" problem! You can thank me later.

Tres Leches Soak

One 14-ounce can sweetened condensed milk (for dulce de leche, if making your own)
¼ cup heavy cream
½ cup milk

Brown Butter Cake

13 tablespoons unsalted butter
4 large eggs
1 cup milk
1 teaspoon pure vanilla extract
1 teaspoon kosher salt
2 cups plus 1 tablespoon all-purpose flour
2 cups sugar
2 teaspoons baking powder

Dulce de Leche Buttercream

One recipe French Buttercream (page 32) or American Frosting (page 34)
One 14-ounce can sweetened condensed milk (if making your own dulce de leche) *or* one jar of commercially prepared dulce de leche
Pinch sea salt

Caramel Shards
¼ cup water
½ cup sugar

DULCE DE LECHE (IF MAKING YOUR OWN)

Matt says: *For this recipe, you'll need to make what is called a bain-marie, aka a water bath. The term comes from the medieval Latin term* balneum Mariae, *meaning "Mary's bath," named after the chick who invented it. Making a bain-marie for the oven is a lot less intimidating than the scary French name implies: You'll need a small baking dish (a loaf pan works well), a larger baking dish that it can fit in to, leaving at least one inch of room on each side, and a kettle full of almost-boiling water. That's it—no special equipment needed!*

Preheat the oven to 400°F.

Empty the sweetened condensed milk into the smaller pan, then cover with aluminum foil.

Place the small pan in the larger one, then place both in the oven. Carefully fill the space between the two pans with water until it comes up three quarters of the way.

Close the oven door and walk away for at least 1 hour. Seriously—don't open the oven door! Go watch some Netflix or something.

Once the hour is up, peel off the foil and check your dulce de leche for color. You want it to be a rich golden brown, like a prizewinning golden retriever. If it's not there yet, put the foil back on and put the pans back in the oven for 15 more minutes. Repeat until the desired color is reached.

Remove from the oven and set aside to cool. Turn down the oven temp to 350°F to bake the cupcakes.

BROWN BUTTER CAKE
Preheat the oven to 350°F. Line cupcake pans with 24 baking cups.

In a skillet over medium heat, melt the butter, stirring occasionally, until the butter becomes a nutty brown color, about 5 minutes.

In a stand mixer with the paddle attachment, beat the eggs on medium-low speed for 2 minutes until light yellow and lightly foamy.

Increase the mixer speed to medium-high. Pour the hot brown butter into the eggs slowly, so that the mixture tempers and the eggs do not scramble. Once the butter is added, reduce the speed to medium-low.

With the mixer running, add the milk, vanilla, and salt. Mix for 1 minute until well combined.

BROWNING BUTTER

Sift together the flour, sugar, and baking powder and add to the butter bowl. Mix on medium until just combined, about 30 seconds. Remove the bowl and paddle from the mixer and, once again, use the paddle to scrape the bottom and sides of the bowl, ensuring that everything is well mixed.

Place the batter in the refrigerator for 10 minutes to allow the flour to hydrate.

Scoop the batter into the prepared baking cups, filling them two thirds of the way.

Bake for 20 to 25 minutes, rotating the pans halfway through. The cupcakes are done when the centers spring back when you touch them.

Prepare the milk soak while the cupcakes are in the oven. Set up a baking sheet with a wire rack.

Remove the cupcakes from the oven. Let cool for 5 minutes.

Take the cupcakes out of the pans and place faceup on the wire rack. Using a fork, dock —or stab—each cupcake three times.

Spoon 1½ teaspoons milk mix onto each cupcake. Let cool completely.

MILK SOAK
Combine the condensed milk, cream, and whole milk in a glass jar. Microwave, uncovered, on high for 1 minute.

Place a lid on the jar and shake vigorously until well mixed. Remove the lid and set the soak aside.

DULCE DE LECHE BUTTERCREAM

Prepare the recipe for French buttercream as directed on page 32 or American frosting on page 34. Add ½ cup dulce de leche and a pinch of salt, and mix well. Taste for flavor. Add more dulce de leche, 1 tablespoon at a time, until the desired flavor is reached.

CARAMEL SHARDS

Place a sheet of parchment paper on a baking sheet, allowing it to overhang the edges.

Mix the water and sugar in a small saucepan until it resembles wet sand.

Cook over high heat, stirring occasionally, until the mixture begins to color. Carefully begin to swirl the pan, continuing to cook until the sugar is a rich amber color.

Immediately pour the molten caramel over the parchment-lined baking sheet. Tilt the sheet back and forth until the caramel cannot spread anymore. Let cool until hardened, about 5 minutes.

ASSEMBLY

Using a pastry brush, give the cupcakes one more quick swipe of the milk mix.

Fill a pastry bag fitted with a fluted tip with the dulce de leche buttercream and pipe onto each brown butter cupcake.

Roll up the parchment paper with the poured caramel, pressing firmly to help the caramel break up into small pieces. Push the larger shards into the buttercream and finish by sprinkling smaller shards across the top of each cupcake.

HALF-ASSED CORNER

If you can buy prepared dulce de leche, feel free to use it. No sense in making your own if you can buy it.

We add the caramel shards because they look sexy and add a nice crunch, but it's completely fine if you want to omit them and save yourself a step. No one will hate you for it.

Tiramisù

Have you ever been to a great Italian restaurant and had tiramisù so good that you just want to start scooping it out of the pan with your hands and shoveling it straight into your mouth? And did you know that apparently doing this in public is considered "gross" and "socially unacceptable," and people will ask you things like "My God, were you raised by wolves?" I thought it would be considered a compliment. Lesson learned.

One of the things I love about cupcakes is that, with enough practice, you *can* shovel an entire cupcake into your mouth while screaming, "Oh, sweet Jebus, just rub this all over my thighs!" in the privacy of your own home. Or you can sit back and savor it like a "mature" human being. If that's your thing.

Espresso Cake

12 tablespoons (1½ sticks) unsalted butter

4 large eggs

2 tablespoons instant espresso powder

1 cup milk

1 teaspoon pure vanilla extract

1 teaspoon kosher salt

2 cups all-purpose flour

1¾ cups sugar

2 teaspoons baking powder

Espresso Syrup

½ cup water

½ cup sugar

3 tablespoons instant espresso powder

Espresso Ganache

1 cup chopped semisweet chocolate

1 cup heavy cream

1½ tablespoons instant espresso powder

Mascarpone Buttercream

One recipe French Buttercream (page 32) or American Frosting (page 34)

½ cup (4 ounces) mascarpone

To Finish
Dutch-process cocoa powder

ESPRESSO CAKE

Preheat the oven to 350°F. Line cupcake pans with 24 baking cups.

Melt the butter in a microwave at 60 percent power for 1½ to 2 minutes. Keep the butter warm—do not allow it to sit and cool off.

In a stand mixer with the paddle attachment, beat the eggs on medium-low speed for 2 minutes until light yellow and lightly foamy. Add the espresso powder.

Increase the mixer speed to medium-high. Pour the warm butter into the eggs slowly, so that the mixture tempers and the eggs do not scramble. Once butter is added, reduce the speed to medium-low.

With the mixer running, add the milk, vanilla, and salt. Mix for 1 minute until well combined.

Sift together the flour, sugar, and baking powder and add to the batter. Mix on medium until just combined, 10 to 20 seconds. Remove the bowl and paddle from the mixer and use the paddle to scrape the bottom and sides of the bowl, ensuring that everything is well mixed.

Scoop the batter into the prepared baking cups, filling them two thirds of the way.

Bake in the middle of the oven for 20 to 25 minutes, rotating the pan halfway through. The cupcakes are done when the centers spring back when you touch them.

While the cupcakes are baking, prepare the espresso syrup. Set up a baking sheet with a wire rack.

Remove the cupcakes from the oven. Let cool for 5 minutes.

Take the cupcakes out of the pan and place faceup on the wire rack. Using a fork, dock each cupcake three times.

Spoon 1 teaspoon espresso syrup onto each cupcake. Let cool completely.

ESPRESSO SYRUP

In a microwave-safe bowl, combine the water, sugar, and espresso powder. Stir gently.

Microwave on high for 1 to 2 minutes until all the sugar is melted. Stir again and set aside.

ESPRESSO GANACHE

Place the chocolate in a bowl and shake the bowl back and forth until the chocolate flattens out on top.

Heat the cream and espresso powder in a medium saucepan until it comes to a boil.

Immediately pour the hot cream mixture over the chocolate, and let sit for 2 minutes to allow the chocolate to melt.

Using a heatproof spatula, stir the cream mixture and chocolate together until completely smooth.

While the ganache is still warm, put 1 teaspoon on the top of each cupcake and spread to coat using the back of a spoon.

MASCARPONE BUTTERCREAM

Prepare the recipe for French buttercream as directed on page 32 or American frosting on page 34. Add the mascarpone and beat until fluffy. (Note that this is additional mascarpone for the American frosting recipe.)

ASSEMBLY

Soak each cupcake with espresso syrup (see page 000 for photographs).

Cover the top of each cupcake with espresso ganache. Let cool in the refrigerator until the ganache is set, 5 to 10 minutes.

Fill a pastry bag fitted with a fluted tip with the mascarpone buttercream and pipe onto each espresso cupcake.

Dust the top of the cupcakes with cocoa powder.

SO YOU HAVE EXTRA . . .
Espresso ganache

- Scoop with a melon baller and roll in Dutch-process cocoa powder or chopped nuts for truffles.
- Squish between store-bought shortbread cookies to make cookie sandwiches.
- Heat with additional cream to make fondue.

Pecan French Toast

We need to start being honest about most breakfasts: they're really dessert. Pancakes? They're cakes made in a pan. It's right there in the title. Muffins? Cake. Danish? Cake glazed in sugar. Doughnuts? Crossiants? Turnovers? All dessert. And then there's French toast—day-old bread soaked in custard, griddled, then drowned in sugary maple syrup and other stuff that's bad for you (no, that side of bacon doesn't make it healthy). I mean, really, who the hell have we been kidding?

Cinnamon Cake
12 tablespoons (1½ sticks) unsalted butter

4 large eggs

1 cup milk

1 teaspoon pure vanilla extract

1 teaspoon kosher salt

2 cups all-purpose flour

1¾ cups sugar

2 teaspoons baking powder

1½ teaspoons ground cinnamon

Maple "Custard" Soak
¼ cup milk

2 tablespoons heavy cream

2 tablespoons grade A maple syrup

Maple-Glazed Pecans
2 tablespoons (¼ stick) unsalted butter

½ cup pecans, roughly chopped

½ cup grade A maple syrup
1 teaspoon kosher salt

Maple Cinnamon Buttercream
One recipe French Buttercream (page 32) or American Frosting (page 34)
¼ cup grade A maple syrup
1 teaspoon ground cinnamon
1 teaspoon pure vanilla extract

CINNAMON CAKE

Preheat the oven to 350°F. Line cupcake pans with 24 baking cups.

Melt the butter in a microwave at 60% power for 1½ to 2 minutes. Keep the butter hot—do not allow it to sit and cool off.

In a stand mixer with the paddle attachment, beat the eggs on medium-low speed for 2 minutes until light yellow and lightly foamy.

Increase the mixer speed to medium-high. Pour the hot butter into the eggs slowly, so that the mixture tempers and the eggs do not scramble. Once the butter is added, reduce the speed to medium-low.

With the mixer running, add the milk, vanilla, and salt. Mix for 1 minute until well combined.

Sift together the flour, sugar, baking powder, and cinnamon and add to the batter. Mix on medium until just combined, 10 to 20 seconds. Remove the bowl and paddle from the mixer and use the paddle to scrape the bottom and sides of the bowl, ensuring that everything is well mixed.

Scoop the batter into the prepared baking cups, filling them two thirds of the way.

Bake in the middle of the oven for 20 to 25 minutes, rotating the pan halfway through. The cupcakes are done when the centers spring back when you touch them.

While the cupcakes are baking, prepare the maple custard soak. Set up a baking sheet with a wire rack.

Remove the cupcakes from the oven. Let cool for 5 minutes.

Take the cupcakes out of the pan and place faceup on the wire rack. Using a fork, dock each cupcake three times.

Take a teaspoon of the maple custard soak and pour it over each cupcake, a small amount at a time, letting it absorb a bit before adding more (if you just dump it, it will run off the top of the cupcake and onto the baking sheet below). Let cool completely.

MAPLE "CUSTARD" SOAK

Combine the milk, cream, and maple syrup in a glass jar. Microwave, uncovered, on high for 30 seconds.

Place a lid on the jar and shake vigorously until well mixed. "Custard" is best absorbed into the cupcake when the cupcake it is still warm, so heat in the microwave in 15-second intervals as needed.

MAPLE-GLAZED PECANS

Melt the butter in a sauté pan over medium heat.

Add the pecan pieces and stir continuously until you can begin to smell them, about 3 minutes.

Add the maple syrup and salt, reduce the heat to low, and continue to cook until all the pecans are uniformly coated. Place the nuts on a dish to cool.

Matt says: *Stay alert! No one wants to burn their nuts! When your nuts get hot, they're going to get fragrant. You'll know when it happens—no one can miss the distinctive smell of hot nuts. If you can smell your nuts, that means the natural oils have gotten good and toasted, and you bet your ass that those nuts are going to be the best damn thing you've ever put in your mouth. Store these glazed pecans in a sealed container in a cool, dry place so the humidity can't get to them and make them too moist—no one wants to be munching on slimy nuts. If you've ever heard someone refer to the summer as "sticky nut season," that's where the phrase comes from.*

MAPLE CINNAMON BUTTERCREAM

For French buttercream (recommended): Prepare the recipe as directed on page 32. After the hot sugar is added, add the maple syrup. Proceed with the recipe as usual. Once the butter is fully incorporated, add the cinnamon and vanilla and beat until mixed. Taste and season with more maple syrup, cinnamon, or vanilla, according to your preference.

For American frosting: Prepare the recipe as directed on page 34, reducing the powdered sugar by ½ cup and omitting the heavy cream, instead replacing it with the maple syrup. Add the cinnamon and vanilla, mix, and taste for seasoning.

ASSEMBLY

Soak each cupcake with maple "custard."

Fill a pastry bag fitted with a fluted tip with the maple cinnamon buttercream and pipe onto each cinnamon cupcake.

Top each cupcake with a generous portion of the maple-glazed nuts.

If that's not enough maple for you (like if you're an elf or something), feel free to drizzle the tops with some more pure grade A maple syrup.

HALF-ASSED CORNER

Replace the candied pecans with chocolate chips and a drizzle of maple syrup to make chocolate chip pancake cupcakes. This can also be done with blueberries, candied bacon (see page 65), or whatever else you like on your pancakes.

Butterbrew

This cupcake started, of course, with my love for a certain fictional boy wizard "who-must-not-be-named" lest we are violently attacked by the lawyers of his publisher, movie studio, various shameless merchandisers, theme parks, and assorted foreign subsidiaries. We were having a party to celebrate the release of one of the movies, and I wanted to serve the beverage that they drink in the novels, henceforth called butterbrew so as to avoid ceding 75 percent of our book royalties to whatever eastern syndicate is currently picking apart this recipe like vultures. There was no known recipe for it, so I just made up my own—a classic New York egg cream, but replacing the chocolate syrup with lots of homemade butterscotch. And *hot damn* was that good. So good, in fact, that we decided that we needed to start making cupcakes out of it.

Instead of making just a butterscotch-flavored cake, we opted instead to make a vanilla cupcake, then soak it with hot butterscotch straight off the stove because great butterscotch needs to be ooey and gooey in addition to sweet and buttery. The main texture component is in the inside of this cupcake, so we garnish the top with a little bit of real edible gold. Sometimes, the inside of your intestines needs to feel fancy, too.

Vanilla Cake

- 12 tablespoons (1½ sticks) unsalted butter
- 4 large eggs
- 1 cup milk
- 1 teaspoon pure vanilla extract
- 1 teaspoon kosher salt
- 2 cups all-purpose flour
- 1¾ cups sugar
- 2 teaspoons baking powder

Butterscotch

- 12 tablespoons (1½ sticks) unsalted butter
- 1¼ cups brown sugar (we use light, but dark is fine too)
- 1 teaspoon corn syrup
- 1 teaspoon kosher salt
- 1 cup heavy cream
- 2 teaspoons pure vanilla extract
- 1 teaspoon bourbon (optional)

Butterscotch Buttercream
One recipe French Buttercream (page 32) or American Frosting (page 34)
½ cup butterscotch (from above)

To Finish
Edible gold leaf

VANILLA CAKE

Preheat the oven to 350°F. Line cupcake pans with 24 baking cups.

Melt the butter in a microwave at 60 percent power for 1½ to 2 minutes. Keep the butter hot—do not allow it to sit and cool off.

In a stand mixer with the paddle attachment, beat the eggs on medium-low speed for 2 minutes until light yellow and lightly foamy.

Increase the mixer speed to medium-high. Pour the hot butter into the eggs slowly, so that the mixture tempers and the eggs do not scramble. Once the butter is added, reduce the speed to medium-low.

With the mixer running, add the milk, vanilla, and salt. Mix for 1 minute until well combined.

Sift together the flour, sugar, and baking powder and add to the batter. Mix on medium until just combined, 10 to 20 seconds. Remove the bowl and paddle from the mixer and use the paddle to scrape the bottom and sides of the bowl, ensuring that everything is well mixed.

Scoop the batter into the prepared baking cups, filling them two thirds of the way.

Bake in the middle of the oven for 20 to 25 minutes, rotating the pan halfway through. The cupcakes are done when the centers spring back when you touch them.

While the cupcakes are baking, prepare the butterscotch. Set up a baking sheet with a wire rack.

Remove the cupcakes from the oven. Let cool for 5 minutes.

Take the cupcakes out of the pan and place faceup on the wire rack. Using a small paring knife, cut a 1-inch slit in the middle of the cupcake, going about halfway down. Then poke the cupcake a few more times on top with a fork.

Lightly pinch the top of a cupcake to open the slit a bit. Take 1 teaspoon of the warm butterscotch and just slide it right in. Unpinch the cupcake and let all that gooey goodness just soak right into the center. Take another ½ teaspoon of the butterscotch, pour it on top of the cupcake, and swirl it over the surface with the back of a spoon. Let cool completely.

BUTTERSCOTCH

Melt the butter in a medium heavy-bottomed, nonreactive saucepan, over low to medium heat.

When the butter is melted, immediately dump in all the brown sugar, corn syrup, and salt and increase the heat to medium-high. Using a wooden spoon, stir the mixture near constantly,

making sure you get into those corners so there's nothing hiding, just waiting to burn and ruin all your hard work.

We're going to keep cooking and stirring this for about 5 minutes, and we're going to be judging our next move based on sight. Initially, the sugar mixture will look like wet sand. In a few moments, it's going to start looking like molten lava, bubbling up and spitting at you. This is good! Just don't forget to keep stirring! Shortly, it's going to stop looking like lava and stop feeling heavy like wet sand. This means the sugar is melting and we're ready to add the cream.

Matt says: *You read our whole bit about mise en place on page 4, right?! And you've been doing it for every single recipe so far, yes? And you're absolutely doing it when you make butterscotch so you don't mess up the entire recipe or end up with third-degree burns, correct?*

Remove the saucepan from the heat and, standing back a bit so you don't burn your face off, slowly pour in all the cream. Slowly stir with your wooden spoon (corners! Don't forget!), making sure all the sugar mix gets incorporated with the cream.

Turn the heat to low and return your pan to the stove. Replace your trusty wooden spoon with a sturdy wire whisk (well done, spoon).

Simmer the butterscotch for 8 minutes, whisking occasionally.

Remove from the heat, transfer to a heatproof bowl, and stir continuously for 1 minute off the heat. Add the vanilla and bourbon, if using, and continue to stir until well combined. When it is cool enough to the touch, taste the butterscotch for seasoning and add more salt, vanilla, or bourbon to taste.

BUTTERSCOTCH BUTTERCREAM

For French buttercream (recommended): Prepare the recipe as directed on page 32. After the hot sugar is added, add the butterscotch. Proceed with the recipe as usual.

For American frosting: Prepare the recipe as directed on page 34, reducing the amount of powdered sugar by ½ cup and omitting the heavy cream, replacing it instead with butterscotch sauce. Taste for seasoning, and add more butterscotch, if desired.

ASSEMBLY

Soak each cupcake with butterscotch (see page 123 for photographs).

Fill a pastry bag fitted with a fluted tip with the butterscotch buttercream and pipe onto each vanilla cupcake.

Using a sharp paring knife, cut off a bit of edible gold leaf and place it on top of each cupcake. Alternately, you may drizzle the top of each cupcake with a tad more butterscotch sauce (but it won't be as fancy).

SO YOU HAVE EXTRA . . .

Butterscotch

- Keep in a jar in the refrigerator—it lasts for several weeks.
- Pour over vanilla ice cream.
- Make our "butterbrew" egg creams. Fill a glass one third of the way full with milk, then pour in the butterscotch until the milk now comes up to the glass's halfway point. Use a butter knife to briskly and repeatedly "stab" the liquid straight to the bottom, while you slowly pour seltzer up to the top of the glass. When the glass is full, stop stabbing and gently stir five or six times to ensure all the butterscotch is incorporated.

HALF-ASSED CORNER

Use store-bought butterscotch.

Omit the edible gold leaf (it's just there to look pretty) and drizzle more butterscotch on top instead.

A Love Letter to Christopher Guest

Many people can pinpoint the exact moment they met "the one." For some it's as instant as a first glance, the electricity of that initial kiss, hearing his or her voice and immediately feeling the air crackle.

I knew Matt was "the one" the second he quoted a Christopher Guest movie to me. My initial instinct whenever I'm feeling sad or hurt is to curl up in bed, throw on *Best in Show* or any of the rest of Guest's flicks, and laugh until finally I feel better. Never before had I met a man who could both randomly insert lines from these films into conversations and also enjoyed having sex with women. Christopher Guest quotes have become the longest-running in-joke of our marriage, a joke only Matt, I, and the entire gay community can understand.

Once we had relaunched ourselves as a bakery, we were having trouble explaining to the press and potential customers our "corporate mission statement." We found ourselves trying to find a way to articulate to a blogger the nature of our creations—how, yes, we used things like fried chicken, blue cheese, and various pork products; how it wasn't meant to be a gimmick; and that everything we did had a distinct reason. She didn't seem to get it, asking us instead if we would make turkey and gravy or brussels sprouts cupcakes for Thanksgiving.

In exasperation, I blurted out, "It's such a fine line between stupid, and, uh . . ."

"Clever," finished Matt.

Spinal Tap.

By that point we'd been together five years, written two business plans, done countless interviews with the media, spent tons of late nights in bed discussing who we were and what our plans were—and after all that soul-searching and self-discovery, the answer all along had been a quote from the Christopher Guest tour de force *This Is Spinal Tap.* The essence of Robicelli's, both personally and professionally, is operating in the gray area between insanely clever and incredibly stupid.

Matt says: *With me being the clever one. I'm also the sexy one.*

The key to our recipes (and in our honest opinion, *all* cooking) is *knowing our ingredients*: tasting them on their own, analyzing the different facets of their flavors, noting their textures, thinking what other things they'll play nice with. Once you know what you're working with, then you can go be clever with it. But if you think you can just take a bunch of "wacky" stuff like Mountain Dew and Doritos, slap them together, and think it's going to work, you're out of your fucking mind.

Food is all about balance. When you have something sweet, temper it with something a little salty or acidic. When you have soft, you want something crunchy or chewy to keep you interested. Something hot? Add something cold. Balance wakes up your tongue, making all your taste buds rise to attention, making you 110 percent present when you're eating. And let's be honest with one another, good dessert isn't remotely good for you. If you're going to put all those calories into your body, you should *really* enjoy them and remember every single freaking one, right?

Don't walk away thinking this philosophy applies only to how enjoyable your food is—keeping true love alive is hard work, and the same principles apply. I don't know if Matt and I would still be together if we didn't understand how important balance is. If we hadn't lost our first store and experienced all the failure and defeat that went with it, how could we appreciate the enormity of all we've been able to accomplish since? If he didn't leave his filthy underwear all over the floor after he showered, how would I truly appreciate what the floor looks like when it's underwear free? If he didn't occasionally get me so angry that I wanted to repeatedly smack him in the face with a tackhammer, how would I appreciate the days where I don't feel like smacking him in the face with a tackhammer?

True love, like food, is about ups and downs, pros and cons, yin and yang. It's about loving someone's faults because those faults do nothing but amplify how amazing someone's strengths are. It's holding someone up through their failures so that you can both bask in their successes.

It's about talking and not talking. Matt and I could not talk or talk forever and still find things to not talk about. Also, we both love soup. And snowpeas.

The Laurenzano

This cupcake, named for Matt's favorite teacher, is a perfect example of the stupid/clever philosophy in action in our kitchen. We're going to stop being silly or dismissive or "OMG bacon cupcakes. LOLOLOLZ!" We're going to act like grown-ups and think like any chef does when writing a recipe: analytically and logically. Grab a pipe and smoking jacket, because you're about to feel smarter.

Picture fresh figs, goat cheese, balsamic vinegar, and prosciutto. Think of them on a salad or maybe a pizza—amazing, right? Slap them on a cupcake? *Stupid*.

Now, analyze: During that small window when figs are perfectly ripe, they're one of the sweetest, most perfect fruits nature can offer. Mashing them up into a cake has been a Brooklyn tradition for ages, because every Italian or Greek worth their salt (us included) has a fig tree in their backyard. Come September, every single fig on that tree turns ripe at the same time, and you need to figure out how to use all seven hundred of them as quickly as possible.

Matt says: Besides Italians and Greeks, know who else loves fig trees? Asshole raccoons. They mysteriously started moving to Brooklyn a few years ago, right after the hipsters showed up, then started invading our fig tree and pelting us with fresh fruit whenever we tried to get rid of them. Am I insinuating that hipsters are really raccoons in disguise? Yes.

Goat cheese is rich and creamy and has a nice tang that always complements sweet things—we can whip the goat cheese into our French buttercream, which is lightly sweet and will accentuate the brightness of the chèvre. Now, with tart and sweet in the picture, we had to introduce one of my favorite secret ingredients in pastry: salt. We could have sprinkled sea salt straight onto the cupcake as we often do, but why not honor a classic culinary pairing by using salty prosciutto we've roasted into crispy little bits?

Sugar? Check. Tart? Check. Salt? Check. We could have stopped there, but it really wouldn't have felt right if we didn't pull the whole thing together with some balsamic. We opted to make a sauce we used in our savory careers—gastrique. In simplest terms, gastrique is a thick vinegar-sugar syrup. It gets slutty on top of pork, but it gets just as slutty on vanilla ice cream. It's the Greta Garbo of vinegar-based pan sauces.

Now look at it again with fresh eyes: *moist fresh fig cake, topped with a whipped*

chèvre French buttercream, accented with crispy bits of imported Italian prosciutto, and drizzled with a balsamico di Modena gastrique.

It is a very fine line between stupid and clever indeed.

Fig Balsamic Gastrique

¼ cup fig jam
½ cup balsamic vinegar
¼ cup granulated sugar

Fig Cake

1½ cups fresh figs, pureed until smooth
1 cup granulated sugar
1 cup brown sugar
1¼ cups canola or grapeseed oil
2¼ cups all-purpose flour, sifted
1 teaspoon baking powder
1 teaspoon baking soda
1 teaspoon kosher salt
4 large eggs, beaten

Crispy Prosciutto

½ pound very thinly sliced imported prosciutto

Goat Cheese Buttercream

One recipe French Buttercream (page 32) or American Frosting (page 34)
½ to ⅔ cup (4 to 6 ounces) goat cheese (chèvre)

FIG BALSAMIC GASTRIQUE

Combine the fig jam, balsamic vinegar, and granulated sugar in a small nonreactive saucepan over medium heat. Stir until the jam is dissolved.

Continue cooking until the mixture is slightly reduced and thick enough to coat the back of a spoon, about 5 minutes.

Pour the sauce into a bowl and refrigerate until thick and syrupy, about 15 minutes.

FIG CAKE

Preheat the oven to 350°F. Line cupcake pans with 24 baking cups.

Matt says:
Buy balsamic the same way you buy cooking wine: Get something nice, but not too nice. Maybe a bottle in the $5 to $10 range.

In a stand mixer with the paddle attachment, combine the fig puree, granulated sugar, and brown sugar and mix on medium-low until well combined, about 1 minute.

With the mixer running, slowly pour in the oil. Continue mixing until combined. Stop the mixer, remove the bowl and paddle, and use the paddle to scrape the insides of the bowl, making sure everything is fully incorporated.

Sift together the flour, baking powder, baking soda, and salt and add to the batter. Reattach the bowl and paddle to the mixer and mix on medium until just combined, then add the eggs and continue mixing on low until the batter is smooth, about 30 seconds. Remove the bowl and paddle from the mixer and, once again, use the paddle to scrape the bottom and sides of the bowl, ensuring that everything is well mixed.

Refrigerate the batter for 10 minutes.

Scoop the batter into the prepared baking cups, filling them three quarters of the way.

Bake in the middle of the oven for 20 to 25 minutes, rotating the pan halfway through. The cupcakes are done when the centers spring back when you touch them.

Remove the cupcakes from the oven and let cool completely while you make the crispy prosciutto and buttercream.

CRISPY PROSCIUTTO

Turn down the oven to 250°F. Line three baking sheets with parchment paper.

Lay the prosciutto slices out on the baking sheets, being careful not to overlap.

Place in the oven and bake for 15 minutes. Check for crispiness—the prosciutto should be crispy enough that it can snap into pieces. If not, bake for an additional 2 minutes, then check again.

Remove the prosciutto from the oven and set aside to cool. Using a chef's knife, dice into small pieces.

GOAT CHEESE BUTTERCREAM

For French buttercream (recommended): Prepare the recipe as directed on page 32. While adding the butter, also add ½ cup of the goat cheese. Add more to taste.

For American frosting: Prepare the recipe as directed on page 34, replacing the mascarpone with ½ cup of the goat cheese. Add more to taste.

ASSEMBLY

Fill a pastry bag fitted with a fluted star tip with the goat cheese buttercream and pipe onto each fig cupcake.

Refrigerate for 5 minutes to allow the buttercream to set a bit.

Spoon about ½ teaspoon of the balsamic gastrique onto each cupcake. Sprinkle crispy prosciutto on top.

SO YOU HAVE EXTRA . . .

Balsamic gastrique

- Keep as a condiment in a jar in the refrigerator.
- Make a panini with a nice Italian Taleggio, some arugula, and gastrique.
- Drizzle on top of pork chops after grilling.
- Toss with freshly cut strawberries and serve over vanilla ice cream or whipped mascarpone.

El Melocotón de la Muerte

Bhut jolokia, aka the ghost chile, is one of the *hottest* chile peppers on earth—four hundred times hotter than Tabasco sauce. In its native India, the peppers are smeared on fences to ward off wild elephants, and the government has been formulating nonlethal hand grenades filled with pepper gas to combat terrorism. Obviously, we hear "weaponized food" and think "Let's make a cupcake out of this!"

We set out to find a way to coax out the actual flavor of the chile, rather than merely focusing on the searing, burning pain that occurs when you eat them straight (go to YouTube "Ghost Pepper" to see what we're talking about). Cupcakes are already full of the usual heat-tempering suspects—dairy, fat, and sugar. We tried to think of what food would be considered the polar opposite of the brutal chile, which led us to the sweet, vulnerable peach. By balancing these two elements against each other, the heat not only becomes a bit more tolerable, but allows the complex flavors and smokiness of the chiles to shine through.

Even though the end result isn't the face-melting experience you'd expect, it is *very important* you exercise extreme caution when working with the bhut jolokia! Wear latex gloves when handling it; do not touch your skin or eyes with anything that has had contact with the chile; keep your kitchen well ventilated; do not inhale any steam produced in either cooking or washing the pot. You may want to wear some sort of eye protection and tie a bandana around your face as insurance. If you think that last part is just a practical joke to get all of you looking ridiculous, I assure you it's not (though feel free to post pictures up on our Facebook page). This chile pepper is a literal monster to work with. But if you take the right precautions, your bravery will be handsomely rewarded.

Matt says: *We use both whole dried and powdered ghost peppers in this recipe, neither of which is more likely to be available in any stores near you. Fortunately, you have the Internet, where everything is always available! (Seriously. I just bought Allison a koala for her birthday. I have no idea how I'm going to hide this thing.)*

In the event you can't find ghost peppers or are too chicken to try using them (bwak bwak bwak!), feel free to substitute cayenne pepper or any dried chile of your choice. Do not use "chili powder," which is dried pepper that is also mixed with garlic, cumin, salt, and other spices.

Peach-Ghost Chile Compote

¾ cup peach juice

1 large or 2 small dried whole ghost chiles

One 1-pound bag frozen peaches, thawed and chopped, or 6 medium, ripe peaches, peeled and chopped

½ cup honey

¼ cup sugar

1 teaspoon kosher salt

Peach–Ghost Chile Cake

12 tablespoons (1½ sticks) unsalted butter

4 large eggs

¾ teaspoon ghost chile powder (use less if you're a scaredy-cat, or more if you're insane)

½ cup peach juice (we like Ceres or Looza)

½ cup half-and-half

1 teaspoon kosher salt

2 cups all-purpose flour

1¾ cups sugar

2 teaspoons baking powder

Ghost Chile Buttercream

One recipe French Buttercream (page 32) or American Frosting (page 34)

½ cup reserved peach–ghost chile compote, pureed

¼ teaspoon guar gum (optional)

PEACH–GHOST CHILE COMPOTE

Matt says: *Remember all the protection we talked about in the recipe intro? Gloves? Eye protection? Bandana? Get that stuff on now. Open your kitchen windows, put on the fan, expel children and small animals from the premises. Overcautious, yes, but we ourselves have gotten a bit lax before, and have suffered horribly for it.*

And for the love of God, do not use the bathroom after handling ghost chiles with your bare hands. You don't want to explain that one at the emergency room (trust me on that). Better yet, just don't touch the stuff at all without wearing gloves unless you want a bunch of strange hospital employees laughing while pointing to your junk.

Now let's have fun and make some cupcakes!

Place the peach juice and whole ghost chiles in a medium heavy-bottomed, nonreactive saucepan with a lid. Bring to a boil, then remove from the heat and let stand, covered, for 30 minutes so the chiles can rehydrate.

Use a fork to remove the hydrated chiles from the peach juice. Set aside.

Add the chopped peaches, honey, sugar, and salt to the pan. Cook over medium heat, stirring occasionally, until the compote is thick and most of the liquid has evaporated, about 10 minutes.

Taste for heat. If you can handle it, chop up the hydrated ghost chile (removing the stem) and add to taste. We use about one entire chopped-up large ghost chile in our compote, but then again, we like ours hot. The majority of the heat is in the seeds, and the majority of the flavor is in the flesh (though there's plenty of heat in there too). Remember that you can always add more heat, but you can't easily take it away, so taste as you go.

Place the peach compote in a bowl to cool. Reserve one half for the topping. Puree the other half in a food processor to add to the buttercream.

PEACH–GHOST CHILE CAKE
Preheat the oven to 350°F. Line cupcake pans with 24 baking cups.

Melt the butter in a microwave at 60 percent power for 1½ to 2 minutes. Keep the butter warm—do not allow it to sit and cool off.

In a stand mixer with the paddle attachment, beat the eggs on medium-low speed for 2 minutes until light yellow and lightly foamy. Add the ghost chile powder.

Increase the mixer speed to medium-high. Pour the warm butter into the eggs slowly, so that the mixture tempers and the eggs do not scramble. Once the butter is added, reduce the speed to medium-low.

With the mixer running, add the peach juice, half-and-half, and salt. Mix for 1 minute until well combined.

Sift together the flour, sugar, and baking powder and add to the batter. Mix on medium until just combined, 10 to 20 seconds. Remove the bowl and paddle from the mixer and use the paddle to scrape the bottom and sides of the bowl, ensuring that everything is well mixed.

Taste the batter for heat. Add more chile powder if you'd like it to taste a bit stronger.

Scoop the batter into the prepared baking cups, filling them two thirds of the way.

Bake in the middle of the oven for 20 to 25 minutes, rotating the pan halfway through. The cupcakes are done when the centers spring back when you touch them.

Remove the cupcakes from the oven. Let cool completely.

PEACH–GHOST CHILE BUTTERCREAM
For French buttercream (recommended): Prepare the recipe as directed on page 32. Once completed, add the ½ cup pureed compote and beat on high until well incorporated. Taste for seasoning and add more compote, 1 tablespoon at a time, if

desired. If the buttercream breaks, add the guar gum and continue beating on high for 2 minutes until the mixture comes back together.

For American frosting: Prepare the recipe as directed on page 34. Add the compote and mix well. If any separation occurs, add more powdered sugar.

ASSEMBLY

Mix any remaining peach–chile puree back into the compote.

Fill a pastry bag fitted with a plain tip with the peach–ghost chile buttercream and pipe onto each peach–ghost chile cupcake.

Using the back of a teaspoon, make an indent in the center of the buttercream. Fill with the cooled peach–ghost chile compote.

SO YOU HAVE EXTRA . . .

Peach-ghost chile compote

- Mix with softened cream cheese and spread on crackers.
- Smear on biscuits with ham.
- Puree and brush onto ribs after grilling.

El Guapo

Corn isn't a vegetable—it's dessert food. Seriously! That sweet corn that we're all so fond of during the summertime? Each kernel is a little bit of starch and a lottabit of pure sugar (*hellooo* corn syrup!), which we slather in butter. Starch with sugar and butter? That's every frikking recipe in this book. It's like corn is really just a cob filled with dozens of miniature cupcakes, all lined up in pretty little rows.

Even though when I explain it corn seems pretty obvious as a sweet, I always have to sell people on the cilantro angle. No, this isn't a savory cake at all. Yes, I know cilantro goes on tacos, and tacos aren't sweet, unless you count those Choco Tacos they used to sell at Taco Bell. Go taste cilantro on its own—it's sort of bright and citrusy, like sunshine in a little green leaf. I wouldn't go making a pie out of it, but then again, you're not eating a fistful of mint leaves at the dessert table either, and I don't see anyone fighting with old minty about his place in the kitchen.

Sweet Corn Cake
¾ cup sweet corn kernels, freshly shucked, or frozen sweet corn
½ cup half-and-half
12 tablespoons (1½ sticks) unsalted butter
4 large eggs
1 teaspoon pure vanilla extract
1 teaspoon kosher salt
2 cups all-purpose flour
1¾ cups sugar
2 teaspoons baking powder

Cilantro Lime Buttercream
One recipe French Buttercream (page 32) or American Frosting (page 34)
⅓ cup fresh cilantro, finely chopped
Zest of 2 limes

To Finish
Plain salted popcorn
2 limes

SWEET CORN CAKE
Preheat the oven to 350°F. Line cupcake pans with 24 baking cups.

Matt says:
In case you were wondering, yes, this was named after ¡Three Amigos! We require all our prospective employees to audition with a rousing rendition of "My Little Buttercup," in addition to surviving the gun-spinning challenge and submitting a résumé.

Place the sweet corn and half-and-half in a blender and puree for 2 minutes. Strain the mixture through a sieve into a 4-cup measuring cup—you should have about 1 cup of liquid. If you're slightly short, add a bit more half-and-half.

Melt the butter in a microwave at 60 percent power for 1½ to 2 minutes. Keep the butter warm—do not allow it to sit and cool off.

In a stand mixer with the paddle attachment, beat the eggs on medium-low speed for 2 minutes until light yellow and lightly foamy.

Increase the mixer speed to medium-high. Pour the warm butter into the eggs slowly, so that the mixture tempers and the eggs do not scramble. Once the butter is added, reduce the speed to medium-low.

With the mixer running, add the corn liquid, vanilla, and salt. Mix for 1 minute until well combined.

Sift together the flour, sugar, and baking powder and add to the batter. Mix on medium until just combined, 10 to 20 seconds. Remove the bowl and paddle from the mixer and use the paddle to scrape the bottom and sides of the bowl, ensuring that everything is well mixed.

Scoop the batter into the prepared baking cups, filling them two thirds of the way.

Bake in the middle of the oven for 20 to 25 minutes, rotating the pan halfway through. The cupcakes are done when the centers spring back when you touch them.

Remove the cupcakes from the oven. Let cool for 5 minutes, then remove the cupcakes from the pan and place on a baking sheet.

CILANTRO LIME BUTTERCREAM

Prepare the recipe for French buttercream as directed on page 32 or American frosting on page 34. Add the chopped cilantro and lime zest and mix well.

ASSEMBLY

Fill a pastry bag fitted with a fluted tip with the cliantro lime buttercream and pipe onto each corn cupcake.

Crush the popcorn over the top of each cupcake for garnish. Using a Microplane grater, zest the limes over the finished cupcakes.

HALF-ASSED CORNER

Omit the popcorn and top with a single cilantro leaf as garnish.

Root Beer Float

Have you ever had a root beer float and thought, "This is nice and all, but it would be *amazing* if only it were a solid instead of a liquid"?

No? Well, we made a cupcake out of it anyway. Enjoy.

Root Beer Custard

½ cup milk

½ cup heavy cream

1 cup root beer

1 large egg

2 large egg yolks

⅓ cup cornstarch

¼ cup sugar

2 teaspoons root beer extract

2 tablespoons (¼ stick) unsalted butter

Root Beer Cake

12 tablespoons (1½ sticks) unsalted butter

4 large eggs

½ cup root beer

½ cup half-and-half

1½ teaspoons root beer extract

1 teaspoon kosher salt

1¾ cups plus 2 tablespoons all-purpose flour

2 tablespoons cocoa powder

1½ cups sugar

2 teaspoons baking powder

Vanilla Buttercream

One recipe French Buttercream (page 32) or American Frosting (page 34)

2 teaspoons pure vanilla extract

To Finish
    24 maraschino cherries

ROOT BEER CUSTARD

Combine the milk, cream, and root beer in a medium saucepan and bring to a boil.

Whisk together the egg, egg yolks, cornstarch, and sugar in a medium bowl until well combined.

While whisking continuously, slowly pour the boiling root beer mixture into the egg mixture. Pour the contents of the bowl back into the saucepan and cook over medium heat until the liquid thickens and comes back to a boil, about 3 minutes.

Pour the custard back into the bowl through a strainer, pushing it through with a spatula. Stir in the root beer extract and butter.

Cover with plastic wrap pressed onto the surface of the custard and set aside to cool as you bake the cupcakes.

ROOT BEER CAKE

Preheat the oven to 350°F. Line cupcake pans with 24 baking cups.

Melt the butter in a microwave at 60 percent power for 1½ to 2 minutes. Keep the butter warm—do not allow it to sit and cool off.

In a stand mixer with the paddle attachment, beat the eggs on medium-low speed for 2 minutes until light yellow and lightly foamy.

Increase the mixer speed to medium-high. Pour the warm butter into the eggs slowly, so that the mixture tempers and the eggs do not scramble. Once the butter is added, reduce the speed to medium-low.

With the mixer running, add the reduced root beer, half-and-half, root beer extract, and salt. Mix for 1 minute until well combined.

Sift together the flour, cocoa powder, sugar, and baking powder and add to the batter. Mix on medium until just combined, 10 to 20 seconds. Remove the bowl and paddle from the mixer and use the paddle to scrape the bottom and sides of the bowl, ensuring that everything is well mixed.

Scoop the batter into the prepared baking cups, filling them two thirds of the way.

Bake in the middle of the oven for 20 to 25 minutes, rotating the pan halfway through. The cupcakes are done when the centers spring back when you touch them.

Remove the cupcakes from the oven. Let cool completely.

VANILLA BUTTERCREAM

Prepare the recipe for French buttercream as directed on page 32 or American frosting on page 34. Add the vanilla and beat well.

ASSEMBLY

Using a pastry tip, hollow out the center of each root beer cupcake (see page 13).

Place the root beer custard in a squeeze bottle or piping bag with a small tip snipped off. Fill the center of each cupcake.

Fill a pastry bag fitted with a fluted tip with the vanilla buttercream and pipe onto each cupcake.

Place a cherry on top. Done!

SO YOU HAVE EXTRA . . .

Root beer custard

- *Eat it.*

Pecan Potato Chip

I can't take credit for the wackiness of this flavor because I totally ripped it off from Immaculate Baking Company. Back when I was pregnant with Atticus, I was head chef of a fancy gourmet market, and we had cases upon cases of their pecan–potato chip cookies that just wouldn't sell. Finally, I opened a box to cut up and sample out, and tried a small piece. And another small piece. And another. And we didn't have to worry about moving those cases, because my fat pregnant ass bought every single one of them.

A mere seven months after Atticus was born I got pregnant with Toby (because we figured "who actually gets pregnant on the first try? The next one will take a few months *at least*!"). Soon enough I started craving the pecan–potato chip cookies like nobody's business, and couldn't find a single box anywhere. The store I had been running had closed, every gourmet shop I called had no clue what I was talking about, and there was no way I was going to haul myself into a hot kitchen in the middle of June to bake some myself while carrying one of Matt's gigantic babies inside my body (something I should have taken into account before marrying a six-foot six-inch former high school linebacker).

I was eight months' pregnant when we attended the Fancy Food Show, looking for products for our original store. My first item of business was to make a beeline to the Immaculate Baking booth, where I intended to eat all their samples and order ten cases of cookies to take home with me that day. And when I got there, I was told the cookies had been "discontinued due to low sales," then "ma'am, please stop crying, it's only a cookie," then "we understand you're upset and hormonal, but there's no need for that kind of language."

This was one of the first flavors we ever sketched out, and I do my best to make it at least once a month, because there will always be a pregnant or otherwise hormonal woman out there who is miserable in her own body and just doesn't know what she needs. And it's *this*. This cupcake is exactly what she needs, all day, every day. Gentlemen, make this for the special lady in your life when the time is right, and you will become a king among men. You have my word.

Salted Butterscotch

4 tablespoons (½ stick) unsalted butter

⅓ cup brown sugar (we use light, but dark is fine too)

½ teaspoon corn syrup

1 tablespoon kosher salt

⅓ cup heavy cream

½ teaspoon pure vanilla extract

½ teaspoon bourbon (optional)

Pecan–Potato Chip Cake

1½ cups all-purpose flour

½ cup potato chips, crushed finely

1 cup granulated sugar

1 cup brown sugar

2 teaspoons baking powder

10 tablespoons (1¼ sticks) unsalted butter

4 large eggs

1 large egg white

1 cup milk

2 teaspoons pure vanilla extract

1 teaspoon kosher salt

1 cup chopped pecans

Vanilla Buttercream

One recipe French Buttercream (page 32) or American Frosting (page 34)

2 teaspoons pure vanilla extract

To Finish

¼ cup roasted pecans, chopped

¼ cup potato chips, crushed

SALTED BUTTERSCOTCH

Follow the directions for Butterbrew on page 121, using the quantities specified in this recipe.

PECAN–POTATO CHIP CAKE

Preheat the oven to 350°F. Line cupcake pans with 24 baking cups.

Place the flour and potato chips in a food processor and process until the chips are finely ground. Add the granulated sugar, brown sugar, and baking powder and continue to pulse until well mixed. Set aside.

Melt the butter in a microwave at 60 percent power for 1½ to 2 minutes. Keep the butter warm—do not allow it to sit and cool off.

In a stand mixer with the paddle attachment, beat the eggs and egg white on medium-low speed for 2 minutes until light yellow and lightly foamy.

Increase the mixer speed to medium-high. Pour the warm butter into the eggs slowly, so that the mixture tempers and the eggs do not scramble. Once the butter is added, reduce the speed to medium-low.

With the mixer running, add the milk, vanilla, and salt. Mix for 1 minute until well combined.

Add the potato chip mixture. Mix on medium until just combined, 10 to 20 seconds. Add the pecans.

Remove the bowl and paddle from the mixer and use the paddle to scrape the bottom and sides of the bowl, ensuring that everything is well mixed.

Place the bowl in the refrigerator for 20 minutes to allow the batter to hydrate.

Scoop the batter into the prepared baking cups, filling them two thirds of the way.

Bake in the middle of the oven for 20 to 25 minutes, rotating the pan halfway through. The cupcakes are done when the centers spring back when you touch them.

Remove the cupcakes from the oven. Let cool completely.

VANILLA BUTTERCREAM

Prepare the recipe for French buttercream as directed on page 32 or American frosting on page 34. Add the vanilla and beat well.

ASSEMBLY

Fill a pastry bag fitted with a fluted tip with the vanilla buttercream and pipe onto each pecan–potato chip cupcake.

Sprinkle the tops with roasted pecans and crushed potato chips.

Drizzle the salted butterscotch over the cupcakes. Refrigerate for at least 10 minutes to set up.

A Love Letter to Old Brooklyn Bakeries

I think Matt and I belong to the last generation of Brooklynites who have any recollection of buying food from several different stores. We didn't go to big-box stores or megamarts when we were kids—we went to butchers and fishmongers and bakers. Why? Because you could count on these people to know what they were doing. Not only that, they knew *you*! These people saw you day in and day out, knew what you liked, knew what items were good that day. Working in these shops wasn't a part-time minimum-wage job to them; it wasn't even just a career. It was a craft, a calling. An art form you learned from people who did it before you, who also taught you how to respect the food and take pride in the quality of your work.

This was in the days before celebrity chefs, rock-star butchers, cheesemonger debutantes, major league produce buyers, pickle luminaries, or majordomo microdistillers. This wasn't considered "artisan"—it was considered a *job*. And if you were the type of person who cared about your customers and what you did, who came to work every day and tried to make the absolute best product you could, then you became a legend.

Brooklyn's sweets all had roots in the old country—the entire reason the baked goods of yore existed was to give people the ability to eat their feelings. Baked goods alleviated homesickness for immigrants. They allowed tradespeople to put their stamp on a burgeoning culture, united expat communities, made people feel a little less lost in a new world. First there were the Germans: Drake's (RIP Ring Dings), Entenmann's, Ebinger. Then came the Jews of eastern Europe, turning out babkas and rugelach at places like Weiss' and Schuller's. The Scandinavians brought Danishes to America. The Poles brought *paczki* to Greenpoint; the Mexicans, tres leches cake to Sunset Park; the Russians, blintzes to Brighton Beach. Every neighborhood had its own distinct ethnic

flavor, and in each you could find a bakery that would, for a few short moments, give people the comfort of being back in their homeland. And for kids like us who were born here, we got to eat our way around the world without paying for airfare. How lucky were we?

For my family, our little slice of heaven was the Italian bakeries of Dyker Heights and Bensonhurst. Dessert in most Italian American households on a daily basis was fresh fruit, but if you were a very good girl that day, there might have been cookies from Rispoli, and if it was a *really* special occasion, someone went to Alba. Alba was so good that if you wanted pastries for Christmas Eve, you could expect to wait in line for one to two hours in the freezing cold. Even though every miserable, little old Italian woman in line would be bitching incessantly about the wait and her fears of impending hypothermia, no one dared get off the line and go somewhere else. One look at Alba's window display would keep you firmly in place: the seemingly countless layers of their delicate *sfogliatelle,* the Kiwanis cakes rotating on their stands like naughty chocolate-drizzled ballerinas, or the pièce de résistance—the legendary Alba cannoli. This is where words fail me, because there is no way to describe the ecstasy of having eaten an Alba cannoli that can truly do it justice. The erotic tango that would occur inside your mouth was so electric, all nipples within a four-block radius would mysteriously spring to attention. Plus, the freaking *pope* used to order his cannolis from Alba! Who the fuck is arguing with the pope?

Then things began to change. Ethnic enclaves started to break up, people began to identify more as being American. Big-box stores and warehouse clubs began to open everywhere. People stopped shopping at bakeries—why bother paying a skilled baker a little more to use quality ingredients and keep traditions going when you could buy a cheap cake slathered in sweetened colored shortening for a third of the price at the chain pharmacy? Please say, "I bought your birthday cake at the pharmacy," and tell me you're okay with that.

One by one, the bakeries, the butchers, the fishmongers—all our great small businesses—began shuttering. Ebinger closed before I was even born, in 1972. Schuller's, Olsen's, Quattlander's, Frances, and even my beloved Alba—all gone. Those are the places we grew up idolizing. I never wanted to be Jean Georges or Thomas Keller. I wanted to be one of those people who made something so good that Brooklynites for generations would argue loudly over it.

"Villabate has the best cannoli? Fuhgeddaboudit—they ain't never had nuttin' on Alba!"

"Why the hell would you go to Mona Lisa for lard bread when you could go to Royal Crown? What do you mean Mona Lisa is better? Go fuck yourself, you fucking stoonad!"

"You think you know good blackout cake? You don't know what the fuck blackout cake is! Ebinger's, now that was a blackout cake! They closed before you were born, so you wouldn't know. All this shit you see everywhere, those assholes couldn't lick Ebinger's ass."

Matt says: *See, you really ain't nothin' in Brooklyn until people are cursing each other out over you. Everyone's got "a guy" for everything—baker, lawyer, whatever you need—and their guy is always "the best." That's what our goal has always been with Robicelli's—to one day become "a guy," until one day we are the guy for just about everyone in Brooklyn. And that, of course, would inevitably lead to people saying "Robicelli's? Everyone says fuckin' Robicelli's! You think they'd cured cancer the way everyone fucking talks about them. Who the fuck do they think they are?"*

For Matt and me, and many kids who grew up in Brooklyn at the tail end of the golden age of small business, we could not forget. Perhaps the resurgence of bakeries and specialty stores here is, in essence, reactionary—as we lose those original generations who came over, as our unique cultural identities disappear, as our parents and grandparents sell off the Brooklyn we love piece by piece to the highest bidder and gentrification slowly erases our history, maybe many of us are returning to our roots in a last-ditch effort to save our culture, to respect the pride and dedication our ancestors built this country with.

Wherever you live, take it from me: It's worth it to spend a few extra dollars at the local butcher, to walk a few extra blocks to the fishmonger, drive a bit farther to the farm stand, or wait in line in the freezing cold at that special bakery. Because honestly, I would kill for just one final Alba cannoli.

Brooklyn Blackout Cake

You say the name Ebinger to any Brooklynite born before 1965 and a smile a mile wide will spread across their face. Ebinger's was *the* bakery in Brooklyn for the better part of the twentieth century, at one point having more than fifty-four locations in the borough—all the more remarkable considering that geographically, Brooklyn really ain't that big. They closed in 1972, shattering the hearts of millions, but having left us with one of the greatest creations in the American culinary canon—the legendary Brooklyn blackout cake.

When Matt and I decided to make a blackout cupcake, we didn't want to make just *any* cupcake. We wanted to make Ebinger's—a legend that was a household name for almost one hundred years, yet today isn't even remembered enough to have a Wikipedia entry. We grilled my parents, my aunts, anyone who was lucky enough to remember what blackouts were supposed to taste like, for painstakingly detailed descriptions. Is this an exact replica? Of course it isn't—this cake hasn't existed for more than forty years, and no one can remember exactly what it tastes like. Is it good enough that my dad can eat one and say he doesn't miss Ebinger's anymore? Yup!

Chocolate Cake
- ¾ cup cocoa powder
- ⅔ cup scalding-hot coffee
- ⅔ cup buttermilk
- ⅓ cup canola or grapeseed oil
- 1 teaspoon pure vanilla extract
- 1 large egg
- 1 large egg yolk
- ½ teaspoon kosher salt
- 1⅓ cups all-purpose flour

1¾ cups sugar

¾ teaspoon baking powder

½ teaspoon baking soda

Chocolate Custard Base

½ cup milk

½ cup heavy cream

⅓ cup sugar

¼ cup Dutch-process cocoa powder

1 large egg

1 large egg yolk

⅛ cup cornstarch

1 tablespoon unsalted butter

1½ teaspoons pure vanilla extract

Chocolate Custard Buttercream

One recipe French Buttercream (page 32) or American Frosting (page 34)

Chocolate custard base (from above)

Chocolate Fudge Glaze

1½ cups semisweet chocolate, chopped

4 tablespoons (½ stick) unsalted butter

2 tablespoons corn syrup

½ teaspoon pure vanilla extract

To Finish

Chocolate cake crumbs

CHOCOLATE CAKE

Preheat the oven to 350°F. Line two cupcake pans with 24 baking cups.

Place the cocoa powder in the bowl of a stand mixer with the paddle attachment and pour the hot coffee over. Mix on low speed until a thick paste forms and the mixture stops steaming, about 1 minute.

Increase the mixer speed to medium. In a 4-cup measuring cup, combine the buttermilk, oil, vanilla, egg, egg yolk, and salt and mix lightly with a fork, ensuring the yolks are broken. Slowly pour into the mixer bowl.

Stop the mixer, detach the paddle, and scrape the bottom of the bowl well to loosen any caked-on cocoa. Reattach the paddle and turn the mixer to medium, letting it run for 1 minute. Stop the mixer again.

Sift together the flour, sugar, baking powder, and baking soda and add to the batter. Mix on low speed until just combined. Remove the bowl and paddle and use the paddle to scrape down the sides of the bowl, ensuring everything is mixed.

Scoop the batter into the prepared baking cups, filling them two thirds of the way.

Bake in the middle of the oven for 20 to 25 minutes, rotating the pans halfway through. The cupcakes are done when the centers spring back when you touch them.

Remove the cupcakes from the oven. Let cool completely. Set 1 cupcake aside for crumbs.

CHOCOLATE CUSTARD BASE

Set out a mixing bowl, a whisk, a medium heavy-bottomed saucepan, a heatproof spatula, and a strainer.

Place the milk, cream, and half of the sugar in the saucepan and cook on medium-high heat.

In the mixing bowl, combine the remaining sugar, the cocoa powder, egg, egg yolk, and cornstarch. Whisk well until pale yellow.

When the milk mixture comes to a boil, immediately remove it from the heat, leaving the stove on. While whisking vigorously, *slowly* pour the hot milk mixture into the egg mixture. Pour it all back into the saucepan and return to the heat, stirring constantly with the heatproof spatula (make sure you get into those corners!).

Bring the mixture back to a boil. The custard will be *very* thick.

Place in a food processor and process until smooth.

Place the custard base in a small bowl and whisk in the butter and vanilla. Refrigerate until cold and set, 30 to 60 minutes.

Matt says: *In the event the custard is too thick for you to manage, or you accidentally get some lumps, you can run the custard through a food processor before refrigerating. And don't feel awful about yourself—every professional pastry chef has messed up a custard at one point in their life.*

Chocolate Custard Buttercream

Prepare the recipe for French buttercream as directed on page 32 or American frosting on page 34. Once the butter is added, add the chocolate custard base and mix on high to combine.

CHOCOLATE FUDGE GLAZE

Place the chocolate, butter, and corn syrup in a microwave-safe bowl. Microwave at 60 percent power at 1-minute intervals until the butter and chocolate are completely melted.

Add the vanilla and stir until combined. Let sit out at room temperature to cool. Do not refrigerate or the glaze will become solid.

ASSEMBLY
Fill a pastry bag fitted with a plain tip with the chocolate custard buttercream and pipe onto each chocolate cupcake. Place the cupcakes in the refrigerator and allow to set, about 20 minutes.

Take the reserved cupcake, place in a processor, and pulse to make cake crumbs. Alternately, you can rip the cupcake into pieces, then rub them between your hands (though this gets messy).

Remove the cupcakes from the refrigerator and dip the tops in the chocolate glaze, letting the excess drip off back into the bowl. Place right side up and sprinkle with chocolate cake crumbs.

SO YOU HAVE EXTRA . . .
Chocolate fudge glaze
- Pour over ice cream for a "magic shell."
- Coat one side of graham crackers to use for campfire s'mores.

Pastiera di Grano, aka Pizza Grana

You know what I don't understand? How we will take an incredible food, attach it to a holiday, and then eat it *only* on that holiday. Like turkey. Turkey's insanely delicious! In fact, stuffing, creamed onions, all that jazz is insanely delicious! Before Thanksgiving, how pumped does everyone get that you're going to get to eat those things? Now, this begs me to ask the question, Why am I eating this only once a year? I mean, I'm a grown-up—I can really do whatever the hell I want *whenever the hell I want*. Not like turkey's going out of season or anything. I could, and *should,* be sitting in a pool in the middle of July, chowing down on turkey legs smeared with mashed potatoes and cranberry sauce. But for some reason that would feel weird. Though for one day it's a rock star, the other 364 days of the year turkey just absolutely does not get the love it deserves.

That's exactly how I feel about *pastiera di grano,* or in our bastardized Brooklyn dialect, "pizza grana." I know many of you may have never heard of this dish, as it's an Italian American staple around Easter. But because this is new to you, you will not be shackled by the harsh chains of tradition. You can totally eat this on Arbor Day, or Lincoln's birthday, or just because.

Wheat Berries and Ricotta

¼ cup dried soft white wheat berries

½ cup fresh ricotta

¾ cup milk

2 tablespoons granulated sugar

Pie Dough

¾ cup powdered sugar, plus additional for dusting

½ cup all-purpose flour

¼ teaspoon baking powder

Scant pinch kosher salt

3 tablespoons unsalted butter, softened

½ teaspoon lemon zest

1 large egg yolk

Italian Citrus Cake
12 tablespoons (1½ sticks) unsalted butter
4 large eggs
½ teaspoon lemon zest
½ teaspoon orange zest
1 cup milk
1 teaspoon orange flower water
1 teaspoon kosher salt
2 cups all-purpose flour
1¾ cups granulated sugar
2 teaspoons baking powder
⅓ cup finely diced candied citron or candied orange zest (optional)

Wheat Berry–Ricotta Buttercream
One recipe French Buttercream (page 32) or American Frosting (page 34)
Wheat berries (from above)
Drained ricotta (from above)
⅛ teaspoon orange flower water
⅛ teaspoon ground cinnamon
⅛ teaspoon freshly grated nutmeg
Guar gum (optional)

To Finish
Powdered sugar

WHEAT BERRIES AND RICOTTA

Place the wheat berries in a bowl, cover with at least 2 inches of water, wrap the bowl with plastic wrap, and let sit overnight to hydrate.

Place a fine-mesh strainer over a bowl and line with a nonprinted paper towel. Add the ricotta, cover with another paper towel, then weight down the cheese with a saucer. Cover the top with plastic wrap and refrigerate overnight.

The next day, drain the wheat berries and place in a small saucepan with the milk and granulated sugar. Simmer on low heat until the wheat kernels are al dente and nearly all the liquid is absorbed, about 25 minutes. While the wheat berries are cooking, preheat the oven to 300°F.

Spread the cooked wheat berries out onto a baking sheet and place in the oven for 5 minutes. Remove from the oven, give a stir, spread out again, and return the sheet to the

oven for another 5 to 10 minutes. (We're not cooking the wheat berries—we're just trying to dry off any surface moisture.) Remove from the oven when the wheat berries are no longer wet on the outside.

PIE DOUGH

Line a baking sheet with parchment paper and dust with powdered sugar.

In a small bowl, combine the flour, powdered sugar, baking powder, and salt and blend with a fork.

Matt says:
You can find wheat berries at health food stores or in the bulk section of some Middle Eastern markets. They're very good for you—you should try them sometime! Outside of this recipe, of course, because there's no way this is remotely healthy.

Add the butter and lemon zest and work them in with your fingertips or the back of a fork until the mixture is pebbly.

Make a well in the center of the mixture, add the egg yolk, and begin to work in the flour mixture. Turn the dough out onto the prepared baking sheet and knead with your hands until smooth. Pat out into a rectangle about 1 inch thick.

Sprinkle the top with powdered sugar and roll the dough out to a 1/8-inch thickness.

Using a pizza cutter, score the dough into batons that are 1/4 x 2 inches.

Place the baking sheet in the refrigerator to rest while you prepare the cupcakes. We'll be baking both of them off at the same time.

ITALIAN CITRUS CAKE

Preheat the oven to 350°F. Line cupcake pans with 24 baking cups.

Melt the butter in a microwave at 60 percent power for 1½ to 2 minutes. Keep the butter warm—do not allow it to sit and cool off.

In a stand mixer with the paddle attachment, beat the eggs on medium-low speed for 2 minutes until light yellow and lightly foamy. Add the lemon zest and orange zest.

Increase the mixer speed to medium-high. Pour the hot butter into the eggs slowly, so that the mixture tempers and the eggs do not scramble. Once the butter is added, reduce the speed to medium-low.

With the mixer running, add the milk, orange flower water, and salt. Mix for 1 minute until well combined.

Sift together the flour, sugar, and baking powder and add to the batter. Mix on medium until just combined, about 30 seconds. Remove the bowl and paddle from the mixer and use the paddle to scrape the bottom and sides of the bowl, ensuring that everything is well mixed.

Stir in the candied citrus, if using.

Scoop the batter into the prepared baking cups, filling them two thirds of the way.

Bake in the middle of the oven for 20 to 25 minutes, rotating the pan halfway through. The cupcakes are done when the centers spring back when you touch them.

While the cupcakes are baking, also bake the pie dough for 10 minutes, rotating the pan once, until golden brown.

Remove the cupcakes from the oven. Let cool completely.

WHEAT BERRY–RICOTTA BUTTERCREAM

For French buttercream (recommended): Prepare the recipe as directed on page 32. Once completed, add the cooked wheat berries, drained ricotta, orange flower water, cinnamon, and nutmeg and beat on medium-low until well combined. The buttercream is meant to be heavily textured with the wheat berries and should not be smooth. If it shows any of the telltale signs of "breaking," add the guar gum ⅛ teaspoon at a time with the mixer on low.

For American frosting: Prepare the recipe as directed on page 34, replacing the mascarpone with the ricotta, and adding the orange flower water, cinnamon, and nutmeg. Fold in the wheat berries. If the buttercream is not stable, add more powdered sugar, 1 tablespoon at a time, until it is sturdy enough to be piped.

ASSEMBLY

Following the score lines, break off the pie dough batons.

Fill a pastry bag fitted with a plain tip with the wheat berry buttercream and pipe onto each citrus cupcake.

Crisscross two batons, on top of each cupcake. Dust with powdered sugar.

HALF-ASSED CORNER

If you can't find wheat berries, you can replace them with cooked white rice instead.

Replace the wheat berry buttercream entirely with the cannoli buttercream from our Dom DeLuise cupcake (page 43). Not as authentic, but still quite delicious.

Use refrigerated pie dough instead of making your own.

Kiwanis

I've had a Kiwanis cake at almost every major event of my life—my christening, my communion, my engagement party. It's a large layered cake filled with vanilla custard, chopped bananas, and roasted walnuts; frosted with mocha buttercream; and then decorated with alternating chocolate-dipped strawberries and cream puffs. It is, in my opinion, *the greatest cake in the history of mankind,* and absolutely the only cake with which to celebrate a major milestone.

I designed this cupcake to celebrate the first birthday of Robicelli's. I'm going to be totally honest. Even though I am head over heels in love with this cake and it is very likely the single most amazing cupcake in our repertoire, it is *highly* labor intensive and a *gigantic* pain in the ass to make—so much so that I forced Matt to swear he'd ensure I'd never make it again, no matter how much I insist on putting it on the menu. Therefore, I am putting the recipe in this cookbook in the hope that *you* will make it, then invite me over for coffee and cupcakes. I make a delightful houseguest.

Pâte à Choux (Cream Puffs)

8 tablespoons (1 stick) unsalted butter
1 cup water
2 teaspoons sugar
½ teaspoon kosher salt
1¼ cups all-purpose flour
4 large eggs
1 large egg white
2 cups vanilla custard

Vanilla Custard (need 3 cups)

1 vanilla bean
1 cup milk
1 cup heavy cream
⅔ cup sugar
1 large egg
2 large egg yolks
¼ cup cornstarch
3 tablespoons unsalted butter

Vanilla Cake

12 tablespoons (1½ sticks) unsalted butter

4 large eggs

1 cup milk

1 teaspoon pure vanilla extract

1 teaspoon kosher salt

2 cups all-purpose flour

1¾ cups sugar

2 teaspoons baking powder

Mocha Buttercream

One recipe French Buttercream (page 32) or American Frosting (page 34)

2 tablespoons instant espresso powder

1 tablespoon hot water

⅓ cup Dutch-process cocoa powder

Pâte à Glacer (Dipping Chocolate)

1 cup finely chopped semisweet chocolate

3 tablespoons canola oil

Cupcake Filling

1 cup vanilla custard (from above)

1 banana, diced

½ cup walnuts, roasted and chopped

To Finish

6 large fresh strawberries, hulled and quartered (plus a few extra for mistakes/ eating)

½ cup chopped roasted walnuts

PÂTE À CHOUX

Preheat the oven to 425°F. Line two baking sheets with parchment paper.

Melt the butter with the water, sugar, and salt in a medium saucepan. Bring to a boil.

Remove the pan from the heat and add the flour, stirring well with a wooden spoon. The dough should become a thick ball. Place the pan back over low heat and continue stirring vigorously—we're making all the moisture in the dough evaporate, so it will take a few minutes. When you see a film of dough begin to coat the bottom of the pan, it's ready.

Move the dough to either a large work bowl or the bowl of a stand mixer with the paddle attachment, and beat on high until all the steam releases from the dough.

MAKING THE PÂTE à CHOUX

Add the eggs and egg white, one at a time, beating well between each addition.

Beat on high for 2 to 3 minutes until the dough becomes elastic when pinched between your fingers.

Using a sturdy piping bag with a 1-inch opening, pipe small cream puffs. Alternately, using a teaspoon dipped in cold water, drop small acorn-size drops of the dough onto the baking sheets, leaving at least 2 inches between them. It's okay if they're not pretty—we're going to fix that.

Dip your fingertips into cold water and gently form each puff into a nicer-looking shape. It doesn't need to be perfectly round, but you don't want any jagged edges.

Bake in the middle of the oven for 10 minutes, then, without opening the oven, turn down the heat to 350°F. Bake for an additional 10 to 15 minutes. The puffs are done when you tap them and they sound hollow.

Turn off the oven. Remove the puffs and immediately cut slits in the bottom of each and pinch slightly to allow the trapped steam to escape. Return the puffs to the baking sheets and place them in the "off" oven to allow them to dry out completely, about 15 minutes. Set aside.

Matt says: *Puffs can be stored, unfilled, in an airtight container at room temperature for 48 hours. Just make sure you loosely wrap them in a paper towel before sealing to prevent them from getting soft.*

VANILLA CUSTARD

Set out a mixing bowl, a whisk, a medium heavy-bottomed saucepan, a heatproof spatula, and a strainer.

Split the vanilla bean and scrape out the seeds. Place both in the saucepan with the milk, cream, and ⅓ cup of the sugar, and cook on medium-high heat.

In the mixing bowl, combine the rest of the sugar, the egg, egg yolks, and cornstarch. Whisk well until pale yellow.

When the milk mixture comes to a boil, immediately remove from the heat, leaving the burner on. Remove the vanilla bean. While whisking vigorously, *slowly* pour the milk mixture into the egg mixture. Then pour it all back into the saucepan and return to the heat, stirring constantly with the heatproof spatula (make sure you get into those corners!).

Bring to a boil and turn off the burner. Place the strainer over a bowl and dump in the custard, pushing it through with the spatula. When the custard is completely strained, add the butter and stir in.

Remove 1 cup of custard to use as filling, leaving the rest for the cream puffs. Cover both portions with plastic wrap placed directly onto the surface of the custard and set aside to cool.

VANILLA CAKE

Preheat the oven to 350°F. Line cupcake pans with 24 baking cups.

Melt the butter in a microwave at 60 percent power for 1½ to 2 minutes. Keep the butter warm—do not allow it to sit and cool off.

In a stand mixer with the paddle attachment, beat the eggs on medium-low speed for 2 minutes until light yellow and lightly foamy.

Increase the mixer speed to medium-high. Pour the warm butter into the eggs slowly, so that the mixture tempers and the eggs do not scramble. Once the butter is added, reduce the speed to medium-low.

With the mixer running, add the milk, vanilla, and salt. Mix for 1 minute until well combined.

Sift together the flour, sugar, and baking powder and add to the batter. Mix on medium until just combined, 10 to 20 seconds. Remove the bowl and paddle from the mixer and use the paddle to scrape the bottom and sides of the bowl, ensuring that everything is well mixed.

Scoop the batter into the prepared baking cups, filling them two thirds of the way.

Bake in the middle of the oven for 20 to 25 minutes, rotating the pan halfway through. The cupcakes are done when the centers spring back when you touch them.

Remove the cupcakes from the oven. Let cool completely.

MOCHA BUTTERCREAM

Prepare the recipe for French buttercream as directed on page 32 or American frosting on page 34. Make a thick paste with the hot water and espresso powder. Add the cocoa powder and half of the paste to the buttercream and beat until light and fluffy. Taste and add more espresso paste according to your personal preference.

PÂTE À GLACER/CHOCOLATE DIP

Place the chocolate in a microwave-safe bowl and microwave on high in 15-second intervals, stirring each time until completely melted.

Add the canola oil, ½ tablespoon at a time, stirring well between each addition. Use immediately to dip the cream puffs and strawberries into.

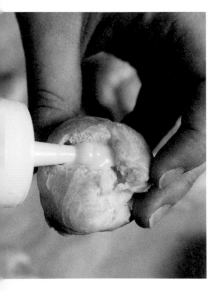

ASSEMBLY

Using a paring knife, make a hole about 1½ inches in diameter in the top of each vanilla cupcake, going about 1 inch down to a point at the bottom. Pop the center out with a spoon. Discard (into your belly).

In a small bowl, mix the reserved 1 cup vanilla custard with the chopped bananas and the walnuts. Stuff the filling into the middle of each cupcake.

Fill a piping bag fitted with a fluted tip with the mocha buttercream and pipe on to each cupcake.

Place the remaining vanilla custard in a squeeze bottle or piping bag with a small tip snipped off. Fill the center of each cream puff with the custard.

Skewer everything with toothpicks to make this next part easier for you: Dip 1 cream puff and strawberry quarter halfway into the pâte à glacer and arrange on top of the first cupcake. Before the chocolate sets, sprinkle with the chopped walnuts. Repeat until all the cupcakes are completed. Refrigerate until ready to use.

Matt says: *Told you it was a pain in the ass.*

SO YOU HAVE EXTRA . . .

Cream puffs

- Freeze for midnight snacks.

Banana walnut custard

- Eat.

Pâte à glacer

- Dip everything in your house in chocolate. Everything. Even the cat.

The Hinsch

Our apartment in Brooklyn is the size of a large dog crate, yet we refuse to move because around the corner is one of the last old school ice-cream joints in all of New York City—Hinsch's. Every generation of my family that has lived in America has been a Hinsch's customer, going back nearly one hundred years. I remember going there with my great-aunt Josie after school many a time, when we'd split a gigantic malted hot fudge sundae made with homemade vanilla ice cream, as long as I "didn't tell my mother."

Today, Hinsch's is a decidedly more modern place, with flat-panel televisions and WiFi, but the latter has made it possible to write chunks of this book while eating many of those flawless homemade hot fudge sundaes, which, thank God, are still exactly the same as they have always been. (In addition, with this paragraph, I've established that thousands of dollars in ice cream is indeed a necessary business expense for tax purposes.)

Malted Milk Balls
2 large egg whites
⅓ cup granulated sugar
¼ cup malted milk powder
½ cup powdered sugar
2 teaspoons Dutch-process cocoa powder

Malted Chocolate Cake
¾ cup cocoa powder
¼ cup malted milk powder
⅔ cup scalding-hot coffee
⅔ cup buttermilk
⅓ cup canola or grapeseed oil
1 teaspoon pure vanilla extract
1 large egg
1 large egg yolk
½ teaspoon kosher salt
1⅓ cups all-purpose flour
1¾ cups granulated sugar
¾ teaspoon baking powder
½ teaspoon baking soda

Malted Milk Hot Fudge

One 14-ounce can sweetened condensed milk

6 tablespoons Dutch-process cocoa powder

3 tablespoons unsalted butter

¼ teaspoon kosher salt

½ cup water

½ cup malted milk powder

½ teaspoon pure vanilla extract

Vanilla Buttercream

One recipe French Buttercream (page 32) or American Frosting (page 34)

2 teaspoons pure vanilla extract

MALTED MILK BALLS

Preheat the oven to 250°F. Line two baking sheets with parchment paper.

In a stand mixer with the whisk attachment, beat the egg whites until frothy. Increase the speed to high and slowly add the granulated sugar, a little bit at a time. Keep whisking until stiff glossy peaks form. Turn the mixer to low and add the malted milk powder. Mix until just combined.

Sift the powdered sugar and cocoa powder over the egg white mixture and fold together with a flat spatula. Transfer to a squeeze bottle or piping bag with ¼ inch tip snipped off.

BEATING EGG WHITES FOR MALTED MILK BALLS

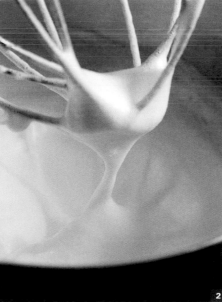

Pipe pea-size balls in rows, leaving at least ½ inch between them. Bake in the middle of the oven for 60 minutes. After an hour, turn off the oven and allow the balls to cool inside, about 30 minutes.

MALTED CHOCOLATE CAKE

Preheat the oven to 350°F. Line two cupcake pans with 24 baking cups.

Place the cocoa powder and malted milk powder in the bowl of a stand mixer with the paddle attachment and pour the hot coffee over. Mix on low speed until a thick paste forms and the mixture stops steaming, about 1 minute.

Increase the speed to medium. In a 4-cup measuring cup, combine the buttermilk, oil, vanilla, egg, egg yolk, and salt and mix lightly with a fork, ensuring the yolks are broken. Slowly pour into the mixer bowl.

Stop the mixer, detach the paddle, and scrape the bottom of the bowl well to loosen any caked-on cocoa. Reattach the paddle and turn the mixer to medium, letting it run for 1 minute. Stop the mixer again.

Sift together the flour, granulated sugar, baking powder, and baking soda, and add to the batter. Mix on low speed until just combined. Remove the bowl and paddle and use the paddle to scrape down the sides of the bowl, ensuring everything is mixed.

Scoop the batter into the prepared baking cups, filling them two thirds of the way.

Bake in the middle of the oven for 20 to 25 minutes, rotating the pans halfway through. The cupcakes are done when the centers spring back when you touch them.

Remove the cupcakes from the oven. Let cool completely.

MALTED MILK HOT FUDGE

Place the sweetened condensed milk, cocoa powder, butter, salt, and water in a small saucepan and bring to a boil, stirring occasionally.

Remove the pan from the heat, pour the fudge into a bowl, and let cool for 5 minutes. Add the malted milk powder and vanilla and whisk to combine. Let cool at room temperature until you're ready to assemble the cupcakes.

VANILLA BUTTERCREAM

Prepare the recipe for French buttercream as directed on page 32 or American frosting on page 34. Add the vanilla and beat well.

ASSEMBLY

Fill a pastry bag fitted with a fluted tip with the vanilla buttercream and pipe onto each malted chocolate cupcake.

Generously drizzle the top of each cupcake with the malted milk hot fudge sauce. Decorate the tops with the homemade malted milk balls.

SO YOU HAVE EXTRA . . .

Malted milk balls

- Keep in an airtight container for 2 weeks. Snack on them as necessary.

Malted milk hot fudge sauce

- Store in a jar in your refrigerator to use over ice cream or cut fruit. Personally, we'd double the recipe to guarantee that you end up with too much.

HALF-ASSED CORNER

Skip making the homemade malted milk balls. You can substitute a maraschino cherry, or just leave it at the malted milk hot fudge. Alternately, you can use store-bought malted milk balls. To make it extra fun, smash them to bits with a hammer first!

A Love Letter to
The Golden Girls

Picture it: Brooklyn, 2008. A young bride and groom with a few dollars and a dream are opening their own business on Bay Ridge's main street. They write press releases and send them out to every newspaper, Web site, and blog they read, only to have them ignored. They toiled in obscurity, working their hands to the bone every day, unable to sleep at night lest they interrupt their hours upon hours of riotous passionate lovemaking.

That bride was me. That groom was Liam Neeson. And the intensity of that lovemaking was responsible for a small series of earthquakes in Perth, Australia, which led to the iron ore shortage of the late aughts.

Okay, maybe that last part didn't happen. And maybe the truth was that after days of Matt toiling at the shop in obscurity, and me at home wrangling two children under the age of two, the hours of passionate lovemaking were more like passing out in each other's arms while watching *Golden Girls* reruns on the Hallmark channel, with occasional high fives tossed in (*passionate* high fives—we know how to keep the magic alive). I had almost no "me" time that year, but after I'd put the boys to bed, I always blocked off at least thirty minutes a night with my girls, even if I was barely conscious for most of the time. As much as they were a constant for me for more than twenty years, I don't think I realized the enormity of their presence in my life until April 2009. I was just a girl who casually liked to watch the show whenever it was on, which, thanks to cable television, was a lot. I wasn't a total nut bag getting tattoos of them or anything incredibly stupid like that. Unlike our friend Eliot Glazer.

By that April we had accepted we'd never be in the newspaper unless something tragic occurred. Then, the cupcakes happened. Holy shit, do people pay attention to cupcakes. No one had cared about a gourmet shop, but make a few cupcakes and in a matter of weeks we were all over the Internet. Soon our front window was full of so many reviews you could barely see inside. And I didn't have to send out press releases anymore—the media began calling *us*. Which, you know, was nice.

I'll never forget April 25, 2009, as long as I live. We had our first packed Saturday in *months*. I must have entertained at least six bloggers that day and learned we'd be featured in Brooklyn's largest newspaper. People were coming into our store from all over the tristate area. Our fortunes were turning. We knew that if we kept this momentum going, then we'd have a shot at keeping our business. At 7:00 p.m. we locked our doors and had begun walking home when my cell phone went off. A text from my friend Andrea contained three simple words: "Bea Arthur died."

And just like that, all the endorphins that had been coursing through my body disappeared as I began tearing up in the middle of the street. Matt groaned, thinking I probably had some leftover pregnancy hormones floating around somewhere that were once again turning me into a whiny little bitch. "Jesus, Al, who the fuck cares? She was old, and you didn't know her. She didn't care about you. I'm not listening to you cry all night!"

He was right—there was no reason for me to be as devastated as I was. Bea Arthur was an actress on a TV show I watched. She could have been a horrible woman who ate baby seals. Yet still, I ran home and searched the channels for whatever network would inevitably be airing a *Golden Girls* marathon. I settled into bed and watched all night, eating junk food and tearing up every now and then, still not understanding why I was so miserable. And when one is that miserable, there's really only one logical thing you can do: go on Facebook and bitch about it so everyone can be miserable too.

I posted a quick "Miss you already, Bea," and someone responded, "You should make a Bea Arthur cupcake as a tribute." Obviously. Matt and I had been accomplished chefs for years at that point. We make cupcakes for three weeks, and all of a sudden everything's "You should make a cupcake out of it."

Matt says: *This became a problem, because Bea Arthur effectively ushered in what was to become known as "The Summer of Death." Two weeks later, Dom DeLuise died, and as he was from our neighborhood, he got a cupcake too. We thought it was a harmless tribute. Then Michael Jackson and Farrah Fawcett went. Then Natasha Richardson, Ed McMahon, Billy Mays, Steve McNair, Walter Cronkite, Ted Kennedy, DJ AM, Patrick Swayze, and the Taco Bell Chihuahua died, along with about five hundred other celebrities. People began posting on our Facebook page, hoping that this one or that one would die because they had a great idea for a memorial cupcake. We had no intention of owning a dead celebrity bakery, nor were we looking forward to watching the news one night and seeing that one of our customers had murdered Jennifer Aniston because "she looked like she'd be delicious."*

Taking their advice, I posted up "Making a Bea Arthur cupcake next weekend—what is it?" and it started getting amazing. *Everybody* I knew started chiming in. People who'd never met each other were talking about their favorite moments from the show, sharing

quotes and videos, making suggestions. Women in their twenties, men in their forties, girlie girls and butches, plumbers, stoners, stockbrokers—the most eclectic group of people I could possibly imagine, all uniting for the common cause of making a cupcake that encapsulated the magic that was Bea Arthur. Cheesecake was a must, a nod to the show (though Bea actually detested it in real life). For the rest, everyone felt she was the living embodiment of a black cup of coffee: strong, bold, no-nonsense, and a force to be reckoned with. And that became the Bea Arthur: a black coffee chocolate cake with cheesecake buttercream, drizzled with espresso ganache.

The next weekend we sold twice as many cupcakes as the previous one, with Matt having to run downstairs midshift to make more. It was like a wake for all of Brooklyn to attend, but instead of viewing a body, people were shoving cupcakes into their mouths. Strangers were striking up conversations with each other about how they'd watched *Maude* with their mothers, how they'd seen her on Broadway in *Mame*, how they wanted to be a teacher one day because of Dorothy Zbornak.

That night while locking up, I was thinking of all the new people I had met that day, thought how we'd all been touched by a celebrity none of us ever knew. The Golden Girls taught me more as a young girl in the 1980s than many adults were willing or able to. They taught me about being, and loving, yourself. That you could be friends with people different than you, and honestly, it was a lot more fun to be different from everyone else anyway. They were the best virtual grandmothers any child could have.

I had always assumed they'd live forever. They were there when I went through adolescence and felt like I didn't belong anywhere. They were there in my late teens when I was figuring out what I wanted to do with my life. They were there when I was going through chemotherapy to show me how pain and fear are human, and okay. They were there in my early twenties when I went through my "Blanche" years. And while I was growing up, watching them frozen in time on my TV screen, they were getting older, and one by one they started to leave us.

Soon we developed cupcakes for all of them, all topped with that famous *Golden Girls* cheesecake, baking them on their birthdays and Mother's Day every year. Our little hat tip to four women we never knew, but who changed all our lives for the better.

There's only one way we can end this. It may seem cheesy, but it's necessary:

Thank you for being a friend, girls. To this day, every night after I tuck my kids into bed, I put on *The Golden Girls* and laugh as I drift off to sleep. And every day ends exactly how it should—with a smile.

Bea Arthur

After being forced to watch every single episode of *The Golden Girls* multiple times, Matt finally developed a love for them as well, with Dorothy being his favorite character. Dorothy was incredibly funny, caring, and nuturing—she was the type of person who constantly got kicked in the teeth by life, but it only made her stronger and more resilent. Most of all, she was the type of person who had no problem allowing herself to be the butt of the joke, and always laughed at herself the hardest.

Matt says the reason she's his favorite is that Dorothy reminds him of me, and our similarities might explain why I love Bea Arthur so much. Which is funny because I thought I loved her because she reminds me so much of Matt—the quick wit, the selflessness, the compassion. And also because of his affinity for gold lamé and shoulder pads.

Black Coffee Chocolate Cake
- ¾ cup cocoa powder
- ½ teaspoon instant espresso powder
- ⅔ cup scalding-hot coffee
- ⅔ cup buttermilk
- ⅓ cup canola or grapeseed oil
- 1 teaspoon pure vanilla extract
- 1 large egg
- 1 large egg yolk
- ½ teaspoon kosher salt
- 1⅓ cups all-purpose flour
- 1¾ cups sugar
- ¾ teaspoon baking powder
- ½ teaspoon baking soda

Cheesecake Buttercream
- One recipe French Buttercream (page 32) or American Frosting (page 34)
- One 8-ounce package cream cheese
- 1 teaspoon pure vanilla extract
- ¼ teaspoon guar gum (optional)

Espresso Ganache

- ½ cup chopped semisweet chocolate
- ½ cup heavy cream
- 2 teaspoons instant espresso powder

BLACK COFFEE CHOCOLATE CAKE

Preheat the oven to 350°F. Line two cupcake pans with 24 baking cups.

Place the cocoa powder and espresso powder in the bowl of a stand mixer with the paddle attachment and pour the hot coffee over. Mix on low speed until a thick paste forms and the mixture stops steaming, about 1 minute.

Increase the speed to medium. In a 4-cup measuring cup, combine the buttermilk, oil, vanilla, egg, egg yolk, and salt and mix lightly with a fork, ensuring the yolks are broken. Slowly pour into the mixer bowl.

Stop the mixer, detach the paddle, and scrape the bottom of the bowl well to loosen any caked-on cocoa. Reattach the paddle and turn the mixer to medium, letting it run for 1 minute. Stop the mixer again.

Sift together the flour, sugar, baking powder, and baking soda and add to the batter. Mix on low speed until just combined. Remove the bowl and paddle, and use the paddle to scrape down the sides of the bowl, ensuring everything is mixed.

Scoop the batter into the prepared baking cups, filling them two thirds of the way.

Bake in the middle of the oven for 20 to 25 minutes, rotating the pans halfway through. The cupcakes are done when the centers spring back when you touch them.

Remove the cupcakes from the oven. Let cool completely.

CHEESECAKE BUTTERCREAM

For French buttercream (recommended): Prepare the recipe as directed on page 32. Once completed, add the cream cheese and vanilla and beat on high until well incorporated. If the cream cheese is particularly liquidy, it could cause the buttercream to "break." If that happens, add the guar gum and continue beating on high for 2 minutes until the mixture comes back together and appears smooth.

For American frosting: Prepare the recipe as directed on page 34, replacing the mascarpone with the cream cheese and adding the vanilla.

ESPRESSO GANACHE

Place the chocolate in a bowl and shake the bowl back and forth until the chocolate flattens out on top.

Heat the cream and espresso powder in a medium saucepan until it comes to a boil.

Immediately pour the hot cream mixture over the chocolate and let sit for 2 minutes to allow the chocolate to melt.

Using a heatproof spatula, stir the cream and chocolate together until completely smooth.

Let cool slightly before drizzling on the cupcakes. The ganache should not be hot to the touch, but still be liquid. If it cools completely and becomes solid, microwave on 50 percent power in 20-second intervals, stirring between each, until the desired consistency is reached.

ASSEMBLY

Fill a pastry bag fitted with a fluted tip with the cheesecake buttercream and pipe onto each black coffee chocolate cupcake.

Drizzle the top of each cupcake with espresso ganache.

SO YOU HAVE EXTRA . . .

Espresso ganache

- Scoop with a melon baller and roll in cocoa powder or chopped nuts for truffles.
- Make a sandwich with ganache and mascarpone, soak in custard, and fry to make tiramisù-stuffed French toast.

Estelle Getty

I love Sophia Petrillo more than just about any sitcom character in history. In most fictional situations, the grandmother is an adorable little old woman who wears an apron, bakes cookies, and says things like "Oh my golly!" My paternal grandmother, however, was just like Sophia—a loud Sicilian woman from Brooklyn who never had a problem telling you exactly what was on her mind. Sometimes this was horrific, like the time she berated a teenage stockboy at Waldbaum's because all the tomato cans that were on sale were dented, then accused the manager of being a "shyster bastard" who was enticing little old ladies into his store with the promise of low, low prices only to attempt to give them botulism. Or the time I watched her shove another grandmother out of the way at Waldbaum's to get her pick of discounted flavored seltzers. Come to think of it, a lot of scary shit went down at Waldbaum's. Everyone make a note: Do *not* fuck with little old Sicilian women when it comes to grocery sales.

Grandmothers like mine or Sophia may not have been the cuddly all-American model, but I'm sure as hell glad they weren't. They were women who came here from poverty, grew up in the Depression, made lives for themselves in a pre-feminist America, raised struggling families in an unglamorous working-class Brooklyn. Those women would give you hell, and you'd come out better for it. Any girl who can crack comeback like it's a whip and takes hell from no one owes broads like them a huge debt.

Amaretti Cookies
- 1¼ cups slivered almonds
- ½ cup powdered sugar, plus extra for dusting
- ⅔ cup granulated sugar
- 2 large egg whites
- ¼ teaspoon cream of tartar
- ¼ teaspoon kosher salt
- ½ teaspoon pure vanilla extract
- 1 teaspoon amaretto

Matt says: *Or if you live by a great Italian grocery like we do, you can just buy a bag of imported cookies from Sicily.*

Amaretto Cake
- 12 tablespoons (1½ sticks) unsalted butter

4 large eggs

¼ cup amaretto

½ cup milk

¼ cup half-and-half

1 teaspoon pure vanilla extract

1 teaspoon kosher salt

2 cups all-purpose flour

1¾ cups granulated sugar

2 teaspoons baking powder

Cheesecake Buttercream

One recipe French Buttercream (page 32) or American Frosting (page 34)

One 8-ounce package cream cheese

1 teaspoon pure vanilla extract

¼ teaspoon guar gum (optional)

AMARETTI COOKIES

Preheat the oven to 325° F, arranging the racks in the lower half of the oven. Line two baking sheets with parchment paper.

In a food processor, combine the almonds, powdered sugar, and ⅓ cup of the granulated sugar. Process until finely ground, using a rubber spatula to occasionally scrape down the sides of the bowl (and don't forget to get into those corners!). Set aside.

Place the egg whites, cream of tartar, and salt in the bowl of a stand mixer with the whisk attachment. Beat on medium speed until the whites are fluffly, then begin to add the remaining ⅓ cup granulated sugar, a spoonful at a time, until stiff peaks form. Remove the bowl from the mixer.

Add the almond mixture, the vanilla, and amaretto and fold together with a rubber spatula until combined.

Drop heaping teaspoonfuls of cookie dough onto the prepared baking sheets, leaving 2 inches between each cookie.

Bake for 15 minutes, then turn off the heat for 10 minutes, leaving the door closed. Crack open the oven door and place a rolled-up kitchen towel in the space to keep the door propped open, letting the heat slowly escape and allowing the cookies to cool inside the oven. The cookies will have a cracked appearance—totally normal.

Remove the cookies from the baking sheet and dust with powdered sugar. Set aside.

AMARETTO CAKE

Preheat the oven to 350°F. Line cupcake pans with 24 baking cups.

Melt the butter in a microwave at 60 percent power for 1½ to 2 minutes. Keep the butter warm—do not allow it to sit and cool off.

In a stand mixer with the paddle attachment, beat the eggs on medium-low speed for 2 minutes until light yellow and lightly foamy.

Increase the mixer speed to medium-high. Pour the warm butter into the eggs slowly, so that the mixture tempers and the eggs do not scramble. Once the butter is added, reduce the speed to medium-low.

With the mixer running, add the amaretto, milk, half-and-half, vanilla, and salt. Mix for 1 minute until well combined.

Sift together the flour, granulated sugar, and baking powder and add to the batter. Mix on medium until just combined, 10 to 20 seconds. Remove the bowl and paddle from the mixer and use the paddle to scrape the bottom and sides of the bowl, ensuring that everything is well mixed.

Scoop the batter into the prepared baking cups, filling them two thirds of the way.

Bake in the middle of the oven for 20 to 25 minutes, rotating the pan halfway through. The cupcakes are done when the centers spring back when you touch them.

Remove the cupcakes from the oven. Let cool completely.

CHEESECAKE BUTTERCREAM

For French buttercream (recommended): Prepare the recipe as directed on page 32. Once completed, add the cream cheese and vanilla and beat on high until well incorporated. If the cream cheese is particularly liquidy, it could cause the buttercream to "break." If that happens, add the guar gum and continue beating on high for 2 minutes until the mixture comes back together.

For American frosting: Prepare the recipe as directed on page 34, replacing the mascarpone with the cream cheese and adding the vanilla.

ASSEMBLY

Fill a pastry bag fitted with a plain tip with the cheesecake buttercream and pipe onto each amaretto cupcake.

Place the amaretti cookies in a zip-top bag and crush them by smacking the bag with the back of a pan. Cover the tops of the cupcakes with crushed amaretti.

HALF-ASSED CORNER

Use store-bought amaretti cookies, or use chopped roasted almonds.

Rue McClanahan

Blanche was, hands down, my favorite of all the Golden Girls. I hope that Matt lives to be a million, but if by chance I do one day find myself a widow, after a proper length of respectful mourning I hope to be banging as many hot, filthy-rich cardiologists as I possibly can.

It's fitting that the character of Blanche Devereaux was from Georgia because there's almost no food that's sexier than a ripe, juicy Georgia peach. And luckily for us, peaches go perfectly with cheesecake! We cook our peaches into a compote with brown sugar and a splash of good ol' Southern Comfort, but if you happen to be making this cupcake during that small sliver of the year where peaches are so ripe and succulent that they're borderline erotic, just lay a few fresh slices across the top—just like Rue McClanahan across a bearskin rug.

Peach Compote

One 1-pound bag frozen peaches, thawed, or 4 medium ripe peaches, peeled and sliced

½ cup brown sugar

1 teaspoon kosher salt

2 tablespoons honey

¼ cup Southern Comfort

Peach Cake

12 tablespoons (1½ sticks) unsalted butter

4 large eggs

½ cup peach juice (we like Ceres or Looza)

½ cup half-and-half

1 teaspoon kosher salt

2 cups plus 1 tablespoon all-purpose flour

1½ cups granulated sugar

2 teaspoons baking powder

Cheesecake Buttercream
   One recipe French Buttercream (page 32) or American Frosting (page 34)
   One 8-ounce package cream cheese
   1 teaspoon pure vanilla extract
   ¼ teaspoon guar gum (optional)

PEACH COMPOTE

In a medium heavy-bottomed, nonreactive saucepan, combine the peaches, brown sugar, salt, honey, and Southern Comfort. Cook over medium heat, stirring occasionally, until the compote is thick and most of the liquid has evaporated, about 10 minutes.

Taste for seasoning, adding more salt, honey, or Southern Comfort according to your desired preference. Set aside to cool.

PEACH CAKE

Preheat the oven to 350°F. Line cupcake pans with 24 baking cups.

Melt the butter in a microwave at 60 percent power for 1½ to 2 minutes. Keep the butter warm—do not allow it to sit and cool off.

In a stand mixer with the paddle attachment, beat the eggs on medium-low speed for 2 minutes until light yellow and lightly foamy.

Increase the mixer speed to medium-high. Pour the warm butter into the eggs slowly, so that the mixture tempers and the eggs do not scramble. Once the butter is added, reduce the speed to medium-low.

With the mixer running, add the peach juice, half-and-half, and salt. Mix for 1 minute until well combined.

Sift together the flour, granulated sugar, and baking powder and add to the batter. Mix on medium until just combined, 10 to 20 seconds. Remove the bowl and paddle from the mixer and use the paddle to scrape the bottom and sides of the bowl, ensuring that everything is well mixed.

Scoop the batter into the prepared baking cups, filling them two thirds of the way.

Bake in the middle of the oven for 20 to 25 minutes, rotating the pan halfway through. The cupcakes are done when the centers spring back when you touch them.

Remove the cupcakes from the oven. Let cool completely.

CHEESECAKE BUTTERCREAM

For French buttercream (recommended): Prepare the recipe as directed on page 32. Once completed, add the cream cheese and vanilla and beat on high until well incorporated. If the cream cheese is particularly liquidy, it could cause the buttercream to "break." If that happens, add the guar gum and continue beating on high for 2 minutes until the mixture comes back together.

For American frosting: Prepare the recipe as directed on page 34, replacing the mascarpone with the cream cheese and adding the vanilla.

ASSEMBLY

Fill a pastry bag fitted with a plain tip with the cheesecake buttercream and pipe onto each peach cupcake.

Using the back of a teaspoon, make an indent in the center of the buttercream. Fill with the cooled peach compote—about 1 teaspoon, though don't worry about being exact.

SO YOU HAVE EXTRA . . .

Peach compote

- Stir into Greek yogurt.
- Make a parfait with the compote, whipped cream, and granola or crushed shortbread cookies.
- Schmear on butter scones or croissants.

HALF-ASSED CORNER

Use store-bought peach jam mixed with a little bit of Southern Comfort or bourbon instead of the compote.

Betty White

Our original idea for this cupcake was to reproduce the traditional St. Olaf friendship cake called "vanskapkaka." It's made with milk, sugar, honey, a whole lot of love, and "just a drop of sunshine." Know what happens when you try putting sunshine in a cake? You end up with third-degree burns. You don't even want to know the carnage that happened once we abandoned that idea and turned our eyes to making "gerflokkenokkin." Stick to our brown sugar–sour cream cake with a touch of lingonberries—just St. Olaf-y enough, while also being safe *and* herring free.

Brown Sugar–Sour Cream Cake

   12 tablespoons (1½ sticks) unsalted butter
   4 large eggs
   ½ cup sour cream
   ½ cup milk
   1 teaspoon pure vanilla extract
   1 teaspoon kosher salt
   2 cups all-purpose flour
   1 cup granulated sugar
   2 teaspoons baking powder
   1 cup brown sugar

Cheesecake Buttercream

   One recipe French Buttercream (page 32) or American Frosting (page 34)
   One 8-ounce package cream cheese
   1 teaspoon pure vanilla extract
   ¼ teaspoon guar gum (optional)

To Finish

   Whole berry lingonberry jam

BROWN SUGAR–SOUR CREAM CAKE

Preheat the oven to 350˚ F. Line cupcake pans with 24 baking cups.

Melt the butter in a microwave at 60 percent power for 1½ to 2 minutes. Keep the butter warm—do not allow it to sit and cool off.

In a stand mixer with the paddle attachment, beat the eggs on medium-low speed for 2 minutes until light yellow and lightly foamy.

Increase the mixer speed to medium-high. Pour the warm butter into the eggs slowly, so that the mixture tempers and the eggs do not scramble. Once the butter is added, reduce the speed to medium-low.

With the mixer running, add the sour cream, milk, vanilla, and salt. Mix for 1 minute until well combined.

Sift together the flour, granulated sugar, and baking powder. Add to the batter, along with the brown sugar. Mix on medium until just combined, 10 to 20 seconds. Remove the bowl and paddle from the mixer and use the paddle to scrape the bottom and sides of the bowl, ensuring that everything is well mixed.

Scoop the batter into the prepared baking cups, filling them two thirds of the way.

Bake in the middle of the oven for 20 to 25 minutes, rotating the pan halfway through. The cupcakes are done when the centers spring back when you touch them.

Remove the cupcakes from the oven. Let cool completely.

CHEESECAKE BUTTERCREAM
For French buttercream (recommended): Prepare the recipe as directed on page 32. Once completed, add the cream cheese and vanilla and beat on high until well incorporated. If the cream cheese is particularly liquidy, it could cause the buttercream to "break." If that happens, add the guar gum and continue beating on high for 2 minutes until the mixture comes back together.

For American frosting: Prepare the recipe as directed on page 34, replacing the mascarpone with the cream cheese and adding the vanilla.

ASSEMBLY
Using a pastry tip, hollow out the center of each brown sugar–sour cream cupcake (see page 13).

Using a very small spoon, fill each cupcake with lingonberry jam.

Fill a pastry bag fitted with a plain tip with the cheesecake buttercream and pipe onto each cupcake.

Using the back of a teaspoon, make an indent in the center of the buttercream. Fill with more lingonberry jam—1 teaspoon or so.

A Love Letter to Compromise

If there's one key to marriage, it's compromise. And a sense of humor—that too. So two keys to marriage: compromise and a sense of humor. And bangarang chemistry in the sack. Sonofabitch.

This fable begins with the most asininely brilliant idea I've ever had. Maybe that's an overstatement as I'm also the person who invented naked rib night. But this one is up there.

Matt says: *You know when you're eating a rack of ribs and you get sauce all over your face and hands? And no matter how many paper towels you use, it still gets stuck under your fingernails and in your hair and you're a total mess? Well here's the solution: Eat them naked. You don't have to worry about getting rib sauce all over everything, meaning you can relax and enjoy the ribs. Then once you're done, you hop into the shower, emerge rib free, and are all ready for bed. Insane? Or brilliant? This is why I married her, folks.*

One of the first ideas we wanted to tackle with our new cupcake line was a series of flavors that celebrated the flavors of Brooklyn's ethnic enclaves, the ones we ate in regularly and drew so much inspiration from. Somewhere in the brainstorming process, I hazily remembered going to an unremarkable greasy spoon in Crown Heights whose name I'll never recall and that probably hasn't existed outside of my memory in more than twenty years. That was the first time I ever had chicken 'n' waffles. It wasn't even particularly good, but even at a young age I was taken by the dish: It was chicken, but with breakfast food. Waffles and syrup with fried goddamn chicken! That's crazy! Then I thought, "But *why* is it so crazy?" Bacon, ham, or sausage with pancakes and syrup, totally normal. Why did fried chicken seem odd? If anything, chicken was even better than the rest of them. It's so mild that *anything* that lacks a strong, distinctive flavor is said to "taste like chicken."

So, why not a chicken 'n' waffles cupcake? I mean, just because people didn't use chicken in dessert didn't mean they *couldn't* use chicken in dessert! A good fried chicken has a nice crispy crust that yields to a meat so tender that you could almost compare it with a custard. It's got a bit of saltiness, a bit of crunch—then paired with some sticky maple syrup, the springiness of the waffle dough, the velvety butter—well, no wonder this dish had stuck with me for twentysomething years. And just because it was considered an "ethnic" dish didn't mean we wouldn't figure out a way to make it popular. Because we're renegades like that. Like Teddy Roosevelt.

Matt says: *Teddy Roosevelt kept five bears and a lion as pets in the White House. Know what Obama's got? A dog. Do we have a petition circulating for more lions in the White House? Maybe.*

I sketched out a recipe, we made our initial prototype, braced ourselves for that first bite—and immediately knew we had created something legendary. Miraculous, even. We knew this cupcake was special, but we couldn't possibly have predicted the media hysteria that would soon ensue once we introduced it. It's inspired knock-offs all over the country. Seriously, four years ago you'd Google this shit and we were the only thing that came up. Now, Google it and you'll find plenty of other entries that aren't TheRobicellisAreOnDrugsAndWeNeedToPlanAnInterventionImmediately.com. Chicken 'n' waffles had officially become a phenomenon.

Then, much as I had suggested the idea for chicken 'n' waffles to Matt a year before, he turned to me and said, "You know what I really want to develop? A Buffalo chicken cupcake." To which I said, "No, that's the stupidest idea I've ever heard."

Remember all that crap I said at the beginning of this story about compromise? If I had just followed my own advice in that exact section, there would be no story here. We'd go straight to the pictures, give you a couple recipes, everyone could go start getting fat. But *noooooo*. . . . I'm an idiot who chose not to listen to my husband and had to endure six months of fighting.

That's right, six months. I thought the idea of a Buffalo chicken cupcake was silly, gimmicky, and disgusting. The chicken 'n' waffles was no gimmick—it was my masterpiece! I could have spent those six months actually listening to my husband like he listened to me, considering his ideas, not dismissing him just like everyone but he had dismissed so many of my ideas. But being part Sicilian gives me a stubborn streak even longer than how it feels to watch any theatrical production that contains children. Also, I'm a wife. We're *never* wrong.

Matt says: *We know you think your seven-year-old redefined the genre with his performance in* The King and I. *He didn't—it was awful. Also, Yul Brynner's ghost is going to haunt your child forever. Especially when he's on the toilet.*

First it started with the eye rolls, then the one-word answers at work, then the muttering under the breath. He claimed I was taking over the company and not valuing his ideas. The Buffalo chicken cupcake discussion grew into the cold war of our marriage. We couldn't even order wings at the bar without getting into a heated screaming match.

"You got to do a chicken cupcake! I want to do *my* chicken cupcake!"

"Nobody can own a chicken cupcake, Matt! Chicken cupcakes belong to everyone!"

"YOU GOT TO NAME THE CHILDREN! ALL I WANT FROM MY LIFE IS TO MAKE A CUPCAKE WITH BUFFALO CHICKEN ON IT!"

Finally, I relented. Not because I believed the cupcake was going to be good, but I just wanted him to shut the fuck up already. We stopped yelling and got to talking seriously about what we were going to do. Matt went in with full-on enthusiasm. I was praying I wasn't going to have to do damage control.

No matter how much I brainstormed, I was pretty certain that this was going to suck, and suck bad. Nothing about this recipe was simple. We spent hours tinkering with the classic recipe for Buffalo sauce, completely baffled as to how this could actually work. Cake after cake after cake ended up in the garbage. Worst of all, my husband was going to fail. While working together again, I realized just how wrong I was about this entire project from the beginning. Not the cupcake—the actual project, and what it had actually been about the entire time.

The store, for better or for worse, had ended up being Matt's, because I was taking care of the kids most of the time. And even though there were a thousand reasons, *good* reasons, why it had gone under, he felt personally responsible. Now, with a failed shop, a struggling company, and a checkbook that was perpetually in the red, he felt that everything he touched was destined for failure. As I've always been the spokesperson for the company, he began to interpret our successes as *my* successes—not mutual successes.

Yes, this was about a lot more than that stupid cupcake. This was his legitimizing himself as the man of the family, as the brilliant chef he was before fortune turned against us. My husband needed to show me that he was still the knight in shining armor that I married, that he could take care of us like he had promised to all those years earlier.

Six months of me not seeing this. Six months of me not compromising, of not listening. Our failures had made me incredibly driven, but also had made me a fucking horrible wife.

Now, all I had to do to make sure my husband didn't totally lose it was to help him figure out a way to make Buffalo sauce taste good on a cupcake. No biggie.

After countless prototypes, and with extreme trepidation, we assembled the final cupcake, tasted it . . . and I didn't hate it. I can't say that I immediately loved it, I can't say it was dessert, and I definitely can't say it was dinner. The more I ate, the more confused I became, but also, the more I began to enjoy it. It was, to coin a genre, "mind-fuck food." It's something you sit down and eat and wonder what the hell is going on, something you are very aware that you are eating and processing. Like a David Lynch movie, but with more frosting.

For Matt, the victory was far more decisive. There was fist pumping, hollering, "whooping." He did it. We put squabbling things aside, worked together again like total equals, like a husband and a wife are supposed to. And to my surprise, the cupcake was an immediate hit. In fact, this is another one of our "you guys are such idiots" ideas that is now copied in bakeries all over the world (though if you're just plopping a wing into a run-of-the-mill supersweet cupcake, it's going to taste terrible. C'mon people, I shouldn't have to tell you that).

Compromise isn't just ceding ground and giving in. Compromise is pulling yourself out of your comfort zone, seeing something from another perspective, thinking differently. Compromise, as hard as it is, helps you grow—whether it's as a chef, a business partner, or a spouse.

Now, ladies and gentlemen, I bring you to what will undoubtedly be the most important part of this book—the part that shall be referenced in this house for, I'm guessing, the rest of my life. As you've gathered by now, I like being right. I really, *really* love being right. So this isn't the easiest thing I've ever done:

Matt, I was wrong. I'm sorry. But thank you for still loving me—even if I suck at being a wife sometimes.

Also, enjoy that last bit, because it's more than likely the last time you'll ever hear it out of me in your lifetime.

Chicken 'n' Waffles

The number-one question we get asked when people see this cupcake is "Is this real chicken?" The second most popular question is "No, *seriously*, is this really chicken?" Fun answers we've come up with:

"No, we just make it look like chicken. It's actually liver."

"Most of them are real chicken, but a few of them are just wadded-up chewing gum—we ran out of chicken late last night with a few cupcakes left to go. Try to guess which ones!"

"We call it chicken 'n' waffles, but it's actually red velvet with a painted rock on top! *Wacky*, right?"

Prepare yourself to answer that question many, many, *many* times.

Fried Chicken

3 thick boneless, skinless chicken breasts (about ¾ pound)

2 cups buttermilk

4 tablespoons kosher salt

Oil for frying (canola, grapeseed, peanut, or other oil with a high smoke point)

2 cups grade A maple syrup

3 cups all-purpose flour

Vanilla Waffle Cake

3 large eggs

1 large egg white

1¼ cups sugar

8 tablespoons (1 stick) unsalted butter

½ cup milk

½ teaspoon pure vanilla extract

¾ teaspoon kosher salt

1⅓ cups all-purpose flour

1¼ teaspoons baking powder

Vanilla Buttercream
> One recipe French Buttercream (page 32) or American Frosting (page 34)
> 1 teaspoon pure vanilla extract

PREPARE THE CHICKEN

Cut the chicken into small chunks, about 1 inch wide. Place in an airtight container with the buttermilk and 2 tablespoons of the salt. Refrigerate for a minimum of 8 hours, preferably 24.

VANILLA WAFFLE CAKE

Preheat the oven to 350°F. Line cupcake pans with 24 baking cups.

Separate the eggs. In a stand mixer with the whisk attachment, beat the egg whites on medium speed until foamy. Increase the speed to medium-high and add half of the sugar, a spoonful at a time, until glossy medium peaks form. Move the egg whites to a large bowl and set aside.

Matt says: Do not be tempted to take a shortcut by using a premade chicken nugget—it won't work. This has to be done from scratch, or not at all.

Melt the butter in a microwave at 60 percent power for 1½ to 2 minutes. Keep the butter warm—do not allow it to sit and cool off.

Add the egg yolks to the now empty mixer bowl and switch to the paddle attachment. Beat the egg yolks on medium speed to the ribbon stage, about 4 minutes.

Increase the mixer speed to medium-high. Pour the warm butter into the eggs slowly, so that the mixture tempers and the eggs do not scramble. Once the butter is added, reduce the speed to low.

With the mixer running, add the milk, vanilla, and salt. Mix for 1 minute until well combined.

Sift together the flour, the remaining half of the sugar, and the baking powder and add to the batter. Mix on medium until just combined, 10 to 20 seconds. Remove the bowl and paddle from the mixer and use the paddle to scrape the bottom and sides of the bowl, ensuring that everything is well mixed.

Using a rubber spatula, divide the egg whites into thirds. Add your first third to the batter and fold in. Once well mixed, repeat two more times with the remaining two thirds of the egg whites until the batter is uniform.

Scoop the batter into the prepared baking cups, filling them two thirds of the way.

Bake in the middle of the oven for 20 to 25 minutes, rotating the pan halfway through. The cupcakes are done when the centers spring back when you touch them.

Remove the cupcakes from the oven. Let cool completely.

FRY THE CHICKEN

Fill a medium heavy-bottomed saucepan halfway full with fry oil, clip on your candy/fry thermometer, and heat to 350°F. Line a baking sheet with three layers of paper towels, then set up an upside-down cooling rack on top of it. Line a 9 × 13-inch baking dish with wax paper. Place the maple syrup in a narrow container with high sides, such as a pint glass or a food-storage container.

In another bowl, mix the flour with the remaining 2 tablespoons salt. Drain the buttermilk from the chicken into yet another bowl.

Take the chicken, a few pieces at a time, and coat completely in the flour. Remove, dip again into the buttermilk, and coat for a second time in flour.

Shake off the excess flour and place the chicken in the hot oil. Fry until golden brown, about 5 minutes.

Remove the chicken from the oil and place on the cooling rack for 1 minute. While still hot, plunge the chicken into the maple syrup and let sit for 10 seconds. Remove the chicken to the wax paper–lined baking dish.

Continue until all the chicken is fried and coated. Let cool completely. Reserve the maple syrup.

VANILLA BUTTERCREAM

Prepare the French buttercream as directed on page 32 or American frosting on page 34. Add the vanilla and beat well.

ASSEMBLY

Fill a pastry bag fitted with a fluted tip with the vanilla buttercream and pipe onto each waffle cupcake.

Top each cupcake with a piece of maple-coated fried chicken. Before serving, drizzle each cupcake with the reserved maple syrup.

Buffalo Chicken

Not that I don't recommend your trying to make this cupcake—you should—but don't make it for dessert. Seriously, if you have guests over and you bring these out after dinner, they're going to be pissed. You make these if you're having people over to watch football, or you're going to some sort of potluck-style picnic scenario where there's going to be tons of other foods for the nonadventurous, or you're really, really fucking stoned. That's legal in a whole bunch of states now, so I don't have to shy away from saying that anymore. We don't smoke ourselves, but we certainly aren't about to judge those who do. We just ask you to remember that ovens are hot, so no matter what cool shit your hand is doing right now, make sure you wear oven mitts.

Matt says: *Again, no shortcuts here! No chicken nuggets, no store-bought Buffalo sauce, no take-out wings from Chicken-on-Wheels.*

Fried Chicken

3 thick boneless, skinless chicken breasts (about ¾ pound)

2 cups buttermilk

4 tablespoons kosher salt

3 cups all-purpose flour

Canola or grapeseed oil for frying

Carrot-Celery Root Cake

1½ cups packed shredded carrots

½ cup celery root, packed

1 cup granulated sugar

1 cup brown sugar

1¼ cups canola or grapeseed oil

2¼ cups all-purpose flour, sifted

1 teaspoon baking powder

1 teaspoon baking soda

1 teaspoon kosher salt

4 large eggs, beaten

Blue Cheese Buttercream
One recipe French Buttercream (page 32) or American Frosting (page 34)
½ cup (4 ounces) fine blue cheese
¼ teaspoon guar gum

Buffalo Sauce
10 tablespoons (1¼ sticks) unsalted butter
⅔ cup brown sugar
½ cup orange juice concentrate or 3 cups orange juice reduced to ½ cup
⅓ cup ketchup
¾ cup Frank's RedHot sauce

PREPARE THE CHICKEN

Cut the chicken into small chunks, about 1 inch in width. Place in an airtight container with the buttermilk and 2 tablespoons of the salt. Refrigerate for a minimum of 8 hours, preferably 24.

CARROT–CELERY ROOT CAKE
Preheat the oven to 350°F. Line cupcake pans with 24 baking cups.

In a stand mixer with the paddle attachment, combine the carrots, celery root, granulated sugar, and brown sugar and mix on medium-low until well combined, about 1 minute.

With the mixer running, slowly pour in the oil. Continue mixing until combined. Stop the mixer, remove the bowl and paddle, and use the paddle to scrape the insides of the bowl, making sure everything is fully incorporated.

Sift together the flour, baking powder, baking soda, and salt and add to the batter. Reattach the bowl and paddle to the mixer and mix on medium until just combined, then add the egg and continue mixing until the batter is smooth, about 10 to 20 seconds. Remove the bowl and paddle from the mixer and, once again, use the paddle to scrape the bottom and sides of the bowl, ensuring that everything is well mixed.

Scoop the batter into the prepared baking cups, filling them three quarters of the way.

Bake in the middle of the oven for 20 to 25 minutes, rotating the pan halfway through. The cupcakes are done when the centers spring back when you touch them.

Remove the cupcakes from the oven and let cool completely while you make the buttercream.

BLUE CHEESE BUTTERCREAM

For French buttercream (recommended): Prepare the recipe as directed on page 32 up to the pâte à bombe stage. After adding the hot sugar to the eggs, wait for 2 minutes, then begin adding the blue cheese in small pieces. Once the mixture is completely cool, add the butter and continue as usual.

For American frosting: prepare the recipe as directed on page 34, replacing the mascarpone with the blue cheese. Beat an additional minute before you begin adding the powdered sugar.

In the event the buttercream breaks, add ⅛ teaspoon of guar gum and beat on high until the buttercream becomes smooth. Add more guar gum pinch by pinch if necessary.

FRY THE CHICKEN

Fill a medium heavy-bottomed saucepan halfway full with canola oil, clip on your candy/fry thermometer, and heat to 350°F. Line a baking sheet with three layers of paper towels, then set up an upside-down cooling rack on top of it.

In a bowl, mix the flour with the remaining 2 tablespoons salt. Drain the buttermilk from the chicken into yet another bowl.

Take the chicken, a few pieces at a time, and coat completely in the flour. Remove, dip again into the buttermilk, and coat for a second time in flour.

Shake off the excess flour and place the chicken in the hot oil. Fry until golden brown, about 5 minutes.

Remove the chicken from the oil and place on the cooling rack. Continue until all the chicken is fried. Set aside to cool.

BUFFALO SAUCE

Melt the butter in a medium nonreactive saucepan over medium heat. Whisk in the brown sugar and orange juice concentrate and bring to a boil. Turn off the heat and add the ketchup.

Using an immersion blender, blend the ingredients while drizzling in the RedHot sauce. (If you don't have an immersion blender, just whisk very well.)

ASSEMBLY

Fill a pastry bag fitted with a fluted tip with the blue cheese buttercream and pipe onto each carrot–celery root cupcake.

Toss the chicken well in Buffalo sauce and place a piece on top of each cupcake. Serve any additional sauce on the side.

SO YOU HAVE EXTRA . . .

Buffalo sauce

- We keep a jar in our house at all times—it's our go-to grilling, burger, hot dog, whatever sauce.
- Don't put on ice cream.

A Love Letter to Columbus Day

My favorite holiday is not St. Patrick's Day or Cinco de Mayo or any other ethnic holiday Americans have co-opted as an excuse to get shitfaced at regular intervals throughout the year; it is Columbus Day. Yes, it's only a matter of time before some frat boys figure out that they can use the day as an excuse to drink limoncello through an ass funnel; but as of now it's still a boring holiday whose main purpose is to inspire all your douchiest friends to take to their MacBook Pros in order to write things on Facebook like "Today we honor a European imperialist who brutally murdered Native Americans with smallpox blankets, so enjoy your day off, fucktards." In the Robicelli home, we decided to take this holiday for ourselves and to celebrate our family. Also, we really didn't want to celebrate Columbus Day the normal way and risk incurring the wrath of any Native American spirits. We've seen *Poltergeist*. We're not stupid.

Because I grew up in Brooklyn, the countryside is a very scary place, potentially filled with swarms of bees and possums and other living things that want nothing more than to see you dead. And by "country," of course I mean New Jersey. Columbus Day in my house meant apple picking. My mother and I would drive to an orchard near my aunt's house in the Garden State and we'd spend a full day picking apples and pumpkins, eating cider doughnuts bought at a rickety little shack, and singing along to Dolly Parton tapes in the car. That one day a year as the sun shone through the leaves, making them twinkle like a canvas of rubies and opals suspended in the sky, I felt like my childhood would last forever.

Then we'd get back to Brooklyn and I'd kiss the floor of my little city dwelling, because even the most spectacular display of fall foliage does not have the power to erase my fear of marauding gangs of murderous bears, or cute little deer that try to lure you in with their adorable doe eyes so they can give you Lyme disease.

As I changed from bright-eyed girl to insufferable adolescent, the apple picking stopped. Columbus Day became just another boring Monday, even though somewhere in the back of my head I knew it was supposed to be special. That's why when I finally met the man of my dreams, I insisted we be married Columbus Day weekend in 2006. The next year we had a six-month-old boy and didn't need pretty leaves to bolster our dreams of a bright future—we were squirreling away any money we had, hoping that soon we'd be able to open our own business. That year, instead of making the trip to the country, we decided to start trying for another baby, so we'd have another set of hands to mine for free child labor when the time came.

By the next year, we did have another baby, and we had opened our business. We had one weekend of incredible success, followed immediately by the stock market crash of 2008 that transformed the main street of our neighborhood from a vibrant thoroughfare into a spooky ghost town. On Columbus Day, Atticus developed a lung infection and spent half the month in the pediatric ICU, hooked up to IVs and monitors and other scary machines that a harried mother of two babies with a new business who was sleeping on a hospital floor cannot accurately remember all these years later. Ten days before Christmas, Matt's mother was struck by a hit-and-run driver in front of her house, leaving her for dead in the street. The months that followed had us juggling the store with our little boys, making trips to the hospital to wait out risky brain surgeries, going to meetings with neurosurgeons, enduring phone calls telling us to drop everything to come say our final good-byes—only to have her miraculously pull through.

None of these events were possible scenarios that were brought up in all those "Be Your Own Boss and Live the Dream!" classes we took.

When the world around you is falling apart and everything you have is invested in a store, you do the one thing that small-business owners do every day: You open your doors and smile. And no matter how bad things got, we did our best to just keep on smiling. Our perfect stuff-fairy-tales-are-made-of marriage began to fall apart. Matt would spend all day at the store, come home just as I put the boys to bed, then I'd either go to the shop to bake or pass out in the exhaustion that comes along with raising two boys under two. During the few moments we saw each other each week, we did nothing but scream at each other out of fear and panic. Our business—our piece of the American dream—was destroying the only thing that truly mattered: our family.

We awoke one Monday, the only day the store was closed, and began our normal day-off routine: cleaning the house, folding the laundry, balancing the checkbook in icy silence in front of the children. Keeping things together and keeping up appearances.

Out of the blue, Matt said, "Let's go apple picking."

Even though I thought of my apple-picking memories constantly, I hadn't actually been to an orchard since I was twelve. I thought he was crazy—we weren't taking a salary, we barely had any money to spend on our basic necessities, and it felt as if it had been weeks since Matt and I had been able to speak to each other for more than twenty minutes without screaming. I could have said that we couldn't afford it, that I could barely stand to be in the same house with him, much less in a car for hours going out to the country. Instead I replied with one word: "Where?"

He said, "I don't care. Away. Away from here, away from Brooklyn, away from our lives, away from this apartment, away from this fucking business. Let's just get in the car and go."

And we did. I dressed the kids and loaded them into the car and Matt found directions to a small town in upstate New York that he had visited as a boy, a town that for him rivaled my memories of my aunt's house in New Jersey. We agreed not to talk about money, not to talk about cupcakes, not to talk about our store or the rent increase, not to talk about Matt's mother, not to talk about fear or pain or desperation.

That day, we would pretend we were millionaires. We'd leave New York City behind and act for only a few hours as if we were once again two people who were just starting out and had their whole lives in front of them, knowing that love could set the world on fire as long as we believed in "us."

We hoisted our sons on our shoulders as they picked apples from the trees—not as giant as they'd seemed when I was a girl, but like redwoods to our kids. We laughed as we rolled down hills and jumped into piles of leaves. We ate apples and doughnuts and handmade fudge. We held hands as we walked down Main Street and peeked into the windows of quaint little shops, and we grinned ear to ear as the boys saw their first real "choo choo train." We stopped fighting. We stopped hurting.

Throughout my life no single sight had given me as much joy as seeing the New York City skyline lit up at night. In this town we'd sacrificed stars in the sky to make our own—millions of windows twinkling in the darkness, an image that could be seen from miles away that always called out to me as my home. As the skyline came into view as we drove home on Columbus Day, for the first time in my life my stomach twisted into knots. I turned to say something to Matt and saw him in the shadows just staring forward with his jaw clenched, tears silently streaming down his face.

The next morning Matt gave me a sweet kiss and a meek smile before heading to our now-despised store, something he hadn't done in weeks. I got out of bed and dressed our children, determined not to let the magic of the previous day be destroyed for them the way it already had been for their mom and dad. I brought them to arguably the most beautiful place in Bay Ridge—Owl's Head Park. Acres of land with hills to roll down, dozens of trees giving up their leaves for jumping piles, and a stunning view of New York Harbor. When it was built in the late nineteenth century, the park was designed to always remain one of the most serene, bucolic spots in all of Brooklyn.

As we built our first leaf pile, I noticed the suffocating odor of poop. I checked my shoes, my kids' shoes—nothing. We moved to another spot, and I kept smelling it—poop. In fact, the scent was getting stronger and more vile. Was it fertilizer? Had a bunch of dogs spent the holiday weekend on a White Castle bender and gone to town on our precious park? Was Owl's Head originally built on a mountain of dinosaur poop, and global warming was finally making its grand reveal?

The answer wasn't quite as logical. Much as when we had designed our quaint mom-and-pop gourmet shop, we had not foreseen a worldwide economic collapse, I doubt the original architect of Owl's Head had foreseen that one day someone would come to the most beautiful spot in that corner of Brooklyn and, upon laying eyes on its magnificent splendor, decided *that* was the right place to build a sewage treatment facility. Nor did the founders of Bay Ridge, Brooklyn, know that the bucolic enclave they were building would be downwind of this eventual plant, meaning that any time we got a good strong breeze off the harbor, the entire neighborhood would reek of hundreds of thousands of pounds of assorted feces from all over New York City.

We headed to a different park, but that too smelled of poop. To the library—more poop. The smell was horrific and inescapable. We went back to our apartment in defeat and closed the windows. As I began to Febreze the furniture, I started crying. Twenty-four hours earlier I was in the most perfect little small town I'd ever seen, having one of the greatest days of my life. Now I was back home in our shoebox apartment, letting my life be destroyed in order to keep a store open in a neighborhood that was ensconced in a thick fog of literal shit. This is what I was sacrificing my family for.

Matt came home and said we'd barely made any money that day—the entire avenue smelled so bad that everyone had apparently stayed indoors. He sat on the bed, stared at the floor, and said, "It's over. There's nothing left. We can't do this anymore. I can't do this anymore. We're closing the store at the end of this month."

And with that, everything was gone. There was plenty of sobbing that day, but unlike every day of the prior year, there was no screaming, no name calling, no tossing blame back and forth. We realized that with the store gone we had our freedom again. People had been traveling from all over New York City for our cupcakes and begging us to open shops in every neighborhood but the one we were in. What if we could keep doing what we loved—the baking—but instead of killing ourselves running a store, we sold cupcakes to shops all over Brooklyn? Then maybe one day we could sell them all over the world! We could grow the company at our pace, spend time with our children, repair our marriage, and keep working together toward our new dream—making millions of people happy.

Losing everything and hitting rock bottom is pretty much the worst possible way to learn what's most important in life. In fact, I highly recommend you never do it, and instead just take my word for it: There is absolutely no amount of money you can make or stuff you can buy that will truly make you happy.

Happiness is as simple as loving with your whole heart, and knowing that in some way you are loved in return. That's all. Everything falls into place after that.

Every year since that day, we spend Columbus Day at an apple orchard somewhere far, far away from Brooklyn, celebrating not the day Robicelli's was born, but the thing that made it all possible. Celebrating the fact that we chose love over all else, and that that choice was the thing that ended up saving it all.

It may not be the intended meaning of the day, but I'm sure that Columbus is up in heaven looking down on our little tradition and smiling, as are all those Native Americans he accidentally murdered with smallpox blankets. I mean really, they can't stay pissed off forever.

Apple Maple Crisp

Every apple-picking day we return with roughly one hundred pounds of apples to be eaten by two adults and two small children. Truthfully, I end up eating about six apples a year, so I don't know who I'm kidding bringing home all these goddamn apples. I tell myself, "I'm going to make a bunch of my famous apple pies," but even if I do find the time between being a mom, keeping up with the house, running a business, and screwing around on the Internet, at best I'm going to use up a small fraction of those apples. Plus for every time I've promised it, I've never actually gotten around to making a single pie (next year, though! For real!). We could make a giant pot of applesauce before the entire lot of it rots, but no one likes applesauce that much. When was the last time you watched someone eat a giant bowl of applesauce?

Apple butter, on the other hand, seems a little more gourmet. It can be put into jars and canned, which can then be stored for ages or given away for Christmas a few short months later. If you're not the canning type, store plastic containers of it in the freezer. Use it throughout the year on your morning toast, on peanut butter or turkey and Brie sandwiches, with pork chops, mixed into oatmeal, poured into a graham cracker crust with some vanilla pudding, or my personal favorite—dollop on top of vanilla ice cream with crushed-up shortbread for a one-minute "deconstructed apple pie à la mode."

Matt says: "Deconstructed" desserts are a fancy way of rearranging ingredients in classic recipes, then charging thirteen dollars for them in a trendy restaurant.

Because apple butter requires a long cooking time at low and slow temperatures, we make ours in the oven, though in a home kitchen, we recommend using a slow cooker because it's going to make your life a hell of a lot easier. Start that at least twenty-four hours before you're going to make the rest of this recipe or, if you can't wait that long, just use store bought.

Slow-Cooker Apple Butter
3 pounds cooking apples
1 cup apple cider

1 cup granulated sugar

½ cup brown sugar

½ cup grade B maple syrup

¼ cup fresh lemon juice

1 teaspoon kosher salt

1 vanilla bean, split

1 teaspoon ground cinnamon

½ teaspoon ground ginger

½ teaspoon ground cardamom

¼ teaspoon freshly grated nutmeg

Apple Cake

2 cups of peeled, shredded, drained, and pressed apples (about 2 large cooking apples; see page 26)

1 cup granulated sugar

¾ cup brown sugar

⅓ cup grade B maple syrup

1 cup canola or grapeseed oil

2¼ cups all-purpose flour, sifted, plus extra if needed

1 teaspoon baking powder

1 teaspoon baking soda

1 teaspoon kosher salt

½ teaspoon ground cinnamon

¼ teaspoon ground cardamom

¼ teaspoon freshly grated nutmeg

4 large eggs plus 1 large egg white, lightly beaten

Maple Oat Crisp

6 tablespoons (¾ stick) unsalted butter, softened

1½ cups quick-cooking oats

¾ cup brown sugar

1 teaspoon kosher salt

¼ cup grade B maple syrup

½ cup all-purpose flour

Vanilla Buttercream

One recipe French Buttercream (page 32) or American Frosting (page 34)

2 teaspoons pure vanilla extract

To Finish
    Grade A maple syrup

SLOW-COOKER APPLE BUTTER

Peel, core, and finely chop the apples, reserving any juices that come out of them. Place in the slow-cooker pot with the apple cider, granulated sugar, brown sugar, maple syrup, lemon juice, salt, vanilla bean, cinnamon, ginger, cardamom, and nutmeg. Set to low for 9 hours. If you want to do this before you go to bed, that would be smart—you'll be using your time wisely, *and* wake up to a house that smells amazing.

Remove the lid of the pot, give the mixture a good stir, then set to high and continue to cook for another 3 hours to allow the excess moisture to evaporate and the flavors to concentrate. If for any reason the apple butter gets too thick, add more apple cider, ¼ cup at a time, until the desired consistency is reached.

Fish out the vanilla bean. Transfer the apple butter to a food processor and blend until smooth. If you don't have a food processor, you can use an immersion blender, or just leave the butter slightly chunky. It's not really "butter" that way, but it is still delicious.

APPLE CAKE

Preheat the oven to 350°F. Line cupcake pans with 24 baking cups.

In a stand mixer with the paddle attachment, combine the apples, granulated sugar, and brown sugar and mix on medium-low until well combined, about 1 minute.

With the mixer running, slowly pour in the maple syrup, oil, and eggs. Continue mixing until combined. Stop the mixer, remove the bowl and paddle, and use the paddle to scrape the insides of the bowl, making sure everything is fully incorporated.

Sift together the flour, baking powder, baking soda, salt, cinnamon, cardamom, and nutmeg, and add to the batter. Mix on medium until just combined, then add the eggs, and continue mixing until the batter is smooth, about 10 to 20 seconds. Remove the bowl and paddle from the mixer and use the paddle to scrape the bottom and sides of the bowl, ensuring that everything is well mixed.

Scoop the batter into the prepared baking cups, filling them three quarters of the way.

Bake in the middle of the oven for 20 to 25 minutes, rotating the pan halfway through. The cupcakes are done when the centers spring back when you touch them.

Remove the cupcakes from the oven and let cool completely while you make the oat crisp and buttercream.

Matt says: Achtung! *Depending on the kind of apples you use, your cake batter may appear a little loose and watery. If this happens to you, add another 2 tablespoons flour, then allow the batter to sit in the refrigerator for 10 minutes or so to allow it to hydrate a bit before baking.*

MAPLE OAT CRISP

Increase the oven temperature to 375° F. Line a baking sheet with parchment paper or a nonstick baking mat.

In the mixer with the paddle attachment, cream the butter, oats, brown sugar, and salt on high speed until well mixed. Drizzle in the maple syrup.

Turn the mixer to low and add the flour, a bit at a time, until the mixture is crumbly.

Crumble the oat crisp loosely across the baking sheet, letting the mixture fall through your fingers in small clumps.

Bake for 5 minutes, remove the pan, stir the crisp to redistribute, then bake for another 5 minutes, or until golden brown. Cool completely before using.

VANILLA BUTTERCREAM

Prepare the recipe for French buttercream as directed on page 32 or American frosting on page 34. While adding the butter, also add the vanilla.

ASSEMBLY

Fill a pastry bag fitted with a fluted tip with the vanilla buttercream and pipe onto each apple cupcake.

Using the back of a teaspoon, make a small divot in the center of each cupcake, about 1 inch wide.

Fill with a generous scoop of the cooled apple butter.

Sprinkle the oat crisp across the top of each cupcake. Serve immediately or refrigerate until 10 to 30 minutes before serving.

Before serving, drizzle each cupcake with a small amount of maple syrup.

SO YOU HAVE EXTRA . . .

Apple butter

- Use on toast, scones, or croissants in the morning.
- Serve as a condiment alongside pork chops.
- Make ice cream sundaes with vanilla ice cream, apple butter, maple syrup, and crushed graham crackers.
- Spread on a ham and cheddar sandwich instead of mayonnaise.

HALF-ASSED CORNER

Use store-bought apple butter.

Replace the oat crisp with crushed granola.

Butternut Spice

At the risk of making all the other cupcakes jealous, I think that this is my absolute favorite of our two hundred (and counting!) flavors. Just try to keep it our little secret, because if that tidbit gets out, the other flavors are likely to get really depressed and, seriously, how pathetic would a depressed cupcake look? Skulking around, listening to Morrissey, writing shitty poetry, posting vague Facebook status updates, sending you text messages all the time about why you're a fucking moron for saying you didn't "get" Morrissey, because *of course* you wouldn't, you filthy corporate capitalist sheep. God, that would be *so annoying*. I really don't want to put up with that, so everyone keep their damn mouths shut.

Candied Pumpkin Seeds

4 tablespoons (½ stick) unsalted butter
¼ cup brown sugar
½ cup raw shelled pumpkin seeds (aka pepitas)
½ teaspoon kosher salt
¼ teaspoon ground cinnamon
¼ teaspoon cayenne pepper
¼ cup butternut squash seed oil

Butternut Squash Cake

1½ cups roasted butternut squash, drained of excess liquid
1 cup granulated sugar
1 cup brown sugar
1¼ cups canola or grapeseed oil
2 cups all-purpose flour, sifted
1 teaspoon baking powder
1 teaspoon baking soda
1 teaspoon kosher salt
½ teaspoon ground cinnamon
½ teaspoon freshly grated nutmeg
4 large eggs, beaten

Vanilla Buttercream
>One recipe French Buttercream (page 32) or American Frosting (page 34)
>2 teaspoons pure vanilla extract

To Finish
>Butternut squash seed oil

Matt says: *Butternut squash seed oil is a relatively rare ingredient, made here in New York State by a company called Stony Brook WholeHearted Foods. Odds are you will have to order this item online. Do it. This is one of our favorite ingredients to have in the kitchen—at home we drizzle it on popcorn or roasted vegetables. If you're not willing to go the extra mile for this cupcake, you can use olive oil in the candied pumpkin seeds, skip the finishing oil portion, and eat your cupcakes knowing we're incredibly disappointed in you.*

CANDIED PUMPKIN SEEDS

Melt the butter in a skillet over medium heat. Add the brown sugar and stir with a heatproof spatula until the sugar is slightly dissolved and the mixture looks like wet sand.

Add the pumpkin seeds and stir continually until all are fully coated. Add the salt, cinnamon, and cayenne and continue stirring for 30 seconds.

Remove the pan from the heat and add the butternut squash seed oil, again stirring to coat. Pour the seeds into a bowl and set aside to cool as you bake the cake.

BUTTERNUT CAKE

Preheat the oven to 350°F. Line cupcake pans with 24 baking cups.

In a stand mixer with the paddle attachment, combine the butternut squash, granulated sugar, and brown sugar and mix on medium-low until well combined, about 1 minute.

With the mixer running, slowly pour in the oil. Continue mixing until combined. Stop the mixer, remove the bowl and paddle, and use the paddle to scrape the insides of the bowl, making sure everything is fully incorporated.

Sift together the flour, baking powder, baking soda, salt, cinnamon, and nutmeg and add to the batter. Reattach the bowl and paddle to the mixer and mix on medium until just combined, then add the eggs and continue mixing until the batter is smooth, about 10 to 20 seconds. Remove the bowl and paddle from the mixer and, once again, use the paddle to scrape the bottom and sides of the bowl, ensuring that everything is well mixed.

Scoop the batter into the prepared baking cups, filling them three quarters of the way.

Bake in the middle of the oven for 20 to 25 minutes, rotating the pan halfway through. The cupcakes are done when the centers spring back when you touch them.

Remove the cupcakes from the oven and let cool completely while you make the buttercream.

VANILLA BUTTERCREAM

Prepare the recipe for French buttercream as directed on page 32 or American frosting on page 34. Add the vanilla and beat well.

ASSEMBLY

Fill a pastry bag fitted with a fluted tip with the vanilla buttercream and pipe onto each butternut squash cupcake.

Sprinkle the candied pumpkin seeds across the tops.

Using a teaspoon, slowly drizzle a little butternut squash seed oil on top of each cupcake, just to garnish (about ½ teaspoon each).

HALF-ASSED CORNER

Omit the butternut squash seed oil and candied pumpkin seeds.

Pear Mascarpone

Pears: kinda like apples, but not as popular. Like if apples were Robert De Niro, pears would be what's his face from *The Sopranos*—the one with the gigantic head. Think that analogy is stupid? Know what else is stupid? Not liking pears. In many apple-based recipes, you can easily substitute pears—just make sure you're using the right pear for the right job. For baking, we like Boscs, which are not overly juicy and shred up nicely for cakes. Making pear sauce, pear butter, or perhaps a delightful spiced pear-parsnip puree to go along with roasted turkey? Use nice juicy Bartletts (also my pear of choice for plain old sloppy eating). For the dried pear chip that tops these beauties, Boscs or Anjous are the way to go—both are sweet and crisp and hold their shape nicely when cooking.

This recipe is really clean, simple, and refined—a flawless combination of sweet pears and cream. Man, you're going to look classy as fuck serving this to your homeowners association or anywhere else where you really want people to know that you're better than them.

Pear Chips

1 Bosc or Anjou pear, cored, peel on

Pear Cake

2 cups of peeled, shredded, drained, and pressed pears
(about 2 large pears; see page 26)

1 cup granulated sugar

1 cup brown sugar

1¼ cups canola or grapeseed oil

2¼ cups all-purpose flour, sifted

1 teaspoon baking powder

1 teaspoon baking soda

1 teaspoon kosher salt

½ teaspoon ground cardamom

½ teaspoon freshly grated nutmeg

4 large eggs, beaten

Mascarpone Buttercream

One recipe French Buttercream (page 32) or American Frosting (page 34)
½ cup (4 ounces) mascarpone

PEAR CHIPS

Preheat the oven to 250°F. Line a baking sheet with parchment paper or a nonstick baking mat.

Using a mandoline, food processor, or very sharp knife, cut the pears into very thin rounds, about ⅛ inch. If you can't get them to be perfectly round, that's fine. Doesn't matter what shape they're in, as long as you get them sliced as thin as you possibly can. Place on the baking sheet.

Bake for 30 minutes. Remove from the oven, flip the slices over (a fork or chopsticks is good for this), then return the sheet to the oven for another 30 minutes, or until dry. Be mindful that it may take slightly longer than an hour if the weather is humid.

PEAR CAKE

Preheat the oven to 350°F. Line cupcake pans with 24 baking cups.

In a stand mixer with the paddle attachment, combine the pears, granulated sugar, and brown sugar and mix on medium-low until well combined, about 1 minute.

With the mixer running, slowly pour in the oil. Continue mixing until combined. Stop the mixer, remove the bowl and paddle, and use the paddle to scrape the insides of the bowl, making sure everything is fully incorporated.

Sift together the flour, baking powder, baking soda, salt, cardamom, and nutmeg and add to the batter. Reattach the bowl and paddle to the mixer and mix on medium until just combined, then add the eggs and continue mixing until the batter is smooth, about 10 to 20 seconds. Remove the bowl and paddle from the mixer and, once again, use the paddle to scrape the bottom and sides of the bowl, ensuring that everything is well mixed.

Scoop the batter into the prepared baking cups, filling them three quarters of the way.

Bake in the middle of the oven for 20 to 25 minutes, rotating the pan halfway through. The cupcakes are done when the centers spring back when you touch them.

Remove the cupcakes from the oven and let cool completely while you make the buttercream.

Matt says: *Achtung! Depending on the kind of pears you use, your cake batter may appear a little loose and watery. If this happens to you, add another 2 tablespoons flour, then let the butter sit in the refrigerator for 10 minutes or so to allow it to hydrate a bit before baking.*

MASCARPONE BUTTERCREAM

Prepare the recipe for French buttercream as directed on page 32 or American frosting on page 34. Add the mascarpone after adding the butter. (Note that we are calling for additional mascarpone in the American frosting recipe—it needs the extra to taste really "mascarponey.")

ASSEMBLY

Fill a pastry bag fitted with a fluted tip with the mascarpone buttercream and pipe onto each pear cupcake.

Place a pear chip straight into the top of each cupcake, like a stately beacon jutting out of a sea of white, asserting its dominance over all the other desserts in its proximity.

Serve immediately or put in the refrigerator to set up a bit. Eat the rest of the pear chips while you wait.

Use store-bought pear chips or omit them entirely.

The Julia

Once you've finally embraced pears, you'll start finding yourself standing a little taller, walking a little more gracefully. I love apples as much as anyone, but truth be told they're a little slutty. Apples climbed into our laps and did a little dance, and suddenly, they *own* pie, not to mention apple cobbler, apple sauce, apple turnovers, apple juice, apple cider doughnuts—all places where pears could easily be a major player as well.

But the pear does not stoop to the apples' level! No, pears are like a special lady, standing strong and dignified with her long sculpted neck and sleek voluptuousness. Pears sit idly by as those slut apples prostitute themselves into every damn dish at Thanksgiving, instead maintaining a quiet dignity in their bin at the produce market, knowing that, eventually, their time will come. Is that time now? Who the fuck knows? Personally, I think this is an incredibly dumb strategy, and it would do the pears well to be a little more aggressive in the market, but you try talking some sense into them. Dignity doesn't get you eaten, dumbasses.

If pears want to make a splash using the highfalutin route, they couldn't ask for a better vehicle than The Juila. Coupling them with brandy and brown butter, and named for the great Julia Child, this cupcake creates a comeback vehicle of *Sunset Boulevard* proportions for them. Then when everyone is back in love with you, pears, I expect a nice thank-you letter. Maybe some flowers. Nice ones.

Brandy Snaps

4 tablespoons (½ stick) unsalted butter

¼ cup grade B maple syrup

¼ cup brown sugar

⅓ cup all-purpose flour

¼ teaspoon kosher salt

2 teaspoons brandy

½ teaspoon pure vanilla extract

Pear Cake

2 cups of peeled, shredded, drained, and pressed Bosc or Anjou pears
   (about 2 large pears; see page 26)

1 cup granulated sugar

1 cup brown sugar

1 cup canola or grapeseed oil

¼ cup brandy

2¼ cups all-purpose flour, sifted

1 teaspoon baking powder

1 teaspoon baking soda

1 teaspoon kosher salt

½ teaspoon ground cardamom

½ teaspoon freshly grated nutmeg

4 large eggs, plus 1 large egg white, lightly beaten

Brown Butter Buttercream

8 tablespoons (1 stick) unsalted butter

¼ cup powdered dry milk

One recipe French Buttercream (page 32) or American Frosting (page 34)

BRANDY SNAPS

Preheat the oven to 350°F. Line a baking sheet with parchment paper or a nonstick baking mat.

Melt the butter, maple syrup, and brown sugar in a small saucepan, stirring constantly with a wooden spoon. Bring to a boil and immediately remove from the heat.

Add the flour and salt and quickly stir to combine. Add the brandy and vanilla.

Use a teaspoon to make small drop cookies on the baking sheet, letting them spread and leaving about ½ inch between each one. If the cookies run together, all is not lost—we're going to break the cookies into pieces, so they don't need to look perfect. However, resist the temptation to just pour all the batter out and make one giant cookie, as the edges will cook while the inside remains raw (we learned this the hard way).

Bake in the middle of the oven for 7 to 10 minutes until golden brown. Remove the cookies from the oven and set aside to cool.

PEAR CAKE

Preheat the oven to 350°F. Line cupcake pans with 24 baking cups.

In a stand mixer with the paddle attachment, combine the pears, granulated sugar, and brown sugar and mix on medium-low until well combined, about 1 minute.

With the mixer running, slowly pour in the oil and brandy. Continue mixing until combined. Stop the mixer, remove the bowl and paddle, and use the paddle to scrape the insides of the bowl, making sure everything is fully incorporated.

Sift together the flour, baking powder, baking soda, salt, cardamom, and nutmeg and add to the batter. Reattach the bowl and paddle to the mixer and mix on medium until just combined, then add the eggs and continue mixing until the batter is smooth, about 10 to 20 seconds. Remove the bowl and paddle from the mixer and, once again, use the paddle to scrape the bottom and sides of the bowl, ensuring that everything is well mixed.

Scoop the batter into the prepared baking cups, filling them three quarters of the way.

Bake in the middle of the oven for 20 to 25 minutes, rotating the pan halfway through. The cupcakes are done when the centers spring back when you touch them.

Remove the cupcakes from the oven and let cool completely while you make the buttercream.

Matt says: Achtung! *Depending on the kind of pears you use, your cake batter may appear a little loose and watery. If this happens to you, add another 2 tablespoons flour, then let the batter sit in the refrigerator for 10 minutes or so to allow it to hydrate a bit before baking.*

BROWN BUTTER BUTTERCREAM

Melt the butter in a small saucepan, then turn down the heat to as low as you can get it. Add the powdered milk and cook, stirring occasionally with a wooden spoon. Continue cooking slowly until the milk solids are golden brown. Pour the super-brown butter into a bowl and place it in the refrigerator to solidify.

Prepare the recipe for French buttercream as directed on page 32 or American frosting on page 34, minus 8 tablespoons (1 stick) butter. Replace the omitted butter in the recipe with the super-brown butter.

ASSEMBLY

Fill a pastry bag fitted with a fluted tip with the brown butter buttercream and pipe onto each pear cupcake.

Break up the brandy snaps and place on top of the cupcakes.

Pumpkin Spice Latte

I'm certain that I am not the only person who stalks a particular coffee chain for the first nine months of the year, waiting for this to come out. In fact, I'm pretty sure this flavor is responsible for taking us from a nation with mildly ambivalent feelings about pumpkin to one that will now ruthlessly ferret out and purchase *anything* pumpkin related—pumpkin spice doughnuts, pumpkin spice beer, pumpkin spice potato chips, pumpkin spice toilet bowl cleaner, pumpkin spice cat litter. While it may not lend itself to everything, pumpkin works extremely well as a cupcake.

Pumpkin Cake

1½ cups packed pumpkin, canned or fresh roasted and pureed

1 cup granulated sugar

1 cup brown sugar

1¼ cups canola or grapeseed oil

1 teaspoon pure vanilla extract

2 cups all-purpose flour, sifted

1 teaspoon baking powder

1 teaspoon baking soda

1 teaspoon kosher salt

1 teaspoon ground cinnamon

½ teaspoon freshly grated nutmeg

4 large eggs, beaten

Espresso Latte Buttercream

One recipe French Buttercream (page 32) or American Frosting (page 34)

½ cup (4 ounces) mascarpone (disregard if making American frosting)

2 tablespoons instant espresso powder

1 teaspoon hot water

Fall-Spiced Espresso Beans
½ cup chocolate-covered espresso beans
¼ teaspoon ground cinnamon or pumpkin pie spice

PUMPKIN CAKE

Preheat the oven to 350°F. Line cupcake pans with 24 baking cups.

In a stand mixer with the paddle attachment, combine the pumpkin, granulated sugar, and brown sugar and mix on medium-low until well combined, about 1 minute.

With the mixer running, slowly pour in the oil and vanilla. Continue mixing until combined. Stop the mixer, remove the bowl and paddle, and use the paddle to scrape the insides of the bowl, making sure everything is fully incorporated.

Sift together the flour, baking powder, baking soda, salt, cinnamon, and nutmeg and add to the batter. Reattach the bowl and paddle to the mixer and mix on medium until just combined, then add the eggs and continue mixing until the batter is smooth, about 10 to 20 seconds. Remove the bowl and paddle from the mixer and, once again, use the paddle to scrape the bottom and sides of the bowl, ensuring that everything is well mixed.

Scoop the batter into the prepared baking cups, filling them two thirds of the way.

Bake in the middle of the oven for 20 to 25 minutes, rotating the pan halfway through. The cupcakes are done when the centers spring back when you touch them.

Remove the cupcakes from the oven and let cool completely while you make the buttercream and espresso beans.

ESPRESSO LATTE BUTTERCREAM

Prepare the recipe for French buttercream as directed on page 32 or American frosting on page 34. Add the mascarpone if making the French buttercream.

In a small bowl, combine the espresso powder and hot water and stir to make a paste. Add to either recipe and mix well until fully combined.

FALL-SPICED ESPRESSO BEANS

Combine the espresso beans and cinnamon in a mini food processor and pulse until roughly chopped.

ASSEMBLY

Fill a pastry bag fitted with a fluted tip with the espresso latte buttercream and pipe onto each pumpkin cupcake.

Sprinkle with chopped espresso beans.

A Love Letter to Emergency Cake

I used to be a typical broad—completely jaded, tough as nails. Then I had kids, and now I cry at fucking *everything*. One time when I was eight months' pregnant with Atticus I dropped a bottle of shampoo in the shower, then proceeded to become a blubbering sobby mess for more than an hour because if I was too incompetent to properly operate shampoo, how the fuck was I going to take care of a baby?

Sometimes I have better reasons for losing it. There are tons of nights I cry because I can't sleep, lying there in the dark, constantly beating myself up in my head over a million things: I can't keep the house clean. We don't have any money. Someone wrote something nasty about us on the Internet. Mostly, I think about how I'm a shitty mom. I'm running and growing an entire company with my children's father as my business partner, so they get double screwed in the parental-neglect department.

During the first two years of Robicelli's we did *everything* ourselves—baking, inventory, cleaning, deliveries, sales, accounting, marketing, everything. Atticus and Toby were right along for the ride . . . literally. We'd make deliveries for hours on end with two toddlers strapped into the backseat of our 2000 Honda Civic, listening to them looking out the window and crying, "Mommy, there's a park! Stop the car and take us to the park!" Then I would scream, "No! Because New York City needs its cupcakes, goddamnit!" and just keep driving, hoping they wouldn't notice I was tearing up over disappointing them. Our "day off" was for inventory, so instead of museums or playgroups, they'd get to go to our local restaurant wholesale warehouse. We'd make games out of it to try to make it fun, but still, I couldn't wonder if they'd be better off at art classes or playing with other kids than helping us.

Eventually our hard work afforded us a few employees to alleviate some of our responsibilities. We did the only logical thing parents with low self-esteem can do—we totally overcompensated for being really shitty parents for two years. We'd take days off and be totally attentive, go on adventures around New York City, be there 110 percent. But then I discovered a new sort of problem: When I'm an awesome mom, I'm a shitty businesswoman. In the age of Yelp and smartphones, you answer e-mails a few hours late because you were having a day at the zoo, or neglect to pick up one person's repeated phone calls because you were too busy playing in a sandbox, someone is all over the Internet telling everyone how bad you suck, and how no one should ever buy your cupcakes again.

The truth of it is, I can't win. Seriously, I can't fucking win. If I'm going to be the best at one thing, I'm going to drop the ball somewhere else, and Lord knows that someone somewhere will call me out on it. Being a "momtreprenuer" (God, I hate that word) is living in a bubble where you are consistently criticized and judged—if not by other moms, customers, or your own kids, then certainly by yourself.

When you sit on your couch and just can't stop thinking of what an abject failure you are as a human being, there's only one thing that can make you feel better: cake. Lots and lots and lots of rich, buttery, delicious cake, packed so tightly inside your mouth that you can't even speak anymore.

Matt says: *Some people say "exercise," but we're pretty sure they're lying.*

As a professional chef, I could get into the kitchen and bake myself up something wonderful. Of course, I won't do that because (a) I want cake *now*, and (b) I just cleaned this place like sixteen times already and really don't want to clean the kitchen. I could walk to the bakery, but of course I always realize I want cake after the bakery is closed. I end up buying a frosting-covered mass-produced cake-in-a-box from a bodega. I come home, curl up on the couch, and immediately . . . *"Mommy, can we have some?"*

I don't want my kids eating cake. I want them to eat their carrots and celery, then maybe drink some low-fat milk for strong bones. Plus, I don't want to share.

I lock myself in the bathroom with the cake. I run the shower in a feeble attempt to drown out the banging on the door and whiny, annoying screams demanding I hand over the cake to them. I grab a hunk from the corner with my bare hands and shove it into my mouth, and it's the waxiest, most God-awful excuse for a cake I have ever tasted. Doesn't really matter at this point—this isn't about cake, it's about principle!

About one third of the way through, I turn my head and catch a glimpse of myself in my bathroom mirror. Twenty-one-year-old Allison wants to know what happened. We used to be so cool. We told ourselves this would never happen to us. But there she is staring back at me: almost-thirty Allison, flat broke with no idea where she's going or what she's doing, in pajama pants and a stained, ripped T-shirt, no makeup, hiding from her children in a bathroom while stuffing her mouth with globs of shitty cake.

There are moments in a woman's life when she knows that she's been pushed too far, where lines must be drawn. I draw lines at cry-eating on the toilet.

I institute a strict policy for myself: I shall *always* have a minimum of three pieces of "emergency cake" in my freezer. They are always my favorite flavors, they are always extraordinary, and they are always available at 1:00 a.m. when I need them. That emergency cake is not for mindless eating, not for making myself feel worse about myself. Emergency cake is for me to have a private moment of celebration with myself on the couch (*never* on the toilet). It's for me to savor and enjoy, to indulge and make myself feel happy and pampered instead of lousy and self-critical.

Matt says: *Also, our freezer is on the top of our fridge, so the kids have absolutely no idea the cake is even in there. Suckers.*

When I get to have my private moments with emergency cake, I have realizations that are far more important than what rooms in the house are appropriate for eating in or my questionable choices in loungewear. I think that maybe I'm not as bad as I've been telling myself. That it's okay that I'm not perfect and that I can't do it all flawlessly, that maybe I should ease up on the unrealistic expectations I have for myself. That the "perfect moms" who go out of their way to make me feel like crap are probably bullying me so that they feel better about not being all that perfect themselves. That even if I had a great nine-to-five job with good pay, I'd *still* think I was a shitty mom because I have never even imagined I could love anything the way I love these kids, and it's nearly heartbreaking in the fact that no matter what I do for them, no matter what I say or what adventures I take them on or presents I buy, it will never be enough to show them all they mean to me.

Then some nights, the boys cuddle up with me and tell me that I'm the best mommy in the whole world. They don't care about all the things I can't give them, they care about the things I *do* give them—or maybe they're just trying to con me into giving them some of my cake, which is totally plausible. Point is, I am the best mom, because I'm *their* mom. And then, there's crying. Lots of it.

Banana Cream Pie

This is a totally selfish recipe developed so that I could have just a little bit of banana cream pie, without making an entire pie. Because, you know, if that happens, I have to eat the entire pie. Because otherwise the bananas will brown and get mushy. Yeah . . . that's it.

However, there's really no way to make only one cupcake. You could put them all in the freezer and eat them just one at a time. Or you could use this as an excuse to invite a bunch of friends over to eat cupcakes and drink wine. Or you could just eat all the cupcakes and drink some wine while watching DVR-ed episodes of *Days of Our Lives* by your lonesome. In my house, we call that "Saturday."

Banana Cake

4 large, not overripe bananas

1 cup granulated sugar

1 cup brown sugar

1¼ cups canola or grapeseed oil

1½ teaspoons pure vanilla extract

2 cups all-purpose flour, sifted

1 teaspoon baking powder

1 teaspoon baking soda

1 teaspoon kosher salt

½ teaspoon ground cinnamon

½ teaspoon freshly grated nutmeg

4 large eggs, beaten

Vanilla Custard

1 cup milk

1¼ cups heavy cream

⅔ cup granulated sugar

1 large egg

2 large egg yolks

½ cup cornstarch

2 tablespoons (¼ stick) unsalted butter

1½ teaspoons pure vanilla extract

Custard Buttercream

One recipe French Buttercream (page 32) or American Frosting (page 34)

1 cup custard (from above)

¼ teaspoon guar gum (optional)

To Finish

Banana chips

Graham cracker crumbs

BANANA CAKE

Preheat the oven to 350°F. Line cupcake pans with 24 baking cups.

In a stand mixer with the paddle attachment, combine the bananas, granulated sugar, and brown sugar and mix on medium-low until well combined, about 1 minute.

With the mixer running, slowly pour in the oil and vanilla. Continue mixing until combined. Stop the mixer, remove the bowl and paddle, and use the paddle to scrape the insides of the bowl, making sure everything is fully incorporated.

Sift together the flour, baking powder, baking soda, salt, cinnamon, and nutmeg and add to the batter. Reattach the bowl and paddle to the mixer and mix on medium until just combined, then add the eggs and continue mixing until the batter is smooth, about 10 to 20 seconds. Remove the bowl and paddle from the mixer and, once again, use the paddle to scrape the bottom and sides of the bowl, ensuring that everything is well mixed.

Scoop the batter into the prepared baking cups, filling them two thirds of the way.

Bake in the middle of the oven for 20 to 25 minutes, rotating the pan halfway through. The cupcakes are done when the centers spring back when you touch them.

Remove the cupcakes from the oven and let cool completely while you make the custard and buttercream.

VANILLA CUSTARD

Set out a mixing bowl, a whisk, a medium heavy-bottomed saucepan, a heatproof spatula, and a strainer.

Place the milk, 1 cup of the cream, and ⅓ cup of the granulated sugar in the saucepan and cook on medium-high heat.

In the mixing bowl, combine the remaining ⅓ cup granulated sugar, the egg, egg yolks, and cornstarch. Whisk well until pale yellow.

When the milk mixture comes to a boil, immediately remove the pan from the heat, leaving the burner on. While whisking vigorously, *slowly* pour the milk mixture into the egg mixture. Then pour it all back into the saucepan and return to the heat, stirring constantly with the heatproof spatula (make sure you get into those corners!).

Bring to a boil. The custard will be *very* thick.

Place the strainer over a bowl and dump in the custard, pushing it through with the spatula. When the custard is completely strained, add the butter and vanilla and stir in.

Remove 1 cup of ultrathick custard and set aside to be used in the buttercream. To the remaining custard, add the remaining ¼ cup cream and whisk well to combine (you may also do this in a food processor). Let cool completely.

VANILLA CUSTARD BUTTERCREAM

Prepare the recipe for French buttercream as directed on page 32 or American frosting on page 34. Once the butter is added, add the reserved 1 cup custard and mix on high to combine.

ASSEMBLY

Using a pastry tip, hollow out the center of each cupcake (see page 13).

Place the remainder of the vanilla custard in a squeeze bottle or piping bag with a small tip snipped off. Fill the center of each cupcake with the custard.

Fill a pastry bag fitted with a fluted tip with the vanilla custard buttercream and pipe onto each banana cupcake.

Top each cupcake with a banana chip. Sprinkle graham cracker crumbs all over the top.

Liddabit 🥄

I remember Atticus's first Halloween so vividly—he was seven months old, yet we still took him trick or treating, because, honestly, what's the point of having an adorable baby dressed as a lobster unless you can use him to score free candy. We still make our kids pay us out at least a third of their haul every year because candy is really bad for kids, and they shouldn't be eating it. Matt and I are totally willing to sacrifice our bodies and eat all the candy to protect them.

We're both incredibly partial to a certain peanuty, nougaty, caramel-y chocolate bar that we're not allowed to say out loud, but we thought it would make an amazing cupcake—and what do you know? It *did* make an amazing cupcake! For legal purposes we couldn't name it after the mego-globocorporation that inspired it. Fortunately, our superclose friends over at Liddabit Sweets were also inspired by it, making their own candy bar version called The Snacker. So this cupcake isn't named after Candy Bar X—it's named after the candy company that makes the tastier knockoff version of Candy Bar X, which gives us three degrees of separation between us and a potential lawsuit.

Salted Caramel
- ½ cup water
- 1 cup sugar
- 1 tablespoon corn syrup
- ¼ teaspoon cream of tartar
- ⅔ cup heavy cream
- 1 tablespoon kosher or sea salt

Chocolate Cake
- ¾ cup cocoa powder
- ⅔ cup scalding-hot coffee
- ⅔ cup buttermilk
- ⅓ cup canola or grapeseed oil
- 1 large egg
- 1 large egg yolk
- 1 teaspoon pure vanilla extract
- ½ teaspoon kosher salt
- 1⅓ cups all-purpose flour
- 1¾ cups sugar
- ¾ teaspoon baking powder
- ½ teaspoon baking soda

Salted Caramel-Nougat Buttercream
One recipe French Buttercream (page 32) or American Frosting (page 34)
⅓ cup salted caramel (from above)
½ cup Marshmallow Fluff
½ teaspoon pure vanilla extract

Matt says: Why Marshmallow Fluff instead of soft nougat? Because it's pretty much the same thing. You can make your own Marshmallow Fluff if you want, but really, aren't you already doing enough? Plus, the most common brand in stores is all natural, HFCS-free, and very much like what you'll end up making yourself.

To Finish
¾ cup chopped roasted peanuts
Salted caramel sauce
Classic ganache (see page 104)

SALTED CARAMEL
In a small nonreactive saucepan, mix the water, sugar, corn syrup, and cream of tartar. Mix with a fork until the mixture resembles wet sand. Bring to a boil.

Continue to cook, leaving the pan undisturbed, until the sugar begins to change color. Over heat, begin gently swirling the pan until the mixture becomes a beautiful golden brown. The darker it gets, the more intense the flavor gets—the French like it practically burned. Us? We go somewhere in the middle.

As soon as your desired color is reached, quickly remove the pan from the heat and *immediately* dump in all the cream. This is going to steam and bubble and really just be generally angry, so stand back and don't keep your face too close to the pan. The cream is going to stop the caramel from cooking any further.

Add the salt. Using a wooden spoon or a heatproof spatula, gently stir until well mixed (and again, don't forget those saucepan corners!).

If any lumps develop, return the pan to the burner over low heat and gently stir until dissolved.

Pour the cream into a bowl and set aside to cool.

CHOCOLATE CAKE
Preheat the oven to 350°F. Line two cupcake pans with 24 baking cups.

Place the cocoa powder in the bowl of a stand mixer with the paddle attachment and pour the hot coffee over. Mix on low speed until a thick paste forms and the mixture stops steaming, about 1 minute.

Increase the mixer speed to medium. In a 4-cup measuring cup, combine the buttermilk, oil, egg, egg yolk, vanilla, and salt, and mix lightly with a fork, ensuring the yolks are broken. Slowly pour into the mixer bowl.

Stop the mixer, detach the paddle, and scrape the bottom of the bowl well to loosen any caked-on cocoa. Reattach the paddle and turn the mixer to medium, letting it run for 1 minute. Stop the mixer again.

Sift together the flour, sugar, baking powder, and baking soda and add to the batter. Mix on low speed until just combined. Remove the bowl and paddle and use the paddle to scrape down the sides of the bowl, ensuring everything is mixed.

Scoop the batter into the prepared baking cups, filling them two thirds of the way.

Bake in the middle of the oven for 20 to 25 minutes, rotating the pans halfway through. The cupcakes are done when the centers spring back when you touch them.

Remove the cupcakes from the oven. Let cool completely.

SALTED CARAMEL–NOUGAT BUTTERCREAM

For French buttercream (recommended): Prepare the recipe as directed on page 32. Once completed, add the salted caramel, Marshmallow Fluff, and vanilla. Beat until fluffy.

For American frosting: Prepare the recipe as directed on page 34, reducing the powdered sugar by ½ cup and increasing the Marshmallow Fluff to ¾ cup. Add the salted caramel and beat until fluffy.

ASSEMBLY

Fill a pastry bag fitted with a plain tip with the salted caramel–nougat buttercream and pipe onto each chocolate cupcake.

Sprinkle a generous amount of peanuts on top of each cupcake.

Drizzle with the reserved salted caramel and the ganache.

SO YOU HAVE EXTRA . . .

Salted caramel

- Keep in a jar in the refrigerator—it lasts forever.
- Spoon over ice cream.
- Microwave until liquid and thin out with some half-and-half to make a dip for fresh fruit.

HALF-ASSED CORNER

Use store-bought caramel sauce.

1¼ cups canola or grapeseed oil

1½ teaspoons pure vanilla extract

2 cups all-purpose flour, sifted

1 teaspoon baking powder

1 teaspoon baking soda

1 teaspoon kosher salt

½ teaspoon ground cinnamon

½ teaspoon freshly grated nutmeg

4 large eggs, beaten

Nutella Buttercream

One recipe French Buttercream (page 32) or American Frosting (page 34)

¾ cup Nutella

½ cup Dutch-process cocoa powder

BANANA HAZELNUT PRALINE

Line a baking sheet with parchment paper. Set aside.

In a large heavy skillet over medium heat, toast the hazelnuts until fragrant, about 4 minutes. Immediately remove from the pan onto a dish; wipe the pan clean with a dry towel.

Place the water, granulated sugar, and corn syrup in the pan, stir to combine, and return to the stove. Increase the heat to medium-high. Cook without stirring until the sugar begins to turn a golden caramel.

Immediately turn the heat to low and add the hazelnuts, banana chips, and salt, and stir to coat.

Spread the praline on the parchment-lined baking sheet to cool. When cool, break the praline into pieces with your hands, or pulse into small pieces in a food processor.

BANANA CAKE

Preheat the oven to 350°F. Line cupcake pans with 24 baking cups.

In a stand mixer with the paddle attachment, combine the bananas, granulated sugar, and brown sugar and mix on medium-low until well combined, about 1 minute.

With the mixer running, slowly pour in the oil and vanilla. Continue mixing until combined. Stop the mixer, remove the bowl and paddle, and use the paddle to scrape the insides of the bowl, making sure everything is fully incorporated.

Banana Nutella

I grew up with Nutella as a constant presence in my house—one of the benefits of growing up Italian American. Nutella began as a product called gianduja, meant to be a cheaper alternative to solid chocolate. During the reign of Napoleon, chocolate became prohibitively expensive, so Italians in the Piedmonte region began cutting it with hazelnut paste to make it stretch. In 1946 a company named Ferrero from that region began making a jarred version, then renamed it Nutella in the 1960s. By the time I was a child in the 1980s, it was a staple for any Italian family, and soon enough the rest of the world remembered that we Italian folk know what the fuck we're talking about when it comes to food. Today, Nutella is deservedly a bona fide phenomenon in the United States.

One of my favorite healthy snacks growing up was a banana dipped into a jar of Nutella. Then I became an adult with a baking company and thought, "How can I make this relatively healthy snack as unhealthy as possible?" Now, once again, I ask you to trust the Italian girl when it comes to food: Go make this and tell me that you don't get all twitterpated by it.

Matt says: *You may recognize the name Ferrero from the famous candy Ferrero Rocher, aka "the candy that never lasts more than ten minutes in our house before we both eat the entire box then complain we have stomachaches, even though we're grown-ups and really should know better by now."*

Banana Hazelnut Praline
- 1 cup hazelnuts, peeled and chopped
- ½ cup water
- ¾ cup granulated sugar
- 2 teaspoons corn syrup
- ½ cup banana chips, crushed
- 1 teaspoon kosher salt

Banana Cake
- 4 large, not overripe bananas
- 1 cup granulated sugar
- 1 cup brown sugar

Sift together the flour, baking powder, baking soda, salt, cinnamon, and nutmeg and add to the batter. Reattach the bowl and paddle to the mixer and mix on medium until just combined, then add the eggs and continue mixing until the batter is smooth, about 10 to 20 seconds. Remove the bowl and paddle from the mixer and, once again, use the paddle to scrape the bottom and sides of the bowl, ensuring that everything is well mixed.

Scoop the batter into the prepared baking cups, filling them two thirds of the way.

Bake in the middle of the oven for 20 to 25 minutes, rotating the pan halfway through. The cupcakes are done when the centers spring back when you touch them.

Remove the cupcakes from the oven and let cool completely while you make the buttercream.

NUTELLA BUTTERCREAM

For French buttercream (recommended): Prepare the recipe as directed on page 32. Once the butter is added, add the Nutella and cocoa powder and mix on high to combine.

For American frosting: Prepare the recipe as directed on page 34, reducing the sugar by ½ cup, replacing the mascarpone with the Nutella, and adding the cocoa powder. Once combined, taste for seasoning.

ASSEMBLY

Fill a pastry bag fitted with a fluted tip with the Nutella buttercream and pipe onto each banana cupcake.

Place pieces of banana hazelnut praline on the top of each cupcake.

HALF-ASSED CORNER

Skip the praline. If you still want a crunchy top, you can sprinkle some crushed banana chips, roasted hazelnuts, or a mixture of the two on top.

Cinnamon Bun

What's more comforting on a cold, rainy day than a warm, gooey cinnamon bun? Maybe curling up in a soft robe with a nice hot cup of tea, watching bad movies on Lifetime starring Valerie Bertinelli as some sort of woman "scorned." Or lying on the couch while an entire litter of kittens sleeps peacefully on your chest. Or sitting in front of a fireplace doing crossword puzzles while listening to Sade's smooth-as-satin voice. Okay, maybe there are a lot of things more comforting than cinnamon buns, but you know what? You can't eat kittens or Sade, so there.

The key part to any worthwhile cinnamon bun, in our opinion, is the sticky "goo" that oozes out. So rather than make just a simple cinnamon cake, we dot ours with a cinnamon sugar mixture that sinks to the bottom during baking and oozes out when you unwrap it. There's no shame in using a knife and fork to eat this one.

Cinnamon Goo
4 tablespoons (½ stick) unsalted butter, melted
⅓ cup brown sugar
2 teaspoons ground cinnamon

Vanilla Cake
12 tablespoons (1½ sticks) unsalted butter
4 large eggs
1 cup milk
1 teaspoon pure vanilla extract
1 teaspoon kosher salt
2 cups all-purpose flour
1¾ cups granulated sugar
2 teaspoons baking powder
Cinnamon goo (from above)

Cinnamon Streusel
6 tablespoons (¾ stick) unsalted butter
½ cup brown sugar
½ cup all-purpose flour

2 teaspoons ground cinnamon
½ teaspoon kosher salt

Cinnamon Butterscotch

½ recipe butterscotch (see page 123)
2 teaspoons ground cinnamon

Cream Cheese Buttercream

One recipe French Buttercream (page 32) or American Frosting (page 34)
One 8-ounce package cream cheese
¼ teaspoon guar gum (optional)

CINNAMON GOO

Mix the melted butter, brown sugar, and cinnamon together in a bowl until the mixture looks like wet sand. Note that this mixture will not come together all the way—that's totally normal. Don't beat yourself up thinking you're doing something wrong. Set aside.

VANILLA CAKE

Preheat the oven to 350°F. Line cupcake pans with 24 baking cups.

Melt the butter in a microwave at 60 percent power for 1½ to 2 minutes. Keep the butter warm—do not allow it to sit and cool off.

In a stand mixer with a paddle attachment, beat the eggs on medium-low speed for 2 minutes until light yellow and lightly foamy.

Increase the mixer speed to medium-high. Pour the warm butter into the eggs slowly, so that the mixture tempers and the eggs do not scramble. Once the butter is added, reduce the speed to medium-low.

With the mixer running, add the milk, vanilla, and salt. Mix for 1 minute until well combined.

Sift together the flour, granulated sugar, and baking powder and add to the batter. Mix on medium until just combined, 10 to 20 seconds. Remove the bowl and paddle from the mixer and use the paddle to scrape the bottom and sides of the bowl, ensuring that everything is well mixed.

Scoop the batter into the prepared baking cups, filling them two thirds of the way.

Using a teaspoon, mix the cinnamon goo once again to reincorporate the butter and sugar. Place random small dollops of the goo over each unbaked cupcake.

Bake in the middle of the oven for 20 to 25 minutes, rotating the pan halfway through. The cupcakes are done when the centers spring back when you touch them.

Remove the cupcakes from the oven. Let cool for 5 minutes. Leave the oven on to bake the streusel.

CINNAMON STREUSEL

Line a baking sheet with parchment paper.

Combine the butter, brown sugar, flour, cinnamon, and salt in a clean bowl of the mixer on medium speed until the mixture looks like small pebbles. If the mixture is still too smooth, add more flour, 1 teaspoon at a time, until the desired consistency is reached.

Sprinkle the streusel over the baking sheet, making sure there are no large clumps. Bake for 8 to 10 minutes, rotating the pan once, until golden brown.

CINNAMON BUTTERSCOTCH

Follow the recipe as directed on page 123. You'll need only half of it for this recipe, but feel free to make a full recipe and store the other half in your refrigerator for another use.

Once the butterscotch is cooked, stir in the cinnamon. Set aside to cool.

CREAM CHEESE BUTTERCREAM

For French buttercream (recommended): Prepare the recipe as directed on page 32. Once completed, add the cream cheese and beat on high until well incorporated. If the cream cheese is particularly liquidy, it could cause the buttercream to "break." If that happens, add the guar gum and continue beating on high for 2 minutes until the mixture comes back together.

For American frosting: Prepare the recipe as directed on page 34, replacing the mascarpone with the cream cheese.

ASSEMBLY

Fill a pastry bag fitted with a fluted tip with the cream cheese buttercream and pipe onto each vanilla cupcake.

Sprinkle the streusel crumbs over each cupcake.

Using a teaspoon, drizzle the cinnamon butterscotch over each cupcake.

HALF-ASSED CORNER

Skip the cinnamon streusel and used crushed cinnamon-flavored cereal instead.

Strawberry Rhubarb Crisp

Along with "flappy," "schmuck," and "persnickety," one of our favorite words to say out loud in the English language is "rhubarb." Say it ten times in a row and tell me it doesn't get funnier every time. Rhubarb. *Rooooooo*-barb. *Rooo*-barbitty-barbitty-barb-barb-barb. And *that*, my friends, is 90 percent of the reason we created this cupcake. The other 10 percent involves the Illuminati, and we're not allowed to discuss it.

Speaking of shadowy conspiracy theories, ever notice how strawberry and rhubarb are a really popular flavor combination, yet rhubarb is in season during the spring and strawberries peak during the summer? *Hmmmmm?!* Okay, maybe we're stretching it a little bit, but we're getting pretty far into this book and I'm sorta running out of ideas for amusing recipe intros—you try doing it and see how easy it is.

Point is: It's okay if you want to use frozen strawberries. No shame in that.

Matt says: *Or if strawberries and rhubarb are out of season, use one of the many, many excellent strawberry-rhubarb jams that are available in a gourmet shop near you.*

Strawberry Rhubarb Compote
2 large rhubarb stalks, split down the middle and cut into ½-inch pieces
    (1½ to 2 cups)
One 16-ounce bag frozen strawberries, thawed with juice reserved
¼ cup fresh lemon juice
⅓ cup water
½ cup brown sugar
1 teaspoon ground cinnamon
½ teaspoon kosher salt

Brown Sugar–Oat Cake
½ cup rolled quick oats
1 cup brown sugar

1½ cups all-purpose flour

1 cup granulated sugar

2 teaspoons baking powder

12 tablespoons (1½ sticks) unsalted butter

4 large eggs

1 large egg white

½ cup milk

½ cup sour cream

2 teaspoons pure vanilla extract

1 teaspoon kosher salt

Oat Crisp

4 tablespoons (½ stick) unsalted butter, softened

1 cup quick-cooking oats

¾ cup brown sugar

½ teaspoon kosher salt

½ cup all-purpose flour

Vanilla Buttercream

One recipe French Buttercream (page 32) or American Frosting (page 34)

2 teaspoons pure vanilla extract

STRAWBERRY RHUBARB COMPOTE

Combine the rhubarb, reserved strawberry juice, lemon juice, water, and brown sugar in a medium nonreactive saucepan and bring to a boil. Immediately reduce the heat to medium-low and simmer until the rhubarb is tender, about 5 minutes.

Add the strawberries and continue to simmer until thick, about 10 minutes. Add the cinnamon and salt and mix.

Taste the compote for seasoning. If the rhubarb is particularly tart, add brown sugar, 1 teaspoon at a time, until the acidity is tempered.

Place the compote in a bowl and set aside to cool.

BROWN SUGAR–OAT CAKE

Preheat the oven to 350°F. Line cupcake pans with 24 baking cups.

Place the oats and brown sugar in a food processor and grind until fine. Add the flour, granulated sugar, and baking powder and pulse to combine.

Melt the butter in a microwave at 60 percent power for 1½ to 2 minutes. Keep the butter warm—do not allow it to sit and cool off.

In a stand mixer with the paddle attachment, beat the eggs on medium-low speed for 2 minutes until light yellow and lightly foamy.

Increase the mixer speed to medium-high. Pour the hot butter into the eggs slowly, so that the mixture tempers and the eggs do not scramble. Once the butter is added, reduce the speed to medium-low.

With the mixer running, add the milk, sour cream, vanilla, and salt. Mix for 1 minute until well combined.

Add the oat mixture. Mix on medium until just combined, 10 to 20 seconds. Remove the bowl and paddle from the mixer and use the paddle to scrape the bottom and sides of the bowl, ensuring that everything is well mixed.

Scoop the batter into the prepared baking cups, filling them two thirds of the way.

Bake in the middle of the oven for 20 to 25 minutes, rotating the pan halfway through. The cupcakes are done when the centers spring back when you touch them.

Remove the cupcakes from the oven. Let cool for 5 minutes, then remove the cupcakes from the pan and place on a baking sheet.

Dip a pastry brush into the strawberry rhubarb compote and lightly brush the top of each cupcake.

OAT CRISP

Increase the oven temperature to 375°F. Line a baking sheet with parchment paper or a nonstick baking mat.

In the mixer, cream the butter, oats, brown sugar, and salt on high speed until well mixed.

Turn the mixer speed to low and add the flour, a bit at a time, until the mixture is crumbly.

Crumble the oat crisp loosely over the baking sheet, letting it fall through your fingers in small clumps.

Bake for 5 minutes, remove the pan, stir to redistribute the crisp, then bake for another 5 minutes, or until golden brown. Let cool completely before using.

VANILLA BUTTERCREAM

Prepare the recipe for French buttercream as directed on page 32 or American frosting on page 34. Add the vanilla and beat well.

ASSEMBLY

Fill a pastry bag fitted with a fluted tip with the vanilla buttercream and pipe onto each brown sugar–oat cupcake.

Using the back of a teaspoon, make a large indent in the center of the buttercream (see page 80).

Place the cupcakes in the refrigerator until the buttercream becomes firm, about 20 minutes. If not serving the cupcakes immediately, store at this point and add the compote just before serving.

Using a slotted spoon, fill the indent generously with the strawberry rhubarb compote.

Generously sprinkle the tops of the cupcakes with the oat crisp.

SO YOU HAVE EXTRA . . .

Strawberry rhubarb jam

- Spread on scones, toast, croissants, or whatever you like at breakfast.
- Fill a prepared graham cracker crust with leftover classic ganache (see page 104), jam, and whipped cream and refrigerate until firm for a delicious icebox pie

HALF-ASSED CORNER

Use crushed granola in place of the oat crisp.

Use jarred strawberry rhubarb jam. If you want to make it a little more "homemade" looking, mix the jam with some freshly chopped strawberries.

Banana
Cashew

It's a universal truth that cashews are the king of all nuts. Cashews are the first thing everyone eats out of a can of mixed nuts (that's as scientific as nut polling gets). Though it costs a bit more, I prefer keeping cashew butter in my house over peanut butter because I enjoy it more when I'm eating spoonfuls out of the jar at 3:00 a.m. We substitute cashews in lots of places where peanuts have developed a false sense of security, like in brittle.

I'm surprised that more candy companies aren't making cashew brittle, but fortunately for all of us, we have good friends who own a candy company and were willing to lend us their recipe. This recipe is ~~stolen~~ adapted from *The Liddabit Sweets Candy Cookbook*. If you're a candy-making novice, you may want to invite a friend over to help you, because it becomes exponentially easier the more hands you have.

And if you don't want to mess with all this crazy fandangled "make your own brittle" jazz, there's no shame in just throwing some chopped roasted cashews on the top for a bit of crunch. You can put anything on top of this cupcake and it'll be amazing. Cashews, chocolate chips, gravel—it's all good!

Cashew Brittle
- 3 cups granulated sugar
- 1 cup water
- 1½ cups light corn syrup
- 4 cups raw cashews, roughly chopped
- 2 tablespoons (¼ stick) unsalted butter
- 1 tablespoon baking soda
- 1½ teaspoons pure vanilla extract
- 2 tablespoons kosher salt

Banana Cake
- 4 large, not overripe bananas
- 1 cup granulated sugar
- 1 cup brown sugar
- 1¼ cups canola or grapeseed oil
- 1½ teaspoons pure vanilla extract

2 cups all-purpose flour, sifted
1 teaspoon baking powder
1 teaspoon baking soda
1 teaspoon kosher salt
½ teaspoon ground cinnamon
½ teaspoon freshly grated nutmeg
4 large eggs, beaten

Cashew Buttercream

One recipe French Buttercream (page 32) or American Frosting (page 34)
½ cup all-natural cashew butter
1 teaspoon kosher salt

CASHEW BRITTLE

Line two baking sheets with parchment paper overhanging the edges, or with nonstick baking mats. Spray sides with nonstick cooking spray.

Combine the granulated sugar, water, and corn syrup in a 4- to 6-quart heavy-bottomed saucepan. Mix well with a heatproof spatula. Clip a candy/fry thermometer onto the side of the pan, making sure the thermometer bulb isn't touching the bottom of the pan.

Bring the mixture to a boil. Cook, without stirring, until the mixture reaches 260°F, 20 to 25 minutes.

Carefully add the cashews and butter. Don't go throwing them in like a maniac, making hot sugar splash all over the place, including on your delicate flesh. Do this slowly and gently, like you're laying down lots of little babies to sleep in a pool of hot, molten sugar lava.

Turn down the heat to medium and stir constantly until the brittle reaches 300° to 305°F, aka hard crack stage, 8 to 10 minutes.

Remove the pan from the heat. Add the baking soda, vanilla, and salt and stir slowly. The baking soda will cause the mixture to bubble up a little bit, lightening up the brittle.

Carefully pour the brittle out onto the prepared baking sheets, using the heatproof spatula to help scrape out the pan.

Spread the mixture as thin as you possibly can using the spatula. Let cool to room temperature, about 25 minutes.

Smashing time! Break the brittle up into small pieces using a hammer, a heavy pan, or the fury of your bare hands. (Note: Do this only if you have *really* strong hands.) Place in an airtight container, layering it with wax paper, and set aside. You'll use much of it for topping the cupcakes, and much more of it for eating while making said cupcakes.

BANANA CAKE

Preheat the oven to 350°F. Line cupcake pans with 24 baking cups.

In a stand mixer with the paddle attachment, combine the bananas, granulated sugar, and brown sugar and mix on medium-low until well combined, about 1 minute.

With the mixer running, slowly pour in the oil and vanilla. Continue mixing until combined. Stop the mixer, remove the bowl and paddle, and use the paddle to scrape the insides of the bowl, making sure everything is fully incorporated.

Sift together the flour, baking powder, baking soda, salt, cinnamon, and nutmeg and add to the batter. Reattach the bowl and paddle to the mixer and mix on medium until just combined, then add the eggs and continue mixing until the batter is smooth, about 10 to 20 seconds. Remove the bowl and paddle from the mixer and, once again, use the paddle to scrape the bottom and sides of the bowl, ensuring that everything is well mixed.

Scoop the batter into the prepared baking cups, filling them two thirds of the way.

Bake in the middle of the oven for 20 to 25 minutes, rotating the pan halfway through. The cupcakes are done when the centers spring back when you touch them.

Remove the cupcakes from the oven and let cool completely while you make the buttercream.

CASHEW BUTTERCREAM

For French buttercream (recommended): Prepare the recipe as directed on page 32. Once the butter is added, add the cashew butter and salt and mix on high to combine. Taste for seasoning. If desired, add more cashew butter, 1 tablespoon at a time, or a pinch more salt. Continue until, after tasting, your eyes roll into the back of your head.

For American frosting: Prepare the recipe as directed on page 34, reducing the sugar by 1 cup, replacing the mascarpone with cashew butter, and adding the salt. Once combined, taste for seasoning.

ASSEMBLY

Fill a pastry bag fitted with a fluted tip with the cashew buttercream and pipe onto each banana cupcake. Place in the refrigerator to set, about 10 minutes.

Just before serving, put as little, or as much, crushed cashew brittle atop each cupcake as you damn well like.

S'mores

We've already established this several times in this book: As a born-and-bred New Yorker, I do *not* do the outdoors. I didn't toast my first marshmallow over a fire or make s'mores until I was well into my thirties, and it was an absolute unmitigated disaster.

When you're in the pitch black and have built a fire pit in the sand, it doesn't actually light up the entire area like the movies will have you believe. No, you're just standing on the beach in the endless darkness, unable to see a single thing except a hole brimming with fire. You know that somewhere on this beach are your two young sons, so you find yourself constantly screaming "DON'T GO NEAR THE FIRE! JUST DON'T MOVE, AND ESPECIALLY DON'T WALK TOWARD THE FIRE! YOU MOVE WHEN I TELL YOU TO MOVE!" Then you realize that sticks that are long enough to toast marshmallows at a safe distance are a rarity in the wild, so you put the marshmallows on shorter sticks and keep quickly jabbing your hands in and out and in and out of this fire pit, hoping that the marshmallow ends up as golden and toasted as your flesh now is.

Once you've accidentally set the marshmallow on fire and blown it out, you need to dig around in the dark to find the graham crackers and unwrap the chocolate, which are now both covered in sand and trace amounts of seawater. Then you thrust your hands in every direction until you finally poke one of your children in the face and hand both of them the results of your struggles—which they proceed to hand back to you saying, "This is icky." Because you *refuse* to have gone through all of it for nothing, you eat every single one of those marshmallowy sand nuggets while nursing your blistered right hand in a small cooler full of ice and fish bait. And somewhere in the infinite blackness, you hear your husband loudly exclaim, "Isn't the outdoors great!"

Better idea? Make these cupcakes, eat them on the couch. Really not hard to make a case for that.

Speculoos Pudding

- ½ **cup sugar**
- 5 **tablespoons cornstarch**
- ⅛ **teaspoon kosher salt**
- 1¾ **cups milk**
- ½ **cup heavy cream**
- ½ **cup speculoos**
- ½ **teaspoon pure vanilla extract**

Chocolate Cake

¾ cup cocoa powder

⅔ cup scalding-hot coffee

⅔ cup buttermilk

⅓ cup canola or grapeseed oil

1 teaspoon pure vanilla extract

1 large egg

1 large egg yolk

½ teaspoon kosher salt

1⅓ cups all-purpose flour

1¾ cups sugar

¾ teaspoon baking powder

½ teaspoon baking soda

Toasted Marshmallow Buttercream

One recipe French Buttercream (page 32) or American Frosting (page 34)

One 16-ounce jar Marshmallow Fluff

BLOWTORCH (yeah, this is going to be awesome)

To Finish

Classic ganache (see page 104)

Graham cracker crumbs

SPECULOOS PUDDING

Combine the sugar, cornstarch, and salt in a medium saucepan. Whisk well to combine.

Slowly pour in the milk and cream, continuing to whisk.

Place the pan on medium heat, switching from a whisk to a heatproof spatula. Cook, continuing to stir, until the mixture thickens and begins to bubble.

Remove the mixture from the heat, add the speculoos and vanilla, and whisk well to combine. Pour the pudding into a bowl, cover with plastic wrap pressed onto the pudding's surface, and place in the refrigerator to cool.

CHOCOLATE CAKE

Preheat the oven to 350°F. Line two cupcake pans with 24 baking cups.

Place the cocoa powder in the bowl of a stand mixer with the paddle attachment and pour the hot coffee over. Mix on low speed until a thick paste forms and the mixture stops steaming, about 1 minute.

Increase the mixer speed to medium. In a 4-cup measuring cup, combine the buttermilk, oil, vanilla, egg, egg yolk, and salt and mix lightly with a fork, ensuring the yolks are broken. Slowly pour into the mixer bowl.

Stop the mixer, detach the paddle, and scrape the bottom of the bowl well to loosen any caked-on cocoa. Reattach the paddle and turn the mixer to medium, letting it run for 1 minute. Stop the mixer again.

Sift together the flour, sugar, baking powder, and baking soda and add to the batter. Mix on low speed until just combined. Remove the bowl and paddle and use the paddle to scrape down the sides of the bowl, ensuring everything is mixed.

Scoop the batter into the prepared baking cups, filling them two thirds of the way.

Bake in the middle of the oven for 20 to 25 minutes, rotating the pans halfway through. The cupcakes are done when the centers spring back when you touch them.

Remove the cupcakes from the oven. Let cool completely.

TOASTED MARSHMALLOW BUTTERCREAM

Grab a baking sheet and a long metal offset spatula. Spread the entire jar of Marshmallow Fluff onto the sheet.

Turn on the blowtorch and toast the Fluff until golden brown, allowing it to burn in a few spots. Using the offset spatula, mix the toasted parts back into the Fluff, respread the Fluff onto the baking sheet, and toast again with the blowtorch. Repeat two more times, then let cool.

Prepare the French buttercream as directed on page 32 or American frosting on page 34. Add ⅓ cup toasted Marshmallow Fluff, beat well, then taste. Add more Fluff according to your personal preference.

Matt says: *Once upon a time in a land far, far away (Europe), a peanut butter alternative was needed. One was made out of the only logical substitute—cookies. A specialty ingredient two years ago, this is quickly becoming available everywhere, marketed as either "speculoos," "Biscoff spread," or "cookie butter." It's such an insane ingredient that we can't tell if it's the greatest thing ever, or an act of evil genius.*

ASSEMBLY

Using a pastry tip, hollow out the center of each chocolate cupcake (see page 13).

Place the speculoos pudding in a squeeze bottle or piping bag with a small tip snipped off. Fill the center of each cupcake.

Fill a pastry bag fitted with a fluted tip with the toasted marshmallow buttercream and pipe onto each cupcake.

Drizzle the ganache across the top of the buttercream. Sprinkle graham cracker crumbs all over.

A Love Letter
to Christmas

Every year I make the same mistake: I spend 359 days of the year getting *ridiculously* excited for Christmas. This is because inside of me, there will always be a five-year-old girl who remembers the potential of what Christmas could be, before I became a grown up and it became the colossal suckfest that I live through now.

Right now, a few people are sitting in abject shock over that last statement. And the following people are smiling and silently nodding their heads in understanding and agreement:

- People who have worked in retail
- People who have worked in the food business
- People who have children
- People who have ever had to shop for presents in their lifetime
- People who are not Jewish

December is, hands down, the absolute busiest month of the year in the food industry, which is convenient for us because it's also the month we're supposed to pull magic out of our asses for the kids. And, idiot that I am, even though for the better part of the past decade I have made it to Christmas Day with barely a shred of sanity and a combined total of fourteen hours of sleep for the entire month, somewhere in the back of my head is that person who still believes in Santa and Christmas miracles and thinks that this is really the year that the *Hallmark Hall of Fame* Holiday Moment is actually going to happen.

In December 2010 we had a total of three days off, meaning we had three chances to "make the magic happen." There was going to be holiday shopping and days wrapped in blankets, drinking cocoa and watching Rudolph, making homemade ornaments and decorating the tree as we listened to my grandfather's LPs of Bing Crosby and Nat King Cole. As charming as all of this sounds, it was merely a teaser to the main event—the biggest, merriest, most holly-est jolly-est moment that was ever going to exist in the history of Robicelli's family Christmases: We were going to take our sons, ages two and three, to see Santa for the very first time.

I would wake up, make a cup of gingerbread spice coffee, and climb into bed with Matt and the boys for a winter-morning snugglefest. Then we'd all put on skull-printed sweaters and plaid shirts, which would both make Matt and me happy as young urban parents, and simultaneously irritate the shit out of my parents, who still don't understand why I can't give my kids proper stockbroker haircuts or tuck in their shirts. I love twofers!

Once we were all dressed up, we'd head out for a big pancake breakfast as a happy family, followed by a subway ride to the original Macy's in the heart of Manhattan, where we'd meet the best department-store Santa in the whole wide world. Then my kids would run into my arms, the arms of the greatest mommy ever, and it would totally make up for all the nights I worked late and playdates I couldn't take them to or the puppy we don't have or the house we can't afford.

Guess how much of this actually happened?

On our first day off, three-year-old Atticus woke up with a 102-degree fever. Matt went to pull the Christmas tree out of storage, only to remember that there were about a thousand boxes piled in front of it. I stayed in bed and tried to lull the boy back to sleep over the din of falling ornaments and the symphony of expletives coming from the next room. Two-year-old Toby took full advantage of the fact that no one seemed to be paying attention to him and drew us a lovely winterscape in crayon on the television screen.

Total disaster. Fine. We still had two more days off. With a few edits and some brilliant time-management skills, I could certainly condense all the joys of Christmas into fewer than forty-eight hours. Plan for day two: Squeeze the magical toy-shopping thing in. Pick up gifts for our parents and friends, each gift thoughtfully selected after months of contemplation. Come home, make a big pot of Matt's extra-special recipe for hot chocolate, throw on some Christmas carols, and finally decorate the tree. Snuggle up in bed all together as we fall asleep in the serene flicker of the tree's lights.

Reality of day two: Toby was now sick and had given the cold back to Atticus. The DVD player was broken because *somebody* put pancakes in it. Stuck with whatever was on television, we were forced to watch Rob Lowe's tour de force *The Christmas Shoes,* the TV movie based on that horrible, horrible country song. Spent the day wondering why God would murder a little boy's mom just to remind Rob Lowe about the true meaning of Christmas. Kids wanted to know why I kept holding them and crying, squeezing them so hard that they, in turn, began to cry. Cats jumped into Christmas tree, knocking it over four times. Kids ended up hogging the whole bed, so I slept curled up like a dog at the foot of the bed. Matt was pushed onto the floor. Cats knocked the tree over for a fifth time at 4:00 a.m., causing us all to jump out of bed thinking storm troopers had broken into the apartment to kill us all.

Fine, another failure. But there was still one more day. *I could do this!*

Plan for day three: Wake up early, run to the store around the corner and buy whatever toys are still available. Come home, throw on clothes, and go to Macy's. See Santa. Skip the thoughtful presents and buy everyone whatever items that are sold closest to the cash register, like umbrellas or the "365 Golf Jokes" day calendar. Come home; listen to Bing Crosby while drinking cocoa; blah, blah, blah magic; go to sleep.

Reality of day three: Children were back to 100 percent and were as energetic as ever. However, Matt and I had fevers, chest colds, and wanted to die. We lay in bed in semiconsciousness as the kids removed all the ornaments from the tree so they could "play" with them (and by "play" I mean "break"). Cats allowed the tree to remain vertical, instead setting their sights on our mantle and knocking down our collection of nutcrackers, nativity set, and stockings. They singled out my stocking as the one to poop on this year. We ended up watching *Bob the Builder Christmas to Remember* on loop. Thanks to my 102.7-degree fever, I believed the apartment was filled with rabid bats and spent the day alternately screaming and hiding under my comforter. Matt passed out on the toilet for an hour. We began drinking liquid cold medicine through a straw as we were now eight days from Christmas and were opening a weeklong pop-up shop in Manhattan the next day. Though our business was set, we had gotten a total of *zero* things accomplished in our personal lives.

I managed to take a fifteen-minute break that week to rush to a store near our commissary to buy toys for the kids, decided everyone would be getting gifts of baked goods for the tenth year in a row, and gave up my dream of having a house that's remotely Christmas-y and not covered in little metal cars and dirty laundry. However, against my better judgment I *refused* to give up my dream of seeing Santa, even though at this point I did not have the time to get the whole family to the Macy's in Herald Square. I *did* have the time to make a quick run in the car to the Staten Island Mall, where I could get some pictures, grab a few little things I needed, and get back to my home in time to help my aunt prepare the next day's Christmas breakfast. In true mommy fashion, I would manage not to let anyone down this year except for myself!

Matt and I woke up extra early and started getting the kids dressed while they were still asleep, which for some bizarre reason they didn't seem to enjoy. Didn't they realize that it was Christmas eve and we were going to see Santa? That every Christmas for the rest of their lives would be held up to these benchmark holidays of childhood? That they should stop biting me and just *put on their goddamn sweaters*???

After a quick coffee stop, we arrived at the mall with cameras in hand and stars in our eyes. Once we saw the line, we were filled with relief that we were, in fact, not the only parents in New York City who waited until the very last second to see Santa. Our children had what we will call a "difference of opinion" about the length of the line and began running away as fast as they could, in opposite directions. I made Matt stay on line, because I'd be damned if we were going to lose our place over this. I snatched Toby out of a handbag display, threw him over my shoulder, and brought him back to Matt, who was busy watching Atticus try to steal one of those kiddie shopping carts that looks like a fire engine. We corralled the kids onto the line and began telling them all about Santa, and how he'd been watching them all year to see if they were good boys. They also needed to tell him the toys they wanted him to bring that night, which had to include the Handy Manny Construction Site Playset and a Sit'n Spin. "I don't *care* if that's not what you want. Santa thinks you'll really like them, and not just because they were the only things left at Costco. No, you don't want that *Toy Story 3* playset—that toy is, *ummm* . . . it'll make you go blind. Santa says the Handy Manny toy is *much* better."

Finally, the moment arrived. We were at the front of the line and the gate to Santa's workshop swung open before us. The paper snowflakes! The thousands and thousands of twinkling lights! The yards of cotton-batting snow and that cheap-crap paper that's supposed to look like bricks but isn't fooling anyone! It was glorious!

And it is at *this* point that I wish there was a little button you could press in this book so you would actually be able to hear the sound of my children's terrified screams as they saw Santa for the first time and started scaling the fence of the workshop in a desperate attempt to escape.

In hindsight, that was the moment I should have just accepted that this wasn't going to happen, but instead I tried picking up my children and dragging them to Santa. "Santa's a good guy! He loves you! He wants to give you presents! HE WON'T BRING YOU PRESENTS IF YOU DON'T SIT ON HIS LAP AND LET MOMMY TAKE A PICTURE!" I begged, pleaded, and bribed my children until eventually I was physically escorted out of Santa's workshop by three teenagers dressed in elf costumes, with my children running ahead in absolute horror, as if they were fleeing a burning building.

I stood steel-faced, staring out into space, trying to hold everything together just as I always did. I have never been a stranger to disappointment or failure—something as small as suffering the indignity of being asked to leave a mall by a fifteen-year-old boy wearing green tights should have been nothing. But, of course, this wasn't nothing. Oh hell no, it was not nothing, not this year. In the calamity and chaos of running a business, of attempting to raise two kids when there were days I felt I could barely take care of myself, of knowing full well that there had been barely enough money to make the bills that year, much less to buy presents, of trying to hide my fear of this from my children so they would never be as scared as I am every single day of my life . . . I *needed* one perfect moment. And without it, I did the only logical thing a woman in my position could do: I had an epic nervous breakdown in JCPenney.

I cried. I screamed. I told my kids that Santa wasn't coming because of what they did. I cursed out several JCPenny employees about the fact they didn't have clear signs pointing to the elevators in case, God forbid, *someone* needed the elevator and didn't want to walk endlessly around housewares for fifteen effing minutes just to end up exactly where they fucking started. I dragged the kids to the car while stifling the urge to be sick in the parking lot; collapsed on the steering wheel, where I cried hysterically until there were no tears left in my body; and then began to drive us all back to Brooklyn in total, complete silence. I dropped Matt and the kids off at my in-laws' house and went back to our apartment to lie in the dark, staring at the ceiling, wondering how exactly I got to this point.

There are not many feelings worse than knowing the two-year-old in the family is a bigger person than you are.

I sat in the blackness of my apartment, completely and utterly alone, watching the minutes pass on my alarm clock, counting down closer and closer to Christmas and waiting for something, *anything,* to happen. Waiting for the miracle countless movies and television specials had promised. Perhaps the bank had made a mistake and we weren't really flat broke. Or I'll turn on the news and they'll say the recession is over, and just like that our business will quadruple overnight.

Or maybe I'll stop crying alone in the dark and become the grown-up I'm supposed to be. Maybe I needed to stop praying and make my own miracle.

I got up. I felt as if there wasn't an ounce of strength left in my entire body, but yet something got me to stand up. I splashed some water on my face to wash away the sediment of my tears, pulled on my favorite sweater, got in the car, and drove to my husband and children. I rang the bell, silently praying they'd forgive me for the way I acted. And when I walked through the door, instead of yelling at me to grow up or giving me the silent treatment like I deserved, they raced to be with me. Atticus handed me a picture he drew, with the words "I'm Sorry" scribbled across the top, half in his childish handwriting and half in Matt's childish handwriting. Toby clung to my leg, looking up at me as if I wasn't his mess of a mother, but as if I were Santa himself. Matt wrapped me in his arms, gently kissing the top of my head as I collapsed into his chest.

Maybe we weren't millionaires, or even thousand-aires. We'll more than likely never be able to get a single photo where Atticus's eyes are open, or where both kids sit totally still, or where I don't look like I'm either eating something or pooping (even though Matt says I look beautiful in all of them). The house will never be perfect, and it's going to take a whole separate miracle for me to ever be able to get it, and keep it, clean. And I doubt Hallmark will ever produce a feel-good movie about a woman losing her mind at the Staten Island Mall, though if they do, I request my part be played by Candace Cameron Bure.

This Christmas story doesn't end with a call from overseas promising us money to save our floundering business, or with Santa giving us a real house to raise our kids in, or with softly hummed carols and twinkling lights. It ends with four people standing in a dingy hallway in Brooklyn, New York, with smudged mascara, knotty hair, and rumpled clothing—wrapped up in one another. And that year, it was more of a miracle than any of us could have ever hoped for.

Crème Brûlée

I find no dessert sexier than crème brûlée. The soft richness of the custard, the crispness of the caramelized sugar, the explicit contrast between the subtle vanilla bean flavor and the char of burned sugar—if the situation ever arises where aliens invade earth and tell me that I have to pick a single dessert for them to turn into human form and force me to make out with in order to save the human race (which can totally happen), I'm going with crème brûlée.

Though this cupcake certainly can be enjoyed at any time during the year, I love the way the sugar on it glistens like an ornament. I bet if the three wise men brought this as a gift to the baby Jesus, he wouldn't have been able to eat it because babies don't have teeth and aren't supposed to be eating a lot of sugar, but everyone who saw the cupcake would have been *really* impressed.

Vanilla Custard Base

- 1 vanilla bean
- ½ cup milk
- ½ cup heavy cream
- ⅓ cup sugar
- 1 large egg
- 1 large egg yolk
- ⅛ cup cornstarch

Vanilla Cake

- 12 tablespoons (1½ sticks) unsalted butter
- 4 large eggs
- 1 cup milk
- 1 teaspoon pure vanilla extract
- 1 teaspoon kosher salt
- 2 cups all-purpose flour
- 1¾ cups sugar
- 2 teaspoons baking powder

Vanilla Custard Buttercream
Vanilla custard base (from above)
One recipe French Buttercream (page 32) or American Frosting (page 34)
1 tablespoon unsalted butter

Caramelized Sugar
2 cups sugar
1 cup water

VANILLA CUSTARD BASE

Set out a mixing bowl, a whisk, a medium heavy-bottomed saucepan, a heatproof spatula, and a strainer.

Split the vanilla bean and scrape out the seeds. Place the milk, cream, half of the sugar, and the vanilla bean in the saucepan and cook on medium-high heat.

In the mixing bowl, combine the remaining sugar, the egg, egg yolk, and cornstarch. Whisk well until pale yellow.

When the milk mixture comes to a boil, immediately remove the pan from the heat, leaving the burner on. Remove the vanilla bean. While whisking vigorously, *slowly* pour the milk mixture into the egg mixture. Then pour it all back into the saucepan and return to the heat, stirring constantly with the heatproof spatula (make sure you get into those corners!).

Bring to a boil. The custard will be *very* thick.

Place the strainer over a bowl and dump in the custard, pushing it through with the spatula. When the custard is completely strained, set it aside.

Matt says: *This custard recipe is particularly tricky because we're not actually making a smooth custard—we're making a thick paste to flavor the buttercream. If you mess up and it looks like a mess of clumps, all is not lost! Try running it in a food processor until smooth.*

VANILLA CAKE

Preheat the oven to 350°F. Line cupcake pans with 24 baking cups.

Melt the butter in a microwave at 60 percent power for 1½ to 2 minutes. Keep the butter warm—do not allow it to sit and cool off.

In a stand mixer with the paddle attachment, beat the eggs on medium-low speed for 2 minutes until light yellow and lightly foamy.

Increase the mixer speed to medium-high. Pour the warm butter into the eggs slowly, so that the mixture tempers and the eggs do not scramble. Once the butter is added, reduce the speed to medium-low.

With the mixer running, add the milk, vanilla, and salt. Mix for 1 minute until well combined.

Sift together the flour, sugar, and baking powder and add to the batter. Mix on medium until just combined, about 10 to 20 seconds. Remove the bowl and paddle from the mixer and use the paddle to scrape the bottom and sides of the bowl, ensuring that everything is well mixed.

Scoop the batter into the prepared baking cups, filling them two thirds of the way.

Bake in the middle of the oven for 20 to 25 minutes, rotating the pan halfway through. The cupcakes are done when the centers spring back when you touch them.

Remove the cupcakes from the oven. Let cool for 5 minutes, then remove the cupcakes from the pan and place on a baking sheet.

VANILLA CUSTARD BUTTERCREAM

Prepare the recipe for French buttercream as directed on page 32 or American frosting on page 34. Once the butter is added, add ½ cup of the vanilla custard base and mix on high to combine. Taste the buttercream. If you'd like it more custardy, turn the mixer back on to medium-low and add more base a few tablespoons at a time. Any additional custard base can be frozen for another use.

CARAMELIZED SUGAR

Prepare an ungreased baking sheet with a large piece of parchment paper that overhangs the sides.

Place the sugar and water in a medium heavy-bottomed, nonreactive saucepan and stir to combine. Put over high heat and bring to a boil.

As the sugar begins to color, swirl the pan so the sugar caramelizes uniformly. When the color is golden yellow, pour one third of the hot sugar onto the parchment paper. Return the remaining sugar to the heat to continue caramelizing. In a few more seconds, the color will be a light brown. Pour half of the remaining caramel out onto another part of the parchment. Return the pan to the heat one last time until the caramel is dark amber, then pour the remainder onto the parchment.

Carefully lift the baking sheet and tilt it back and forth to spread the caramel. Let sit to cool.

ASSEMBLY

Fill a pastry bag fitted with a fluted tip with the vanilla custard buttercream and pipe onto each vanilla cupcake.

Place the cupcakes in the refrigerator until the buttercream becomes firm, about 20 minutes.

Roll up the parchment paper. Repeatedly smack it with something hard to break the caramel into small shards. Pour the tricolored caramel into a pie plate or baking dish.

Remove the cupcakes from the refrigerator. Roll the buttercream in the caramel, pressing slightly so the caramel adheres.

Chocolate Chestnut

How many of you have actually ever roasted chestnuts over an open fire? Though the song may inspire you to set a small fire in your house in order to participate in a beloved Christmas tradition, I implore you, *do not set fires in your house* (unless you have a fireplace, in which case you're okay). You can roast chestnuts in your microwave that will not only taste delicious, but will also taste like safety!

Use a sharp knife to cut large X's into the chestnuts and then arrange them cut side up on a microwave-safe plate. Nuke them in 1-minute intervals until the shells can be peeled—in my microwave it takes about 3 minutes, but it can be anywhere between 2 and 4. Be careful when testing them. They contain a lot of steam and can burn your delicate little hands! Once you've tested one for doneness, let the lot of them cool for a bit before peeling.

If that still seems like a lot of work, you can also buy roasted chestnuts in a jar. But "Chestnuts coming from a *jaaaarrr*" doesn't sound sexy, even if Nat King Cole were singing it. Just tell all your friends you did it the old-fashioned way. No one is going to be fact-checking your cupcakes to figure out if they're filled with lies.

Marrons Glacés (pretentious way of saying candied chestnuts)

- 1 cup roasted chestnuts, cut in half
- ¾ cup sugar
- ¼ cup corn syrup
- ¾ cup water
- 1 teaspoon orange flower water (optional)

Chocolate Cake

- ¾ cup cocoa powder
- ⅔ cup scalding-hot coffee
- ⅔ cup buttermilk
- ⅓ cup canola oil or grapeseed oil
- 1 teaspoon pure vanilla extract
- 1 large egg
- 1 large egg yolk

½ teaspoon kosher salt
1⅓ cups all-purpose flour
1¾ cups sugar
¾ teaspoon baking powder
½ teaspoon baking soda

Chestnut Puree (optional)
½ cup roasted chestnuts
2 teaspoons sugar
2 tablespoons heavy cream

Chestnut Buttercream
One recipe French Buttercream (page 32) or American Frosting (page 34)
Small jar chestnut cream or homemade chestnut puree (from above)

MARRONS GLACÉS
Combine the chestnuts, sugar, corn syrup, and water in a medium nonreactive saucepan over medium heat. Stir and bring to a boil.

Reduce the heat to a simmer and cook for 10 minutes. Remove the pan from the heat and add the orange flower water, if using. Place the chestnut mixture in a bowl and let sit, covered, overnight.

The next day, place the chestnuts and syrup in a medium nonreactive saucepan and bring to a boil. Remove from the heat. Return the mixture to the bowl and let sit at room temperature as you make the cupcakes.

CHOCOLATE CAKE
Preheat the oven to 350°F. Line two cupcake pans with 24 baking cups.

Place the cocoa powder in the bowl of a stand mixer with the paddle attachment and pour the hot coffee over. Mix on low speed until a thick paste forms and the mixture stops steaming, about 1 minute.

Increase the mixer speed to medium. In a 4-cup measuring cup, combine the buttermilk, oil, vanilla, egg, egg yolk, and salt and mix lightly with a fork, ensuring the yolks are broken. Slowly pour into the mixer bowl.

Stop the mixer, detach the paddle, and scrape the bottom of the bowl well to loosen any caked-on cocoa. Reattach the paddle and turn the mixer to medium, letting it run for 1 minute. Stop the mixer again.

Sift together the flour, sugar, baking powder, and baking soda and add to the batter. Mix on low speed until just combined. Remove the bowl and paddle and use the paddle attachment to scrape down the sides of the bowl, ensuring everything is mixed.

Scoop the batter into the prepared baking cups, filling them two thirds of the way.

Bake in the middle of the oven for 20 to 25 minutes, rotating the pans halfway through. The cupcakes are done when the centers spring back when you touch them.

Remove the cupcakes from the oven. Let cool completely.

CHESTNUT PUREE

If making your own chestnut puree, place the chestnuts and sugar in a mini food proccessor and puree for at least 3 minutes, scraping down the sides occasionally. Add the cream, a bit at a time, continuing to process until smooth.

CHESTNUT BUTTERCREAM

Prepare the French buttercream as directed on page 32 or American frosting on page 34. Add ⅓ cup chestnut cream or puree, beat well, then taste. Add more chestnut cream according to your personal preference.

ASSEMBLY

Fill a pastry bag fitted with a fluted tip with chestnut buttercream and pipe onto each chocolate cupcake.

Decorate the cupcakes with the marrons glàces.

SO YOU HAVE EXTRA . . .

Candied chestnuts
- Use as a garnish with some whipped cream on pumpkin pie.
- Sprinkle over vanilla or chocolate ice cream.

Chestnut cream or puree
- Fold into vanilla pudding.
- Schmear on French toast.

HALF-ASSED CORNER

Skip candying the chestnuts. You can either just use roasted and drizzle with some classic ganache (see page 104) or leave the cupcakes plain.

The Hansel
(he's so hot right now)

This began as a project to make the ultimate Christmas cupcake—something so full of joy that the second you put it in your mouth, it would feel like a reindeer threw up in it (not disgusting—reindeer are well known for vomiting pure unadulterated joy, much like unicorns and gnomes do).

Of all the holiday sweets, nothing is more iconic than the gingerbread house—and no other sweet is quite the saucy little minx either. Sitting there in the middle of your Christmas table, all crispy and crunchy and spicy and fragrant, covered in gobs of icing, dotted with all your favorite candies and whimsical little gingerbread men—and once you've been worked up into a sufficient frenzy just by laying eyes on this magical sugar palace, you find out you're not allowed to eat it. What kind of asshole dessert exists just for you to look at and not eat?

But we at Robicelli's don't just sit here and bitch about the issues—we get up and fix them. The house's walls became our supermoist gingerbread cake. The rock-hard, overly sugary icing was replaced with far more indulgent white chocolate custard. The cracker roof became soft, silky speculoos buttercream, and for the gingerbread men? Well, we can't leave those guys out—we make our own, then dip their pretty little heads in white chocolate (except we cut the cookies into squares, because it really is a pain in the ass to cut out all those teensy-tiny little men with our gigantor hands. Just pretend they're little gingerbread SpongeBobs).

Matt says:
Heads up! This recipe needs to be started a day in advance because the cake batter needs to hydrate in the refrigerator overnight.

Gingerbread Cake

- 1 cup canola or grapeseed oil
- 1 cup sugar
- 3 large eggs
- 1 cup molasses
- 2 teaspoons baking soda
- 2 teaspoons hot water
- 2 cups all-purpose flour
- ½ teaspoon kosher salt
- 1 teaspoon ground cinnamon
- 1 teaspoon ground ginger
- 1 teaspoon ground cloves
- 1 teaspoon ground allspice
- 1 cup boiling water

Gingerbread Cookies

1½ cups all-purpose flour, plus extra for dusting

¾ teaspoon baking powder

½ teaspoon baking soda

Pinch kosher salt

Pinch freshly ground black pepper

2 teaspoons ground ginger

1 teaspoon ground cinnamon

¼ teaspoon ground allspice

¼ teaspoon ground cloves

3 tablespoons unsalted butter, softened

⅓ cup brown sugar (we use light, but dark is fine too)

1 large egg

¼ cup molasses

1 teaspoon pure vanilla extract

¾ cup white chocolate

White Chocolate Custard

1 cup half-and-half

⅓ cup sugar

1 large egg

1 large egg yolk

2 tablespoons cornstarch

½ cup white chocolate, chopped

1 tablespoon unsalted butter

½ teaspoon pure vanilla extract

Speculoos Buttercream

One recipe French Buttercream (page 32) or American Frosting (page 34)

¾ cup speculoos (see page 260)

Gingerbread Cake

Preheat the oven to 350°F. Line cupcake pans with 24 baking cups.

Place the canola oil, sugar, eggs, and molasses in the bowl of a stand mixer with the paddle attachment and mix on medium for 1 minute.

In a small bowl, combine the baking soda and the 2 teaspoons hot water. Add to the sugar mixture and mix for another 10 seconds.

Sift together the flour, salt, cinnamon, ginger, cloves, and allspice. With the mixer on low speed, add the flour mixture, a little bit at a time.

Add the 1 cup boiling water, quickly turn the mixer to high for 3 seconds, then immediately turn it off.

Remove the bowl and paddle from the mixer and use the paddle attachment to scrape the bottom and sides of the bowl, ensuring that everything is well mixed.

Refrigerate the batter overnight to allow the flour proteins to hydrate.

Scoop the batter into the prepared baking cups, filling them three quarters of the way.

Bake in the middle of the oven for 20 to 25 minutes, rotating the pan halfway through. The cupcakes are done when the centers spring back when you touch them.

Remove the cupcakes from the oven. Let cool completely.

Gingerbread Cookies

Sift together the flour, baking powder, baking soda, salt, pepper, ginger, cinnamon, allspice, and cloves.

In the clean bowl of the mixer, cream together the butter, brown sugar, egg, molasses, and vanilla.

Gradually mix in the flour mixture until smooth.

Wrap the dough in plastic wrap, smoosh into a flat disk, and refrigerate for at least 1 hour.

Remove the dough from the refrigerator. Preheat the oven to 350°F. Spray a baking sheet with nonstick cooking spray and line with parchment paper.

Roll the dough out to a thickness of ⅛ to ¼ inch. Using a knife or pizza wheel, cut cookies into 1½ x 1½-inch squares (or little gingerbread men if you're a show-off). Place the cookies on the baking sheet at least 1 inch apart.

Bake in the middle of the oven for 10 minutes, rotating once.

Remove the cookies from the oven. Let cool completely.

Line a plate or baking sheet with parchment paper or wax paper.

Melt the white chocolate in a microwave at 60 percent power in 30-second intervals, stirring with a fork intermittently.

Dip half of each cookie into the white chocolate and place on the parchment paper. Put in a cool place and let the chocolate set.

WHITE CHOCOLATE CUSTARD

Set out a mixing bowl, a whisk, a medium heavy-bottomed saucepan, a heatproof spatula, and a strainer.

Place the half-and-half and half of the sugar in the saucepan and cook on medium-high heat.

In the mixing bowl, combine the remaining sugar, the egg, egg yolk, and cornstarch. Whisk well until pale yellow.

When the half-and-half mixture comes to a boil, immediately remove the pan from the heat, leaving the burner on. While whisking vigorously, *slowly* pour the hot half-and-half mixture into the egg mixture. Then pour it all back into the saucepan and return to the heat, stirring constantly with the heatproof spatula (make sure you get into those corners!).

Bring to a boil. Remove from the heat, add the white chocolate, and whisk well.

Place the strainer over a bowl and dump in the custard, pushing it through with the spatula. When the custard is completely strained, add the butter and vanilla and stir in.

SPECULOOS BUTTERCREAM

Prepare the recipe for French buttercream as directed on page 32 or American frosting on page 34. Once the butter is added, add the speculoos and mix on high to combine. Taste, then add more speculoos according to your personal preference.

ASSEMBLY

Using a pastry tip, hollow out the center of each gingerbread cupcake (see page 13).

Place the white chocolate custard in a squeeze bottle or piping bag with a small tip snipped off. Fill the the center of each cupcake.

Fill a pastry bag fitted with a fluted tip with the speculoos buttercream and pipe onto each cupcake.

Place a white chocolate–dipped gingerbread cookie on top of each cupcake.

SO YOU HAVE EXTRA . . .

White chocolate custard and cookie scraps

- Layer the custard and crushed gingerbread cookies in a glass to make a parfait. You can even throw in a little cranberry sauce if you're feeling extra festive.

HALF-ASSED CORNER

Use store-bought gingerbread cookies. You don't have to dip them in white chocolate if you don't want to (but they sure do look pretty that way).

The Blatt

Traditionally, the menu at Hannukah consists mostly of fried foods, which is to commemorate the miracle of the oil in the Maccabees' lamps that lasted eight days and nights. This menu is why non-Jews like Matt and me spend a solid month before Hannukah sucking up to our Jewish friends in order to score the best dinner-party invites. Deep-frying anything in a tiny Brooklyn kitchen with no windows is rough, so when we hear that someone is making latkes and jelly doughnuts, we do what we must to weasel our way in.

And if fried stuff wasn't enough to make Hannukah one of the best food holidays ever, you know what the other food tradition is? Cheesecake. It goes back to the story of Judith and how she saved her people by plying an enemy general with wine and cheese, and then beheading him with his own sword once he was drunk. You didn't think cheesecake could be that badass, did you?

We decided to combine these two traditions to make the ultimate Hannukah cupcake: a handheld hybrid of cheesecake and jelly doughnut. When it came to deciding what jelly to use, we called a good friend of ours to ask what his mother used in her doughnuts. He said that she always used raspberry jam, for no other reason than it was the most expensive of all the jams at the grocery store, and if you used anything less than that, everyone would gossip about how you were cheap. It warms my heart to know that no matter what religion you're a part of, no matter what our differences may be, there will *always* be women talking smack about one another after services.

We named our cupcake for our friend's mother, Mrs. Blatt—it's a vanilla cupcake with rich cheesecake buttercream, covered in fried cookie dough, and filled with lots of the most expensive jam we could possibly find at the supermarket.

Fried Cookies

1 large egg

2 large egg yolks

5 tablespoons unsalted butter, softened

¼ teaspoon kosher salt

1 tablespoon milk

½ teaspoon pure vanilla extract

⅔ cup powdered sugar

¼ teaspoon ground cardamom

1¾ cups all-purpose flour

Canola oil for frying

Vanilla Cake

12 tablespoons (1½ sticks) unsalted butter

4 large eggs

1 cup milk

1 teaspoon pure vanilla extract

1 teaspoon kosher salt

2 cups all-purpose flour

1¾ cups granulated sugar

2 teaspoons baking powder

Cheesecake Buttercream

One recipe French Buttercream (page 32) or American Frosting (page 34)

One 8-ounce package cream cheese

1 teaspoon pure vanilla extract

¼ teaspoon guar gum (optional)

To Finish

Raspberry jam (Nice stuff. Don't go too cheap here.)

Powdered sugar

FRIED COOKIES

In a stand mixer with the whisk attachment, beat the eggs, egg yolks, butter, and salt until thick and light yellow. Add the milk and vanilla and whisk until just incorporated.

Switch to the paddle attachment and add the powdered sugar and cardamom. Mix well on medium speed.

Turn the mixer to low and add the flour, a little bit at a time, until a thick dough ball forms. Place any extra flour on your countertop, remove the dough, and lightly knead by hand for about 1 minute until smooth.

Place the dough on a sheet of plastic wrap and press the dough down as much as you can into a pancake. Wrap entirely in plastic and place in the refrigerator for at least 1 hour.

Time to get your frying setup ready! Fill a medium heavy-bottomed saucepan halfway full with canola oil, clip on your candy/fry thermometer, and heat to 350°F. Line a baking sheet with three layers of paper towels, then set up an upside-down cooling rack on top of it. Once again lightly flour your countertop and grab your rolling pin, a sharp knife, and tongs. Now, let's do this!

Remove the cookie dough from the refrigerator and cut into smaller pieces to make it easier to work with. Roll out as thin as you can get it—about 1/16 inch, but no more than 1/8 inch.

Matt says: *Don't worry about its being pretty—you're going to crumble up the cookies anyway, so you can forgive yourself if your pieces don't look flawless. This isn't a Martha Stewart book—you can breathe a little.*

Using your sharp knife, cut the cookie dough into strips about 1 x 2 inches. Shake off any excess flour left from the rolling process and place the strips in the hot oil. The cookies should sink, then float to the top. Fry the cookies in small batches, being careful not to crowd the pan.

Use the tongs to flip over the cookies, making sure the cookies cook on both sides. When they are golden brown, remove them from the oil and place on the prepared baking sheet.

While the cookies are still hot, dust with powdered sugar. Set aside while you make the rest of the cupcakes. Unused cookies can be stored in an airtight container for a week (if they last that long).

VANILLA CAKE

Preheat the oven to 350°F. Line cupcake pans with 24 baking cups.

Melt the butter in a microwave at 60 percent power for 1½ to 2 minutes. Keep the butter warm—do not allow it to sit and cool off.

In a stand mixer with the paddle attachment, beat the eggs on medium-low for 2 minutes until light yellow and lightly foamy.

Increase the mixer speed to medium-high. Pour the hot butter into the eggs slowly, so that the mixture tempers and the eggs do not scramble. Once the butter is added, reduce the speed to medium-low.

With the mixer running, add the milk, vanilla, and salt. Mix for 1 minute until well combined.

Sift together the flour, granulated sugar, and baking powder and add to the batter. Mix on medium until just combined, 10 to 20 seconds. Remove the bowl and paddle from the mixer and use the paddle to scrape the bottom and sides of the bowl, ensuring that everything is well mixed.

Scoop the batter into the prepared baking cups, filling them two thirds of the way.

Matt says: *Tip—to make sure your jam pipes smoothly, give it a 10-second whirl in the food processor.*

Bake in the middle of the oven for 20 to 25 minutes, rotating the pan halfway through. The cupcakes are done when the centers spring back when you touch them.

Remove the cupcakes from the oven. Let cool completely.

CHEESECAKE BUTTERCREAM

For French buttercream (recommended): Prepare the recipe as directed on page 32. Once completed, add the cream cheese and vanilla and beat on high until well incorporated. If the cream cheese is particularly liquidy, it could cause the buttercream to "break." If that happens, add the guar gum and continue beating on high for 2 minutes until the mixture comes back together.

For American frosting: Prepare the recipe as directed on page 34, replacing the mascarpone with the cream cheese and adding the vanilla.

ASSEMBLY

Using a pastry tip, hollow out the center of each vanilla cupcake (see page 13).

Place the raspberry jam in a squeeze bottle or piping bag with a small opening snipped off. Fill the center of each cupcake.

Fill a pastry bag fitted with a regular tip with the cheesecake buttercream and pipe onto each cupcake.

Pipe squiggles of raspberry jam across the top of the buttercream.

Break the fried cookies into small pieces and sprinkle across the tops of each cupcake.

Before serving, dust with powdered sugar.

HALF-ASSED CORNER

You can buy chrusciki, aka fried angel wing cookies, at many supermarkets and Polish specialty stores. If you can't find them, feel free to use whatever you can get your hands on that makes you happy—like cannoli shells or pizzelles.

Coquito

One of the things I love most about being from Brooklyn is the endless supply of international delights we are gifted with from all our friends during the holidays. Italians make *struffoli*, Jamaicans give rum cake, Syrians bake baklava, and the Irish, Jameson (the ones in Bay Ridge at least have never been much for cooking).

If you're really lucky, like we are, and you've got Puerto Ricans in your life (and trust me, *everyone* needs Puerto Ricans in their life), you've tried *coquito*, aka *Boriqua* eggnog. It's a mixture of coconut milk, rum, sweetened condensed milk, rum, lime, spices, and more rum. See what I'm talking about? Christmastime in New York is known all over the world for lots of things, but our melting pot of insanely good food might be the best reason of all. And the coquito? Why, that's the thing that puts it over the top every single year. So suck on that, small-town America Christmas! Brooklyn's celebrating the baby Jesus by getting fat and wasted!

Coconut Rum Cake

- 12 tablespoons (1½ sticks) unsalted butter
- 4 large eggs
- 1 large egg white
- Zest of 2 limes
- ¾ cup coconut milk
- ¼ cup dark rum
- 1 teaspoon pure vanilla extract
- 1 teaspoon kosher salt
- 2 cups all-purpose flour
- 1¾ cups sugar
- 2 teaspoons baking powder

Milk Soak

- One 14-ounce can sweetened condensed milk
- One 13½-ounce can coconut milk
- ⅓ cup dark rum (optional)

Coconut Lime Buttercream

- 1¼ cups sweetened coconut
- Zest of 3 limes
- One recipe French Buttercream (page 32) or American Frosting (page 34)

COCONUT RUM CAKE

Preheat the oven to 350°F. Line cupcake pans with 24 baking cups.

Melt the butter in a microwave at 60 percent power for 1½ to 2 minutes. Keep the butter warm—do not allow it to sit and cool off.

In a stand mixer with the paddle attachment, beat the eggs and egg white on medium-low for 2 minutes until light yellow and lightly foamy. Add the lime zest.

Increase the mixer speed to medium-high. Pour the warm butter into the eggs slowly, so that the mixture tempers and the eggs do not scramble. Once the butter is added, reduce the speed to medium-low.

With the mixer running, add the coconut milk, rum, vanilla, and salt. Mix for 1 minute until well combined.

Sift together the flour, sugar, and baking powder and add to the batter. Mix on medium until just combined, 10 to 20 seconds. Remove the bowl and paddle from the mixer and use the paddle to scrape the bottom and sides of the bowl, ensuring that everything is well mixed.

Scoop the batter into the prepared baking cups, filling them two thirds of the way.

Bake in the middle of the oven for 20 to 25 minutes, rotating the pan halfway through. The cupcakes are done when the centers spring back when you touch them.

While the cupcakes are baking, prepare the coconut milk soak. Set up a baking sheet with a wire rack.

Remove the cupcakes from the oven. Let cool for 5 minutes. (Leave the oven on for the coconut.)

Take the cupcakes out of the pan and place faceup on the wire rack. Using a fork, dock each cupcake three times.

Spoon 1½ teaspoons of the milk soak onto each cupcake. Let cool completely.

MILK SOAK

In a microwave-safe bowl, combine the sweetened condensed milk, coconut milk, and rum, if using.

Microwave on high heat for 1 minute to thin out the sweetened condensed milk. Using a whisk, mix until well combined.

COCONUT LIME BUTTERCREAM

Place the coconut on a baking sheet and place in the oven for 10 minutes to toast, stirring occasionally to ensure even browning.

Remove the coconut from the oven. Immediately add the lime zest and stir. Set aside to cool.

Prepare the French buttercream as directed on page 32 or American frosting on page 34.

Add half of the coconut lime mixture to the buttercream and beat until well incorporated.

ASSEMBLY

Fill a pastry bag fitted with a fluted tip with the coconut lime buttercream and pipe onto each coquito-soaked cupcake.

Sprinkle the tops of the cupcakes with the remaining toasted coconut mixture.

Fruitcake

If you are disgusted by the mere mention of fruitcake, you obviously have no idea what fruitcake is actually supposed to be. At my first catering job, one of my first tasks was to make the holiday fruitcake. This befuddled me because not only did I wonder who was actually eating something that's the butt of just about every Christmas joke, but also because I was asked to make it in October. My chef taught me to make it the old-fashioned way, the way it was made for hundreds of years before it became an industrialized mess filled with glacéed technicolor cherries and various colored "fruits" of unknown origin.

They called it the Three Wise Men Cake. First, we went to a Middle Eastern import store and bought bags of the best dried figs, dates, currants, cherries, apricots, and raisins money could buy. We chopped them up with plenty of roasted nuts, folded them into cake batter, baked them into loaves, and wrapped them in cheesecloth. Then we put them in the closet where they would be aged for three months with the "three wise men": Johnny Walker, Jack Daniels, and Jim Beam. Each week until Christmas, the cakes would get a healthy dousing of each. By the time they were ready to be served, those six loaf cakes had collectively absorbed a fifth of each. The only way to serve the cake without rendering someone unconscious was in a 1 x 1-inch cube, and even then that person would have to sit down after eating one. How people have managed to downgrade what was pretty much the most awesome cake *ever* into those sad, bricklike monstrosities that are packed into cans and that no one loves, I'll never understand. Matt and I have done our best to try to show people what fruitcake is really supposed to taste like, but it's by far our hardest sell. Once people finally taste it, they're hooked.

Matt says: *You can use whatever dried fruits you're particularly fond of. Because we make this cake in huge batches and own a bakery with a plentiful inventory, we'll add several different types ourselves—figs, dates, cherries, cranberries, currants, apricots, plums, golden raisins, blueberries. There's no need for you to go all out and buy a tablespoon of each type—just make a blend of a few different types that you like. Same goes for booze—this is up to your personal preference. Some like dark rum, some like Scotch, some like bourbon—we're traditionalists and like brandy. Use one or a mix of a few—entirely up to you.*

We cook our alcohol off (see page 24), but feel free to go full strength if you're hoping to throw a Christmas party that involves nudity.

Candied Kumquats
- ¾ cup whole kumquats
- ½ cup granulated sugar
- ½ cup water

Fruitcake
- 3 cups assorted high-quality dried fruits, finely chopped
- 1 cup brandy

1 cup dark rum

2 cups hot water

2 cups all-purpose flour

1 pound (4 sticks) unsalted butter, softened

1 cup brown sugar

1 teaspoon ground cinnamon

1 teaspoon kosher salt

4 large eggs

1 cup molasses

1 teaspoon baking powder

½ cup milk

1 cup chopped walnuts

Vanilla Buttercream

One recipe French Buttercream (page 32) or American Frosting (page 34)

2 teaspoons pure vanilla extract

To Finish

Candied kumquats

¼ cup pomegranate seeds

7 dried figs, rehydrated and quartered (or dried fruit of your choice)

¼ cup walnuts, roasted and chopped

CANDIED KUMQUATS

Cut the kumquats in half and remove as many seeds as possible. The seeds are edible, so don't worry if you miss a few.

Place the sugar and water in a small saucepan and bring to a boil. Add the kumquats, reduce the heat to low, cover, and simmer for 20 minutes.

Remove the kumquats from the syrup and set aside. Increase the heat to high and reduce the syrup until thick, about 4 minutes. Pour the syrup over the kumquats, mix, and set aside to cool.

FRUITCAKE

Preheat the oven to 350°F. Line cupcake pans with 24 baking cups.

Place the dried fruits, brandy, ½ cup of the rum, and the hot water in a bowl and let sit for 24 hours. Drain and toss with 1 cup of the flour.

In a stand mixer with the paddle attachment, cream together the butter, brown sugar, cinnamon, and salt on medium-high speed until light and fluffy. Scrape the sides of the bowl and cream for a few seconds more.

Add the eggs and molasses and mix on medium for 30 seconds.

Sift together the remaining 1 cup flour and the baking powder. With the mixer on low, alternate adding the flour mixture and milk.

Fold in the fruit mixture and chopped walnuts.

Scoop the batter into the prepared baking cups, filling them three quarters of the way.

Bake in the middle of the oven for 20 to 25 minutes, rotating the pan halfway through. The cupcakes are done when the centers spring back when you touch them.

Remove the cupcakes from the oven. While the cupcakes are still hot, brush the tops with some of the remaining ½ cup rum. Set aside to cool. Brush with rum one more time before frosting.

VANILLA BUTTERCREAM

Prepare the recipe for French buttercream as directed on page 32 or American frosting on page 34. Add the vanilla and beat well.

ASSEMBLY

Fill a pastry bag fitted with a fluted tip with the vanilla buttercream and pipe onto each fruitcake cupcake.

Decorate the tops with candied kumquats, pomegranate seeds, dried fruits, and walnuts.

SO YOU HAVE EXTRA . . .

Candied kumquats

- Keep in a jar in the refrigerator for several months.
- Stir into Greek yogurt.
- Use in cocktails, such as a kumquat mule or a kumquat whiskey sour.
- Mix with a little white wine vinegar and serve alongside roast chicken.

HALF-ASSED CORNER

Omit the kumquats and decorate the tops with whatever nuts and dried or fresh fruit you have on hand.

You can also drizzle the tops with some leftover butterscotch (see page 121) spiked with the liquor of your choice.

Acknowledgments

And now ... the book is over! Yup, leaving it right there in December of 2010—everyone loves a good cliffhanger. Want to know what happens next? Well, hopefully we'll sell billions of copies of this book and get a deal to finish the story and give you more delicious recipes in *Robicelli's Episode Two: Attack of the Scones (and Other Tasty Teacakes)*. Right now, you alone have the power to spread the word of this book to all your friends, and put us straight on the path to being the type of family that owns His and Her dune buggies.

Or, I suppose, you could probably Google us. That would fill in a lot of gaps as well.

I guess you could also infer that since we got a book deal, everything ended up fine. Concentrating on the final result wouldn't get you into all the blood, sweat, and tears that went into this book, though. Like how my editor, Lucia Watson, fought to get this book, believed that America was ready to read four-letter words written by a woman, never held me back creatively, and encouraged us to be ourselves instead of trying to fit in. Her assistant, Gigi Campo, has been nothing short of a saint for having to put up with my constant barrage of stupid e-mails and general incompetency in the ways of grammar (apologies to the copy editor as well). There's superpublicist Carrie Bachman, who constantly floors me with her massive, sexy brain, and every single person at Viking Studio who in some way made this book happen.

Then there's Peter Hobbs from NonaBrooklyn who was the one who encouraged me to start writing in the first place, and Charlotte Druckman at Medium.com, who urged me to continue. And dare I forget Molly O'Neill, without whom I never would have met my agent. I know there's something inherently sleazy about being that person who thanks their agent, but mine is nothing like the stereotype (I don't think she even owns Ray-Bans). Melissa Sarver has become so much to me in the past two years: a muse, a teacher, a mom, a sister, a therapist, and one of my best friends. She's made me a better writer and a better person.

Finding her has been one of the best parts of this journey.

I found time to write this book because we found the best goddamn employees in America to take over all the baking, leaving me free to write two-hundred-something pages of abject nonsense with some recipes thrown in. Have you ever watched one of those workplace sitcoms and wondered "whose life is like this? Don't these people have families?" Well, while we do have "other" families, Robicelli's is exactly like that—we've become one of our own. What we'd do without Rachel Anderson, Monique Henry, Lawrence Daggett, Mike Markou, and Andrew Gallegos we don't know. Even though Matt and I get most of the press and accolades, it's these guys who are the heart and soul of this business, and we are incredibly fortunate that they chose to join the Robicelli family.

We also can't forget about the photos in this book—they were gorgeous as fuck, weren't they? I honestly didn't think one could photograph cupcakes fifty times and keep it interesting, but in the hands of the incredible Mr. Eric Isaac, assisted by Fernando he "Savage Koala" Souto, cupcakes became as spine-tingly sexy as Kevin James (I have a particular type). Thank you both for exceeding my expectations and tolerating my mood swings as we shot this book during the NYC school bus strike of 2013, and there was a fair amount of vacillating between hysterical laughter, uncontrollable sobbing, flat out yelling, and between it all, short naps.

We shot a good portion of these photos at some of our favorite businesses in Bay Ridge: Rosco's Pizza in Crown Heights, Blue Apron Foods in Park Slope, ALC Italian Grocery and Tuscany Grill.

Thank you to Jon Greenberg, Allan Palmer & Ted, Louis Collucio, and the Conforti family for allowing us to shoot inside their respective establishments. Please visit these places and spend ridiculous amounts of money there—these guys deserve it.

Then there was the actual physical writing of the book, which for the most part happened at Hôm in Bay Ridge. For the owners Sal and Daymein Forte: thank you for being our muses, our family in entrepreneurship, and our friends. Also thanks to the past and present staff of Starbucks store #11808, where the rest of it was written. If their corporate overlords are reading this, you should know that this is the store with the best staff in your entire company, and you should give them all raises.

I think that about answers all the questions about the physical book itself. But there's also all the other people who essentially held us together between the stories you just read—I mean, without them, this would have been just another generic collection of recipes that you would have attempted once, then put under the corner of your couch to level out that weird droopy bit. The entire story couldn't have happened, and we wouldn't have survived long enough to create a written record of it, if it wasn't for the wonderful people in our lives, like our parents, Allan, Jean, Arlene, and Tony. You couldn't script better parents than these four right here. They're the ones who gave us our love of food, who taught us how to be funny, sent home "leftovers" during the times they knew we didn't have enough to eat, and are helping us raise our children in the grand Italian American tradition of having too many goddamn people involved in their lives, all in the name of helping us follow our dreams. There's Matt's brother Chad, who was his first culinary partner, as they taught themselves to cook such delicacies as store-brand fish sticks as latchkey kids in the 1980s. If you could put down the book and throw all of them some polite applause, that would be appreciated. (Maybe throw in a few claps for my grandmother, Aunt Josie, Aunt Ro, Aunt Joan, and Aunt Regina as well—like I said, Italian kids get raised by a village, and my village is pretty fucking spectacular.)

And what about all the people from Brooklyn past and present—we can't forget about them either! Brooklyn—Bay Ridge, in particular—is for better or for worse who we are. From PS 185 and PS 160 to McKinley and Dyker to Stuyvesant, Kearney, Fort Hamilton, and past that—this book is for every kid who's from our little forgotten section of Brooklyn, and will always be part of it, even when we all inevitably get priced out and are forced to move to Staten Island. This story wouldn't have happened if it wasn't for hanging out in the sandbox with Justin Pooran, hitting L'Amours with Jay Liquori and Dugan, drinking on the stairs and sneaking into bars with the C.B.C., late nights at Bridgeview with Andrea Maniscalco and Claudia Foglia, spending every waking moment of my formative years with Telly Leung, slumber parties with Sarah Shin, and finding a sister like Debbie Aagotnes.

There's some people who aren't from Brooklyn who count, too. People like Rachel Waynberg, Fany Gerson, Liz Gutman, Susan Povich, Ralph Gorman, Rob Blatt, Scott Bridi, Steve Cobb, Josh Meuller, Dan Cohen, Siobhan Wallace, Jeremy Pickett, Amanda Pitts, Peter Shankman (who's from Staten Island, which is close enough) . . . know what? I just realized that if I listed everyone we love, we'll have to make this a two-book set. If you're one of those people who knows us and is looking to see if you're mentioned in this section, then you're probably what I'm talking about right here. We have a pretty incredible life, and that's entirely because of the people who are a part of it.

This story never would have happened if it wasn't for our fans, our customers, our cheering section. I mean, a bakery that went long swaths of time without a physical location? One who's toured the city doing pop-up shops, markets, one-night-only appearances, waiting years before putting down solid roots in the name of their family—what sort of crazy shit is that? But no matter where we were, we'd always see the same familiar faces, growing in numbers every time. Some had been with us since the original store, some traveled across states, some came from overseas, some we only know through the grace of the Internet. But no matter where you're from, know that every single one of you played a bigger part in this story than you know. You were the ones who helped us get out of bed on those mornings when we thought there was just no point anymore.

Above all: this book, and everything in our lives, is because of our sons, Atticus and Toby. We'll never be perfect parents or "have it all," but always know that we love you two in a way we didn't think was humanly possible. Books are nice. Money is nice. Success is nice.

But it's you guys that are the center of our universe, and you always will be.

Index